Henry James Coleridge

The preaching of the Beatitudes

Henry James Coleridge

The preaching of the Beatitudes

ISBN/EAN: 9783743383579

Manufactured in Europe, USA, Canada, Australia, Japa

Cover: Foto ©Lupo / pixelio.de

Manufactured and distributed by brebook publishing software (www.brebook.com)

Henry James Coleridge

The preaching of the Beatitudes

THE LIFE OF OUR LIFE.

PART THE SECOND.

THE PUBLIC LIFE OF OUR LORD JESUS CHRIST.

II.

The Preaching of the Beatitudes.

QUARTERLY SERIES.   VOLUME FOURTEEN.

ROEHAMPTON :

PRINTED BY JAMES STANLEY.

THE PREACHING
OF THE BEATITUDES.

BY

HENRY JAMES COLERIDGE,

OF THE SOCIETY OF JESUS.

FOURTH EDITION.

LONDON: BURNS AND OATES, LIMITED.

—

1892.

✠

HÆC · OMNIA · LIBER · VITÆ
ET · TESTAMENTUM · ALTISSIMI · ET · AGNITIO · VERITATIS
LEGEM · MANDAVIT · MOYSES · IN · PRÆCEPTIS
JUSTITIARUM
ET · HEREDITATEM · DOMUI · JACOB · ET · ISRAEL
PROMISSIONES
POSUIT · DAVID · PUERO · SUO · EXCITARE · REGEM · EX
IPSO · FORTISSIMUM
ET · IN · THRONO · HONORIS · SEDENTEM · IN
SEMPITERNUM
QUI · IMPLET · QUASI · PHISON · SAPIENTIAM
ET · SICUT · TIGRIS · IN · DIEBUS · NOVORUM
QUI · ADIMPLET · QUASI · EUPHRATES · SENSUM
QUI · MULTIPLICAT · QUASI · JORDANIS · IN · TEMPORE
MESSIS
QUI · MITTIT · DISCIPLINAM · SICUT · LUCEM
ET · ASSISTENS · QUASI · GEHON · IN · DIE · VINDEMIÆ
QUI · PERFICIT · PRIMUS · SCIRE · IPSAM
ET · INFIRMIOR · NON · INVESTIGABIT · EAM
A · MARI · ENIM · ABUNDAVIT · COGITATIO · EJUS
ET · CONSILIUM · ILLIUS · AB · ABYSSO · MAGNA
EGO · SAPIENTIA · EFFUDI · FLUMINA
EGO · QUASI · TRAMES · AQUÆ · IMMENSÆ · DE · FLUVIO
EGO · QUASI · FLUVII · DIORYX
ET · SICUT · AQUÆDUCTUS · EXIVI · DE · PARADISO
DIXI · RIGABO · HORTUM · MEUM · PLANTATIONUM
ET · INEBRIABO · PRATI · MEI · FRUCTUM
ET · ECCE · FACTUS · EST · MIHI · TRAMES · ABUNDANS
ET · FLUVIUS · MEUS · APPROPINQUAVIT · AD · MARE
QUONIAM · DOCTRINAM · QUASI · ANTELUCANUM · ILLUMINO
OMNIBUS
ET · ENARRABO · ILLAM · USQUE · AD · LONGINQUUM

(Ecclus. xxiv.)   ·

PREFACE.[1]

I SHOULD have but little to say in the way of preface to the following pages, if I had not to express my thanks for the great kindness with which the first volume of this work has been generally received, and for the encouragement which I have had from private friends as well as from persons of authority. The best way in which gratitude for such kindness can be shown is to endeavour to make the future volumes of the work on which I am engaged less unworthy of their great subject than they might be, if any pains were spared to give them such comparative perfection as lies within the reach of their author and his opportunities.

The present volume might, as I hoped, have contained the whole Sermon on the Mount, as well as the subsequent incidents of our Lord's Public Life during the first year of His Preaching. But I soon found that it was impossible to compress the matter into the small compass necessary, and as the Sermon on the Mount had to be divided, it seemed most natural to divide it at the Beatitudes. I have accordingly endeavoured to

[1] To the First Edition.

give, to some extent, their full importance to these great principles of our Lord's teaching and legislation, which might well occupy, without being exhausted, far larger volumes than those which will be devoted in the present work to the whole Public Life of our Lord. The more they are considered and meditated upon, the more will men become convinced of their deep and Divine philosophy, if I may apply to our Lord's legislation an expression which was used in a higher sense in ancient times than in our own. I need hardly remind Catholic readers of the volume which has been devoted to them—with the rest of the Sermon on the Mount—by Father Salmeron, of the sermons upon them which are to be found in the works of St. Bernardine, or of the beautiful manner in which their teaching, as carried out into practice in the Christian ages, has been illustrated by the author of the *Mores Catholici.* These and other books have been largely used in the following pages, in many cases without any reference to the particular passages, and I hope that this general acknowledgment of obligation to them will suffice. There are few, I fear, in the present day, conversant with such works as those of Father Alvarez de Paz and Father Francis Arias; but those that have the advantage of knowing their writings will often find traces of them, and sometimes more than traces, in the present volume. Not long ago, a great authority among us expressed the hope that leisure might be found by some to edit, among other things, 'portions of St. Bonaventure, St. Thomas, Dionysius the Carthusian, and St. Bernardine of Siena,' and the sermons of the last-named Saint on the Beatitudes were particularly mentioned.[1] I shall rejoice very much if the use which has been here made of St. Bernardine, and of some other later writers such as those named above, should at all events promote the study of these giants of spiritual literature. Their grand folios contain lore enough to furnish whole libraries of the slight and sketchy productions of the present day; and if it be impossible to translate them as they stand, chiefly on account of their great length, it may at all events be useful to abridge them, or to set their materials forth in a new dress, which may suit the readers of our generation, without losing either the solidity or the clearness which they possess in their original form.

It may, perhaps, be as well to add a few words as to the general character of the work of which this volume forms a part. Any writer on the Life of our Lord must necessarily have to decide for himself how far he is to attempt to make his work a commentary or exposition. The words of our Lord form, after all, the largest part of what has come down to us concerning Him. The Gospels, as has already been said more than once, were apparently intended as manuals of doctrine quite as much as historical memoirs, if not much more so. But the words of our Lord are living and pregnant, no commentary can hope to exhaust their meaning, while to record them altogether without commentary is often to leave the reader in much difficulty, and to

1 Cardinal Manning's *Internal Mission of the Holy Ghost*, Dedication, p. viii.

a 2*

deprive him of the light which Christian interpreters have been able to shed upon them. One of the main objects of this book, moreover, is to assist meditation, especially by drawing out the theological and practical meaning of our Lord's teaching. It is therefore, I hope, not unnatural that a comparatively considerable space should be given to exposition, especially in certain parts, the subject-matter of which forms what may be called the foundation of our Lord's practical doctrine, as in the Beatitudes and the Evangelical Counsels, or of His teaching with regard to God's government of the world, as in the Parables. It appears that during the first year of His Public Ministry, our Lord's activity in preaching throughout Galilee was immense and almost uninterrupted, while what remains to us as to that period in the way of history, is comparatively little. But we should form a false estimate of the position in which He stood before the people in general, and particularly before the authorities at Jerusalem at the end of that year, if we were not at least to endeavour to take into consideration the wonderful stirring of hearts and minds which must have been the result of several months of continuous preaching of doctrines such as those which are summed up in the Beatitudes and the rest of the Sermon on the Mount, especially when it is remembered that His preaching was accompanied and enforced by a constant series of His most marvellous miracles. For this reason, to pass over such teaching without at least attempting to draw out the Christian commentary upon it, would be, in truth, to glide over without due attention one of the most important periods of His Public Life. There are many parts of that Life as to which we shall be able to pass onwards with comparative rapidity, but the teaching of the first year was the foundation of the whole, both as to the training of the Apostles and the formation of the large number of disciples who afterwards became the first members of the infant Church. Few people would think, without examining the subject, how deep are the traces of the Beatitudes and the Sermon on the Mount on the first Christian communities, as far as we know them, and how naturally the teaching of the Apostles in their Epistles connects itself by direct descent with this first great publication of the Christian law.

H. J. C.

London,
Feast of the Nativity of St. John Baptist, 1875.

CONTENTS.

CHAPTER I.

General features of our Lord's Preaching.

St. Matt. iv. 12—17; St. Mark i. 14, 15;
Vita Vitæ Nostræ, § 29.

PAGE

Importance of our Lord's preaching 1
Populousness of Galilee . . 2
Our Lord visiting all parts . 3
Connection with the preaching of St. John 4
Three-fold occupations of our Lord 5
Exhortations to penance usually the same . . . 6
Involving great labours . . 7
New instructions . . . 8
Revisiting scenes of preaching 9
The multitudes who followed Him 9
Practice of poverty . . 10
Acceptance of hospitality . 10
Our Lord's prayer at night . 11
Care of the sick . . . 12
Great beneficence . . . 13
Training of the Apostles . 14
All this required a long time . 14
Time of year of His circuits . 15
The Sabbatical year . . 16
Our Lord's immense activity . 16
St. Matthew quoting Isaias . 17
The people sitting in darkness 18
Referred to by St. Zachary . 19

CHAPTER II.

Fishers of Men.

St. Matt. iv. 18—22; St. Mark i. 16—20;
Vita Vitæ Nostræ, § 29.

PAGE

The preaching of our Lord to continue in the Church . 20
Apostles to be familiar companions of our Lord . . 21
They had returned home . 22
Labour and industry in the Christian system . . . 23
Not in dishonour with the Jews 24
Call of the four disciples . 24
Meaning of 'Come after Me'. 25
Our Lord's reference to their fishing 26
Fishing and preaching . . 27
Dangerous occupations . . 27
Dependence on God . . 28
'Weather wisdom' . . 28
The prey of the fishermen . 29
Obedience of the four . . 30
Dangers of the call . . 32
Their diffidence . . . 32
To obey showed their confidence in Him . . . 33
Brotherly love . . . 33
Necessity of charity . . 34

CHAPTER III.

The Synagogue at Capharnaum.

St. Mark i. 21—34; St. Luke iv. 31—41
(compare St. Matt. viii. 14—19);
Vita Vitæ Nostræ, § 30.

Full account of one Sabbath . 35
Contrast with Nazareth . . 36

	PAGE
Synagogue services	37
Our Lady and others present	37
No opposition to our Lord's claim to teach	38
Reason of this	38
Effect of our Lord's majesty	39
Influence of His preaching	40
Power of sanctity	40
Instances in the Church	41
The Preacher as distinct from His words	42
Silence of the Evangelists as to details	42
Astonishment at His 'authority'	43
Explanation of this	44
Authority among the Jews	45
Our Lord speaking in His own Name	46
Obedience of our Lord	47
Our Lord requiring faith	48
Substance of His teaching	48
The 'great light'	49
Effects of our Lord's teaching	50

CHAPTER IV.

The Demoniac in the Synagogue.

St. Mark i. 23—26; St. Luke iv. 33—35; *Vita Vitæ Nostræ*, § 30.

	PAGE
Display of power over devils	51
Exorcisms of the Jews	52
Authority of our Lord	52
Modern disbelief in possession	53
A part of God's system	54
Inconsistency of opponents	55
Christian view of diabolical agency from the beginning	56
Extent of licence allowed to the evil spirits	57
Possession not the worst	58
Limits of 'possession'	58
Not incompatible with grace	59
Reasons for its permission	59
The glory of God	60
To manifest the benefits of the Incarnation	60
Hatred of the devils for the Incarnation	61
Future 'redemption of the body'	62
Possession permitted for punishment and trial	62
The demoniac at Capharnaum	63
Meaning of his words	64
'Art Thou come to destroy us?'	65
'I know Thee'	66
Perhaps a temptation	67
The Presence of God	67
Desire to hinder preaching	68
His witness not accepted	69
Fury of the evil spirit	70
Effect on the crowd	70
Fear and joy	71
Exercise of a new power	72
Spread of the news	73
NOTE I.—*Instances of possession permitted as a trial*	74

CHAPTER V.

Miracles at Capharnaum.

St. Mark i. 29—34; St. Luke iv. 38—41; St. Matt. viii. 16, 17; *Vita Vitæ Nostræ*, § 30.

	PAGE
Our Lord's teaching confirmed by miracles	76
Peter's mother-in-law	77
Incidents of the cure	77
Gathering of the sick at the door	79
Evening of the Sabbath	80
Did the devils know our Lord?	81
Reasons for thinking so	81
Reasons on the other side	82
They were not lawful witnesses	83
Silence often enjoined	84
Fulfilment of prophecy	84
Meaning of the words of Isaias	86

CHAPTER VI.

Preaching throughout Galilee.

St. Matt. iv. 23—25; St. Mark i. 35—39; St. Luke iv. 42—44; *Vita Vitæ Nostræ*, § 30.

	PAGE
The night at Capharaaum	88

	PAGE
Our Lord stealing forth . .	89
The cities of Galilee . .	90
Wide extent of our Lord's preaching	91
Splendid miracles . . .	92
Wonderful teaching . .	93
Comparative scarcity of records	94
Christian contemplations on this time	95
Anne Catharine Emmerich's contemplations . . .	96
NOTE II.—*On the arrangement of the contemplations of Sister Anne Catharine Emmerich on the Life of our Lord*	98

CHAPTER VII.

Illustrations of our Lord's Preaching from the Lives of the Saints.

	PAGE
Our Lord's Life continued in the Church . . .	100
Interior resemblance to Him in the Saints . . .	101
External points of likeness .	102
Great number of miracles .	102
Large crowds of followers .	102
Statements of the Evangelists	102
The missionary saints . .	103
St. Bernard	104
His visit to Germany . .	105
Miracles in the diocese of Constance	105
A chapter by his companions	106
Brunville	106
Juliers	107
Aix-le-Chapelle and Utrecht .	108
St. Servatius and Liege . .	109
St. Vincent Ferrer . .	110
Miserable period in which he lived	111
His apostolate . . .	112
His method	113
His sermons	114
Gift of tongues . . .	115
Companies which followed him	115

	PAGE
Rules of these bands . .	116
Their large numbers . .	117
St. Vincent and St. Bernardine	117
Beginnings of St. Bernardine	118
His method	119
St. John of Capistrano . .	120
His immense successes . .	121
Illustrations of our Lord's preaching	122

CHAPTER VIII.

The Sermon on the Mount.

St. Matt. v. 1 ; *Vita Vitæ Nostræ*, § 31.

	PAGE
A great monument of our Lord's teaching . .	123
Importance of it in St. Matthew's Gospel . . .	124
Unparalleled in the other Gospels	124
The multitudes . . .	125
Different grades of believers .	126
Brevity of the sayings in the Sermon	127
Our Lord may have added developments . . .	128
The Sermon has a character of its own	129
St. Matthew's reference to types	129
The Law of Sinai and the Sermon on the Mount .	130
Solemnity of the occasion .	131
Scope of the Sermon and of the Decalogue . . .	132
Contrast between them . .	132
The disciples already a separate body	134
Our Lord as Legislator .	135

CHAPTER IX.

The Beatitudes.

St. Matt. v. 3—10 ; *Vita Vitæ Nostræ*, § 31.

	PAGE
Brevity and pregnancy of the Beatitudes . . .	136
The new Creation . .	137

	PAGE
Relation of the virtues and rewards	138
What is a ‘ Beatitude ’	139
St. Bernardine’s definition	140
Principles of holiness	141
How far obligatory	142
Contrast with the Decalogue	142
Appeal to hope	143
Beatitudes open to all	144
Their relation to the heavenly state	145
To Christian society	145
The two societies	146
Characteristics and possible effects of the Beatitudes	147
Actual effects	148

CHAPTER X.

The Beatitude of the Poor in Spirit.

St. Matt. v. 3; *Vita Vitæ Nostræ*, § 31.

	PAGE
The Mount of the Beatitudes	149
The Sermon easily heard	150
Our Lord opening His mouth	151
He begins with blessing	152
Poverty of spirit and humility	153
Poverty actual and spiritual	154
Humility connected with Poverty	155
What poverty relates to	157
All may be poor in spirit	158
Truth on which poverty of spirit is founded	159
God as our Father	160
The filial spirit	161
Large-heartedness of the poor in spirit	161
In Christian communities	162
Christian and pagan views of poverty	163
Graces connected with poverty	164
It leads to the other Beatitudes	165
Our Lord’s practice of poverty	166

CHAPTER XI.

Poverty and the Kingdom of Heaven.

St. Matt. v. 3; *Vita Vitæ Nostræ*, § 31.

	PAGE
‘ The Kingdom of Heaven ’	167
A complex idea	168
A kingdom means many things	168
The first and last Beatitudes	169
Riches and power	170
Treasures of the Kingdom for the poor	171
The poor and the angels	172
Fruitfulness of poverty	172

CHAPTER XII.

The Beatitude of the Meek.

St. Matt. v. 4; *Vita Vitæ Nostræ*, § 31.

	PAGE
Meekness healing another concupiscence	173
Conquest of pride and independence	175
Natural meekness	176
Meek saints often naturally wanting in meekness	176
Courage of the truly meek	177
Meekness and firmness	178
Meekness and obedience	178
Meekness and charity	179

CHAPTER XIII.

The Meek possessing the Land.

St. Matt. v. 4; *Vita Vitæ Nostræ*, § 31.

	PAGE
Unexpectedness of our Lord’s blessings	181
The meek ‘ inheriting the land ’	182
The Psalm quoted by our Lord	183
Promise of providential aid to the meek	184
Rules of God’s government	185
St. Chrysostom’s interpretation	186

	PAGE
Abraham and David . .	186
True meaning of inheritance	187
Enjoyment of the physical world . . .	188
Meekness and intellectual enjoyment	189
God's providence and gifts .	19
Meekness the key to God's treasures	191
Three meanings of the land .	192
Meekness and purity . .	193
Empire over hearts . .	194
Influence of meekness . .	195
The ' land of the living ' .	196

CHAPTER XIV.

The Beatitude of the Mourners.

St. Matt. v. 5; *Vita Vitæ Nostræ,* § 31.

	PAGE
Reasonableness of the Beatitudes	197
Foundation of the virtue of mourning	198
Shock to the world . .	198
Worldlings in the Book of Wisdom	199
Intellectual scepticism and the condition of man . .	200
Mr. Mill on ' Nature ' . .	201
Effects of ' mourning ' . .	202
Motives of mourning—God .	203
Treatment of our Lord .	204
The Passion	204
Loss of grace and glory .	205
The world as a ' valley of tears '	206
Our Lord's mournings . .	207

CHAPTER XV.

The Consolation of the Mourners.

St. Matt. v. 5; *Vita Vitæ Nostræ,* § 31.

	PAGE
Truth of the grounds of mourning	208
Our Lord's remedies and the world's . . .	209
Happy effects of sorrow .	210
Satisfaction for sin . .	211
Spirit of prayer . . .	211
Desire of Heaven . . .	211
The concupiscence of the flesh	212
Special consolations . .	213

CHAPTER XVI.

The Beatitude of Hunger and Thirst after Justice.

St. Matt. v. 6; *Vita Vitæ Nostræ,* § 31.

	PAGE
Truthfulness of our Lord .	215
Mourning leads to activity .	216
Practice of justice . .	216
Hunger and thirst which satisfy	217
The reward of justice . .	218
What is due to God . .	219
What is due to ourselves .	219
Purity of heart . . .	219
Custody of tongue . .	220
Discipline of body . .	221
What is due to others . .	222
Other classifications . .	223
First degree of hunger and thirst	224
Desire of pardon . . .	225
Desire for perfection . .	225
Desire for the extension of justice	226
Desire for heavenly justice .	227
NOTE III.—*Other arrangements of the Christian virtues for the purposes of meditation* . . .	228

CHAPTER XVII.

The Hungry and Thirsty filled.

St. Matt. v. 6; *Vita Vitæ Nostræ,* § 31.

	PAGE
Blessedness of craving for justice	231
Restlessness of nature . .	232
Uses of desire . . .	232

PAGE

Pursuit of justice teaches humility 233
Extinguishes tepidity . . 233
Man made for justice . . 234
Great opportunities . . 235
Satisfaction in justice . . 236
The saints 237
Effects of the desire of justice on society 237
Satisfaction hereafter . . 238

CHAPTER XVIII.

The Beatitude of the Merciful.

St. Matt. v. 7; *Vita Vitæ Nostræ*, § 31.

Our Lord's joy in mercy . 240
Power of His words . . 240
His Mission one of mercy . 241
Place of this Beatitude . . 242
Mercy apparently easy . . 243
Natural mercifulness . . 244
The supernatural virtue . 245
God's joy in it . . . 245
Mercy committed to man . 246
God's mercy 'over all His works' 247
'Commandment concerning our neighbour' . . . 248
'Mercy and not sacrifice' . 249
Our own forgiveness dependent on it 251
Mercy needs great grace . 252
Fruits of mercy . . . 252
Four other fruits . . . 254
The last four . . . 256
Mercy a difficult virtue . . 257
Mercy and the Church . . 258
Dangers to mercy . . . 260

CHAPTER XIX.

The Merciful obtaining Mercy.

St. Matt. v. 7; *Vita Vitæ Nostræ*, § 31.

Three rewards for mercy . 261
'The man who understandeth' 262
Differences of glory . . 264

PAGE

Our Lord's promise . . 265
Our Lord Himself the reward 267

CHAPTER XX.

The Beatitude of the Clean of Heart.

St. Matt. v. 8; *Vita Vitæ Nostræ*, § 31.

The soul turned to God . 269
Purity of heart after justice and mercifulness . . 270
Meaning of the heart . . 271
Its capacity for evil . . 272
And for good . . . 273
God alone sees it . . . 275
Purgation from sins . . 275
From lesser sins . . . 276
Different kinds of venial sin . 277
Faults of character . . 278
Instances 279
Study of the Sacred Heart . 280
Free from love of temporal things 280
From worldly delights . . 281
From desire to please men . 281
From imperfect intentions . 282
From useless thoughts . . 283
From superfluous cares . . 284
From all bitterness . . 285
From all vainglory . . 286
From created consolation . 286
From all anxiety . . . 287
From impatience . . . 288
From self-will . . . 288
Purity and the means of grace 289
No vocation excluded . . 290

CHAPTER XXI.

Purity and the Vision of God.

St. Matt. v. 8; *Vita Vitæ Nostræ*, § 31.

Blessedness of purity of heart 291
Degrees of vision of God . 292
Misery of natural blindness . 292
Blindness as to God . . 293
God seen in many ways . 293
In the universe . . . 294

Contents. xix

In providence . . . 294
In conscience . . . 295
The Psalms 295
The creation of grace . . 295
Our Lord and His Saints . 296
Sacred Scripture . . . 296
Extraordinary communications of God . . . 297
Purity of heart the condition 298
Prayer and contemplation . 299
The presence of God . . 300
Higher states of prayer . 301
The intuitive vision . . 302

CHAPTER XXII.

The Beatitude of the Peacemakers.

St. Matt. v. 9; *Vita Vitæ Nostræ*, § 31.

Our Lord might here pause . 303
His Beatitudes not exhausted 304
The work of peace . . 305
Sonship to God . . . 305
Natural love of peace . . 306
Peacemaking and mercifulness 307
Peace and purity . . . 308
Multiplicity of the works of peace. 309
The work of the Church . 310
Antagonistic spirits . . 311
Manifold works of mercy . 311
Ministers of religion peacemakers 312
Forgiveness of injuries and love of enemies . . . 313
A certain sign of the children of God 314
All Christians are peacemakers. 314
Guilt of detraction . . 316
Guilt of heresy and schism . 316

CHAPTER XXIII.

The Sons of God.

St. Matt. v. 9; *Vita Vitæ Nostræ*, § 31.

Blessedness of peacemaking . 319
Special blessing of sonship . 320
Three things make men sons of God 320
Faith 321
Charity 321
Concord of peace. . . 322
The work of the Son of God 322
God's work of peace . . 323
Peace in the universe . . 323
And among rational beings . 324
Peace by law . . . 324
Glory to God in consequence 325
Peace in man . . . 326
Peace in society . . . 327
Defeat of God's designs . 328
Restoration of peace by our Lord 329
Peace the work of His Incarnation 329
Hence the crown of the peacemakers 330

CHAPTER XXIV.

The Beatitude of the Persecuted.

St. Matt. v. 10; *Vita Vitæ Nostræ*, § 31.

The seventh Beatitude seems to end the chain . . 331
Price of the work of peace . 332
Application of the work of peace 333
Must have the same conditions as the work itself . 333
The Passion and suffering . 334
The crown of suffering . 334
The Beatitude dependent on others 335
Hatred of God in persecution 337
The persecuted acknowledge God's supreme majesty . 338
Confession of the Faith . 339
Great faith and virtue required 340
St. Paul's doctrine . . 341
God's special glory . . 342
Fruitfulness 343
Special love of God . . 345

xx

Contents.

CHAPTER XXV.

Persecution and the Kingdom of Heaven.

St. Matt. v. 10—12; *Vita Vitæ Nostræ,* § 31.

	PAGE
Blessedness of persecution	346
Reward identical with that of poverty of spirit	347
Interior Kingdom of Heaven	348
Great trial in persecution	348
It requires great virtues	349
Sanctifies quickly	350
Dignity of the persecuted	350
This Beatitude connected with the preceding	351

CHAPTER XXVI.

Our Lord and the Beatitudes.

St. Matt. v. 1—10; *Vita Vitæ Nostræ,* § 31.

	PAGE
Beatitudes founded on our Lord	352
Direct relation to God and His rights	353
And to the actual condition of the world	354
Double order of Providence	356
Predominance of the order of Redemption	357
Our Lord's own Life	358
The Beatitudes in the Church	359
The Apostles	360
St. Paul	360
Universal imitation of our Lord	361
Power of the Beatitudes	362

APPENDIX.

Harmony of the Gospels.

From *Vita Vitæ Nostræ,* §§ 29—36.

	PAGE
Sect. 29.—Beginning of the preaching in Galilee, and call of four disciples	363
Sect. 30.—The Sabbath at Capharnaum	364
Sect. 31.—The Eight Beatitudes and the Light of the World	367
Sect. 32.—Evangelical Justice	368
Sect. 33.—Alms, Prayer, and Fasting	370
Sect. 34.—Confidence in God our Father	371
Sect. 35.—Against judging others, and of confidence in prayer	371
Sect. 36.—The narrow way to life	372

CHAPTER I.

General features of our Lord's Preaching.

St. Matt. iv. 12--17; St. Mark i. 14, 15; *Vita Vitæ Nostræ*, § 29.

THE Evangelists to whom we owe our chief acquaintance with the ordinary preaching of our Blessed Lord, agree in connecting the beginning of that preaching with the date of the imprisonment of St. John Baptist.[1] The extent to which our Lord's movements were actually influenced by the arbitrary act of Herod Antipas has been already spoken of, and we may proceed at once to examine the character and chief features of the course of preaching on which He now entered, in relation to the condition of the country, which was its scene and the population for whose benefit it was under-

[1] It must be remembered that the Evangelists speak here with the utmost brevity. St. Matthew has omitted everything that intervened between the temptation of our Lord and the beginning of the Galilæan preaching; and when he says that our Lord heard of the imprisonment of St. John, returned into Galilee, left Nazareth and went down to dwell at Capharnaum, his words are to be understood as meaning that the last mentioned incident synchronized with the first, that the final removal to a new scene of action was accomplished about the time of the imprisonment. St. Mark's words are more general, inasmuch as he has never mentioned Nazareth, and so, has not to explain that it was abandoned. St. Luke, as has been seen, gives the immediate occasion on which our Lord left Nazareth as a place of residence; and St. John fills up the story by adding the incident of the miracle of the nobleman's son, which was indirectly connected with the rejection in the synagogue at Nazareth, as well as by explaining that our Lord had actually left Judæa—the early Ministry in which country he alone has related—before the actual arrest of St. John, which probably took place about the time of this journey of our Lord's through Samaria. See *The Ministry of St. John Baptist*, c. xxvii.

B 2

taken. We must try to give ourselves a fair idea of
the kind of work in which so much of our Lord's time
in the course of the three years of His Ministry was
spent, to which He specially trained His Apostles, and
which, it may be added, has ever been the most laborious
and necessary work of the Church since their time—a
work which can never be relaxed or discontinued, while
it requires ever fresh and more energetic exertions, in
proportion as the populations committed to her care
grow in numbers, intelligence, activity, and in the complexity of their moral and religious wants. When we
have formed some notion of what the work must have
been, we shall be better able to understand the passing
hints concerning it which are to be found in the Gospels,
as also to see why it would have been almost impossible
for their writers to furnish us with anything like a narrative in detail of all that our Lord said and did at this
period of His Life.

The province of Galilee was in those days the flourishing and well-cultivated home of a population which even
among ourselves would be considered as sufficiently
teeming, if not overabundant, even for the rich resources
of every kind with which nature had endowed that
favourite corner of Palestine. Josephus tells us, speaking
of a time a little later than this, that Galilee contained
as many as two hundred and four towns or villages, and
that the least of these had more than fifteen thousand
inhabitants.[2] It has been said that the best idea we

---

[2] The number of towns given in his *Life*, c. 45. The other place
in which he speaks of Galilee is *De Bello Jud.* I. iii. c. 2, n. 2, where
he says : ' It is all rich and full of good pasture, planted with trees of
every kind, so as to invite by its promise of good living even the most
indolent of men. It has all been brought into cultivation by its
inhabitants, and no part of it is undeveloped ; it is also thickly strewn
with cities, and has a multitude of villages, everywhere popular on
account of its abundance ; so that the least of them has more than
fifteen thousand inhabitants.'

probably could form of the Galilee of our Lord's time would be to take as its picture some one of the most thickly populated and well-cultivated districts of about the same size in modern Italy. But such a district would still be inferior in climate, and lack some of the advantages of the situation of Galilee, as well as the special charm of the inland sea of which we hear so much in the Gospels. If the statement of Josephus can be depended upon, Galilee must have had a population not far short in numbers of the present inhabitants of Lancashire and Yorkshire put together, and the towns must have stood within very short distances one from the other. Even if the picture has been too highly coloured, we may still be certain that the work which is spoken of as the going 'round' or 'about' or 'through the whole of' Galilee must have been a work requiring very great exertion and perseverance, and a very con-siderable period of time. It seems that our Lord began by teaching in the synagogues on the Sabbath-days; but it is known that there were other days in the week on which the Jews were wont to assemble in the synagogue, and we need not, therefore, limit His opportunities of teaching to the Sabbaths, and, if He arrived at a town on a day on which there would not ordinarily be a service, He might still have the people specially invited to the synagogue.

It must, however, be remembered that it was one of the most essential novelties of His preaching, that it was now brought home to all. St. John had remained mainly in one or two spots, and while our Lord taught in Judæa, before coming into Galilee, it would seem that He also kept to one place. Now, however, instead of drawing people to Him from all quarters—a system of all others, perhaps, the most likely to have moved first the jealousy of the priests at Jerusalem, as mentioned by St. John, and afterwards to have caused possible danger from the agents of Herod—our Lord was to go Himself from place to place, finding people at their homes. We may be sure, therefore, that our Lord's journeys through Galilee were no occasional excursions of a day or two at a time to towns in the immediate neighbourhood of Capharnaum, where He had taken up His abode, but that, on the contrary, whether He visited or not every one of the cities and large villages of which Josephus speaks, He at least went from place to place over a large part of the country, repeating everywhere, in sub·stance, the same preaching, teaching the same doctrine, and confirming His words by the same display of marvellous miracles of mercy. If our Lord had done less than this, He would hardly have justified the language which is used by the Evangelist as to His work at this time, and He would not in His own personal action have laid the foundations of that Apostolical and missionary life which was to be the main occupation of so many who were afterwards to tread in His footsteps and carry on in this respect that work of 'preaching the Gospel to the poor,' in which He was in truth the first labourer as well as the source of all fruitfulness in the future labours of others.

It is easy to see how this missionary work of our Blessed Lord completed and carried on still further the work which had already been done by His Forerunner, St. John Baptist, as well as by Himself in that earlier stage of His teaching which occupied the interval between His own Baptism and this time. The main burden of the preaching of St. John had been penitence for past sin, reconciliation with God through contrition and confession, and a profession of faith, more or less explicit, in the coming Kingdom and the Person of the promised Messias. He had gone further than this, no doubt, in the training of His own personal disciples and He had also given general instructions to several classes of persons as to the discharge of the duties of their station. Our Lord's first teaching is described by the Evangelists in words which show that it was mainly identical with the teaching of St. John. 'From that time,' says St. Mathew,[3] 'Jesus began to preach and to say, Do penance, for the Kingdom of Heaven hath drawn nigh.' St. Mark describes the substance of His preaching in the words: 'The time is now fulfilled, and the Kingdom of Heaven hath drawn near: Do penance and believe the Gospel.'[4] A little later St. Matthew speaks of three things as occupying our Lord in His circuit in Galilee. 'He was teaching in the synagogues, preaching the Gospel of the Kingdom, and healing every sickness and infirmity among the people.'[5] Thus we are led to see that our Lord carried on in the first place the work of arousing men's consciences by reminding them of their sins, of the justice of God, the coming day of account, and the like: that He urged on them the necessity of repentance and of faith in the new Kingdom as the condition of pleasing God: that He added to this preaching a good deal of moral and practical instruction, more like in subject-matter, perhaps, to the ordinary teaching of the Synagogue as suggested by the portions of Sacred Scripture which were first read and then expounded at the time of the public meetings for prayer and devotion, but having a peculiar character of its own, first in the authority with which He taught, and then in the sublimity, purity, and simplicity of His doctrine; and that lastly, He enforced His lessons, and won the love and obedience of His hearers, by His tender care for the sick and suffering of every possible class, who soon came to throng to Him from every side. That is, He roused people to repent-

---

[3] St. Matt. iv. 17.   [4] St. Mark i. 15.   [5] St. Matt. iv. 23.

ance by His preaching, He gave a great deal of instruction, practical and doctrinal, to the people thus roused, and He attended in the most gracious and compassionate manner to the needs of the afflicted.

As to the first of these three divisions into which our Lord's work in Galilee may thus be said to fall, it would be very much a continuation, as has been said, of the preaching already begun by St. John Baptist. Preaching of that kind, which must always form a large part of the work of the Apostolic labourer, when even he has to deal with populations already in possession of the true Faith and living in the communion of the Church, is by its very nature mainly the same everywhere and at all times, save that it receives a special direction, or a peculiar force and power, either from the practical knowledge which the preacher may have acquired of the particular dangers and snares to conscience which prevail in this or that place, or at this or that time, or from the gifts which may be specially vouchsafed to him of eloquence, natural or supernatural, and his own personal influence as a man of extraordinary holiness or penance. But even the more chosen instruments of God in work of this kind will use, as a rule, the usual topics and put forward the usual truths, the difference between their preaching and that of others lying in the energy or simplicity of their words, in their power of character, and, above all, in the abundant supplies of grace, arousing and enlightening the hearts of their hearers, which are the reward with which God crowns their intense prayers and long penances, or carries on His own work in the souls of men by occasion of their ministrations. We do not expect, therefore, to find the exhortations to penance which were used by our Lord, or, again, by the Apostles after Him, recorded in so many words in the narrative which relates to us the other incidents of their preaching. Nor are we, indeed, told with any precision to what an extent our Lord discovered Himself as an object of faith to those whose hearts were brought to contrition by His preaching, or to what extent He administered to them by Himself and others either the simple baptism of penance, or the Christian sacrament which He had already established. We may well suppose that large numbers would be far advanced by Him in these respects, and in any case, the work would be laborious on account of the numbers with whom it would be necessary to deal, not in masses, but one by one. And it is probable that the general instructions, both as to doctrine and practice, which our Lord addressed to His converts, would be such as to ensure them a thorough and solid knowledge in both respects.

General exhortations to repentance, to a change of life, to the abandonment of sin, to reconciliation with God—especially if this has to be sought by means of the Christian practice of confession, or something analogous thereto—to restitution and the reparation of injuries, to works of penance and satisfaction, and a more perfect ordering of man's daily actions, in accordance with the commandments of God and the particular duties of the state of each—all these things imply the need of a very considerable amount of personal intercourse, and of instruction adapted to special circumstances, without which the work of conversion would at best be only half done. We have here, then, a reason for supposing a state of things, as consequent upon our Lord's public preaching of penance, which would involve a very large drain upon His time in any place where His audience had been numbered by hundreds or thousands, and where His words had struck home to the hearts of men. Every contrite sinner, in all the crowds to whom

His words had been addressed, would certainly have been as eager to open to him in private the wounds of his own soul, as were the multitudes who in later times thronged to the Evangelical preaching of great missionaries such as St. Vincent Ferrer or St. Bernardine of Siena. In many cases there would be need of continued personal instruction; there would be many whose souls could not be set right at once, who might be entangled in complicated mazes of sin in which others also were concerned, or lying under burdens imposed on them by their own injustice, from which they must deliver themselves before they could be at peace.

Again, our Lord came not so much to administer a system of grace already in possession, as to introduce a new religious dispensation, in which there were many points requiring proof and argument, many new and more sublime views as to duty and the requirements of God to be illustrated and enforced, many new means of grace to be instituted and explained. When His hearers had become, to some extent at least, His disciples, there would lie open before Him an immense field of new instruction in the Gospel morality, which might naturally form the staple of much of His public teaching in the synagogues, as well as of the private conversations which our Lord would hold with persons more fitted to profit by them, or who, like Nicodemus, thought themselves forced by circumstances to seek Him less openly. It would be to take a very inadequate view of our Lord's work at this time of His Ministry, to suppose that He would content Himself with a perfunctory or superficial discharge of His office as Teacher, and we may see in the Gospel accounts many hints which naturally lead us to suppose that He adopted the plan, which has from time to time been followed in the Church by those who have had the vocation to extraordinary missionary duties, as distinguished from those of the resident and local clergy—the plan; namely, of revisiting more than once at short intervals the places which have been the scenes of their more extensive and continued labours. We have thus another reason given us for supposing that a great many months were occupied by our Lord in the 'circuits' of Galilee, of which the Evangelists speak from time to time.

There are also statements in the Gospels which show that, exactly as multitudes followed the great missionary preachers of later times who have already been named, and others like them—even though, like our Lord, they went about the country from place to place in order to scatter the seed of God's Word as widely as possible—so, as our Lord went about through Galilee, He gathered to Himself large crowds of followers, who were not content with the instructions which He delivered in the places of their ordinary abodes. Many among these would become His closer and more intimate disciples, and be thus capable of higher training and greater perfection in the practice of virtue. It was to a multitude made up in the main of such followers, as we shall see, that the requisite lessons of the Sermon on the Mount were addressed. Here again we have an intimation of a higher range of preaching than that which would be addressed to those whose consciences were in the first instance to be aroused to a sense of their own guiltiness, and on whom the necessity of immediate repentance and conversion was to be urged by the use of the topics natural to such a theme. But to give such higher instruction in details, expanding the heads which are collected and arranged in the Sermon on the Mount, must have required an expenditure of time and labour on the part of our Lord of which it is difficult to form an adequate notion.

One or two other general characteristics of our Lord's manner of life at this time, have their importance here, inasmuch as every detail in His method must have been deliberately adopted from considerations of the greater glory of His Father and the greater profit of the souls for whose salvation He was labouring, and also out of regard to the great outlines of the missionary life in His Church which was to be the continuation of the work on which He was now occupied. We find Him insisting, in the charge to the Apostles, on the strict practice of poverty, chiefly, as it would seem, on account of that absolute dependence upon the providence of His Father, which was to be one of the conditions of great Apostolical success. It cannot therefore be doubted that He practised the same kind of dependence Himself, and that it was a matter of choice with Him to have so little provision for Himself and for His immediate companions, that they might be occasionally driven by hunger to feed upon the ears of corn which they might gather as they went through the fields. In the same way, when He said to one who applied to be received as His follower that 'the foxes have holes and the birds of the air nests, but the Son of Man hath not where to lay His head,' His words do not imply a complaint of want of hospitality or of due provision made for Him by His friends and admirers, so much as a principle of the Apostolical life analogous to that which has just been mentioned, and involving, like that, the most perfect dependence, day after day, upon the providence of His Father. Again, we find our Lord continually accepting the invitations offered to Him, whether by near friends or by those who were not altogether well disposed towards Him, as if it were a principle with Him at this time to put Himself at the beck of all, and to make the acts of kindness or charity which His poverty thus elicited the occasion of the return of great spiritual benefits to His entertainers. Nor can we suppose that those who thus invited Him were always free from the influence of lower motives, sometimes, perhaps, of a kind of ostentation, sometimes, it may be, of a desire to watch Him, and if possible to find some fault in Him or His companions. And we find our Lord so ready to accept calls of this kind as to get the name, among the stricter Jews, of a friend of publicans and sinners, and, towards the end of His Public Life, we are told that He even invited Himself as the guest of Zacchæus, who was the chief of the publicans.

Again, if, as from the Gospel narrative seems most probable, even in the very earliest period of His preaching He had with Him at least a small company of those who afterwards became His Apostles and near followers, He would probably take care that they were lodged in the several towns to which their journeys led them with persons well known for probity and devotion, according to the principle which He afterwards laid down as to such matters in His charge to the Apostles. For Himself, He may have accepted hospitality as well as for them, but it is clear that most of the nights, even when the days had been altogether occupied in the severe labours of His Ministry, were spent in long private prayer to His Eternal Father—a practice in which the Apostles and the great saints of the Church in all ages, especially the missionary saints, have uniformly followed Him, as being one of the most essential, if not actually the most essential, of all the points in which it has pleased God that they should have His example to guide them. Many a night our Lord must have spent on the mountains, or in the nearest place of retirement that was within His reach from the town in which He had been preaching, placing before His Father the needs of the souls among whom He had been toiling, or among whom He was about to toil, taking up into His Sacred Heart all the miseries and dangers to which they were exposed, negotiating by His all-powerful prayer the success of what He was about to establish in the Church for their benefit, winning grace to the end of time for the Apostolate which He was inaugurating, and for the teaching which was to carry on over the whole world the truths and precepts and counsels which He was pouring forth all around. The nightly prayer of the Church is founded upon these nights of our Lord, which were no doubt not spent in intercession only, but in praise and thanksgiving and supplication and contemplation.

There is another feature which, as has been already said, is especially prominent in the short descriptions furnished by the Evangelists of our Lord's preaching tours, as to which it is necessary that a few words should be added. Whether we look at those descriptions themselves, or at the outlines of missionary duties as drawn by our Lord in His charge to the Apostles when they were first sent out, two and two, to labour in the same way—or again, at the accounts given later on in the New Testament of the manner in which the same Apostles carried on our Lord's work after the Day of Pentecost—or once more, at what we know to have been the habits of the great saints who have had the same kind of commission in later centuries—we find the care of the sick quite as marked and as essential a principle in all such cases as the practice of Evangelical poverty or of the most absolute reliance on Divine Providence. In the case of our Lord, of the Apostles, and of a number of the great saints who have laboured in this particular way, we find, indeed, as was to be expected, the gift of miracles very profusely exercised in favour of the sick, it being often in the providence of God that the authority of the missionaries or of the truths which they taught should be thus publicly demonstrated, and that the wonderful operations of His grace which were going on in the souls of men by occasion of such ministrations, should be paralleled and made, as it were, visible by analogous effects of mercy on the bodies of men.

But it must be noted that the very great care which our Lord, and those who have followed most closely in His footsteps, always bestowed upon the sick, was not limited to the cases in which miracles were to be wrought in their favour, and the principle of Evangelical working which is involved in the examples shown us in the Gospels and in the Acts of the Apostles would be to a great measure lost, if the essential necessity of the care of the sick and the poor in all cases were not fully acknowledged. We find our Lord, in some conspicuous instances, breaking off a course of instruction or altering the line of conduct which He had deliberately adopted, at the call to visit the sick, even at inopportune moments. We are at present engaged on what may be called the chief features of the period of missionary activity, on which the history of our Lord's Public Life has now to enter, and we may certainly add to the other main occupations of this time which have been already noted, the constant and most charitable care of the sick in body as well as of the diseased in soul. This was so prominent a feature in our Lord's method at this time, that to many witnesses it may have been the most characteristic of all. Thus we find that when St. Peter, in his address to the Gentile Cornelius and his friends, related in the Acts of the Apostles,[6] has to speak of what they already knew concerning our Lord from common report, and from His period of

6 Acts x. 37, 38.

preaching in Judæa, he selects this feature beyond all others, saying that our Lord was 'anointed with the Holy Ghost and with power, and went about doing good, and healing all that were oppressed by the devil.'

We have thus a number of occupations which must have crowded upon our Lord at the time of which we are speaking, in addition to the care which He would certainly bestow upon the more close and personal training of those of His future Apostles who were already to some extent His habitual companions, as well as to the long hours which He was always wont to occupy in prayer and silent communion with His Father. All these considerations help us to understand the extreme laboriousness of His life at this time, and make it natural to suppose that a very large part indeed of the first year of His Ministry is abundantly accounted for in the simple statement that He went about preaching and teaching, and healing the sick, through the many well-populated towns and villages of the rich, fertile, and prosperous Galilee. To refer to the illustrations which have been already suggested, we should think it no inadequate account to give of nine or ten months of the active life of a great missionary preacher, to say that He spent a space of time of that kind in preaching from town to town through Tuscany, the March of Ancona, or the north of England. When we come to examine in detail the great monument of our Lord's teaching at this period which survives to us in the Sermon on the Mount, we shall find other reasons in abundance for supposing that it must have been addressed to an audience who had already become very familiar indeed with the distinctive principles of the Evangelical teaching, to an extent which can hardly be accounted for except on the supposition that our Lord had already spent many long months in raising at least a very large proportion of those who listened to Him to the high level of Christian intelligence which is taken for granted in that marvellous discourse.

We may also add that it is only natural to suppose that our Lord, in the arrangement of His preaching throughout a country such as Galilee, would choose the time of the year when it would be more convenient for the people to attend His ministrations in large masses, much as it is the custom with modern missionaries to take the months when there is less work to be done in the fields, and when the nights or evenings, which in many countries are the more usual time for the public services, are longer and less occupied. If our Lord, as seems likely, came into Galilee about the time of, or soon after, the feast of Pentecost, just before which the fields at Sychar would be 'white unto the harvest,' and if His missionary course began within two or three weeks of His arrival, He would then have before Him the long and usually fine and dry months up to the feast of Tabernacles in the autumn, a time when the people would be comparatively unoccupied in agriculture and other outdoor pursuits. This period might embrace about six months, a space of time which cannot certainly be considered as in any sense too long for what we are told by the Evangelists of the occupations of our Lord, although, as has already been said, a very few lines are enough to give the main divisions into which those occupations naturally fell. There is also some reason for thinking that the comparatively unoccupied time was longer in the particular year of our Lord's first preaching in Galilee than was usually the case. It has been argued with very great appearance of probability, that the year which seems most likely to have been the year in question was a Sabbatical year, or rather that a Sabbatical year, in which the land was allowed to lie fallow, began at the seed-time in the late autumn of this particular year. Thus the people would have had less occupation in that autumn and in the following spring than was usual, and would be more free to attend to such extraordinary religious opportunities as were afforded them by our Lord's missionary preaching throughout the country. It may be remembered, in connection with this suggestion, that our Lord, when in the synagogue at Nazareth, at the very outset of His course of preaching, applied to Himself the prophecy of Isaias, a part of which contains the words, 'To preach the acceptable year of the Lord, and the day of reward.' These words might seem more naturally to apply to a year of Jubilee than to an ordinary Sabbatical year, but they are at least applicable to the latter. It appears that the Jubilee, which was celebrated every fiftieth year, and which had so many great social advantages attached to it as well as so much spiritual meaning, was not celebrated after the return of the Jews from the Babylonian captivity.[7]

These considerations are enough to suggest the conclusion which has been already more than once stated, that we have now to enter on a period of our Lord's Life which was full of immense and varied activity, although, just as the greatest mysteries of the Faith are expressed in a few simple words, just as the great acts of God and our Lord in the Incarnation and in the economy of Redemption are stated for us in the Gospels with the utmost brevity, so also it is characteristic of Sacred Scripture to relate with the same brevity actions or series of actions of our Blessed Lord which filled a large space of time, and had results both in His own Life and in the after-life of the Church

[7] See Creswell, *On the Harmony of the Gospels*, vol. ii. diss. xxii. pp. 232—239.

which have been most momentous and most lasting in their influence.

The short and general description which the Evangelists give of the beginning of our Lord's preaching in Galilee is supplemented by St. Matthew in his characteristic manner by an application of the prophecy of Isaias.[8] The passage from which the Evangelist quotes is that which immediately precedes the great prophecy of the birth of our Lord, which is familiar to all Christians—'For a Child is born unto us, and a Son is given us,' and the rest. This prophecy is connected by Isaias, as it seems, with some of the circumstances of the conquest of Syria and the kingdom of Israel by the Assyrian King Theglathphalasar, when for the first time a part of the holy nation were transplanted, according to the policy of the Eastern conquerors, from their own country into Assyria itself, the captivity beginning with part of the tribes of Zabulon and Nephtali, to whom what was even then, as it seems, known as Galilee had been allotted. The historical particulars to which Isaias refers are naturally not very clear to us, and the text is obscure, but the point to which St. Matthew's application refers is easily ascertained. This is not the place for a full discussion of this famous prophecy of Isaias, but it is remarkable with regard to this prediction of the birth of a Child and the giving of a Son, which he introduces as a ground of consolation and hope under the calamities which were in his day falling upon the chosen nation, that his method appears to be exactly parallel to that which he seems also to have followed in the very similar and still more famous prophecy of the miraculous conception of our Lord in the womb of a Virgin, which occurs not long before this in the prophetic book, and

[8] Isaias ix. 1, seq.

which has also been quoted by St. Matthew in the first chapter of his Gospel. In both cases it seems that Isaias appeals to the existence of a well-known current of prophetical tradition as to the future coming of our Lord, the great King and Deliverer, as a reason against despondency and despair under the critical circumstances of the holy nation.

As to St. Matthew's use of the passage of Isaias, with which the ninth chapter of the Prophet opens, it is enough for his purpose to connect the rising of the great light with the truth announced in the same passage, that the part of the land which was to be the first on which the beams of that light were to shine was exactly that part which had been the first to suffer. The prophecy, then, as applied by St. Matthew, is in a certain manner a continuation of the series of predictions to which the Evangelist has referred in an earlier place in his Gospel, where he points out that our Lord's dwelling in Nazareth was the fulfilment of the prophecies which said that He should be called a Nazarene. 'Land of Zabulon and land of Nepthalim, the way of the sea beyond the Jordan, Galilee of the Gentiles, the people that sat in darkness hath seen great light, and to them that sat in the region of the shadow of death, light is sprung up.' This passage does not follow the Septuagint version, but it is an independent rendering of the Hebrew text, such as we meet with elsewhere in similar cases in St. Matthew. It may have been a familiar passage in the earlier teaching of the Apostles at Jerusalem, of which early teaching there are so many traces in the work of the first Evangelist, who must often, with the other Apostles, have had to answer objections brought by the Jews against the Galilæan preaching of our Lord. The words of Isaias enabled the Christian disputants to prove that the scene of our Lord's first and most protracted labours had already been fixed, like so many other particulars concerning Him, by the infallible word of God in prophecy. There was also another fitness in the words, inasmuch as they seem to have been in the mind of the Prophet of the New Testament, Zachary, father of St. John Baptist, who concludes his canticle concerning the Incarnation and his own son's part in the manifestation of the truth concerning it, in words which were based upon this very prophecy of Isaias, 'To give knowledge of salvation (or Jesus)[9] to His people, unto the remission of their sins, through the bowels of the mercy of our God, in which the Orient from on high hath visited us; to enlighten them that sit in darkness and in the shadow of death, and to guide our feet into the way of peace.' The Galilæan preaching, therefore, like the sojourn at Nazareth, had been the distinct choice of God, as well as the subject of definite prophecy, and as it had been predicted because it had been decreed, so now it was to be accomplished because it had been predicted.

[9] The Canticle of St. Zachary abounds with allusions to the names of persons concerned in the mystery to which it refers. In verses 72, 73 (St. Luke i.) the words 'to perform *mercy* to our forefathers, and to remember His holy *testament*, the *oath* which He swore to Abraham,' &c., seem suggested by the names John, Elisabeth, and Zacharias.

CHAPTER II.

Fishers of Men.

St. Matt. iv. 18—22 ; St. Mark i. 16—20; *Vita Vitæ Nostræ*, § 29.

It was a part of the counsel of Divine Providence as to the carrying out of His merciful designs in the dispensation of the Incarnation, that the great work of preaching the Gospel to the poor, in the fullest and largest sense of the words, was not to be committed to our Blessed Lord alone and to terminate with His Life upon earth, but to be an abiding and unfailing source of spiritual health, strength, and renovation in the Catholic Church which He came to found. Like everything else of which the divinely appointed system of the Church is made up, the work of this Ministry was to be founded and inaugurated by our Lord Himself, from Whom all its grace and power were to flow in unfailing streams of blessing over the whole world and throughout all the Christian ages, and He was to be not only the Founder of all missionary labours and the meritorious cause of their power and success, but also the perfect example to all those to whom such labours were afterwards to be entrusted, setting before them in the clearest lines and in ample detail the method which they were to pursue and the virtues which they were to practise, in order that their enterprise might have the full blessing of God the Father, and be perfectly pleasing to Him and salutary to their fellow-men.

In order that this rule of God's providence might be carried out, it was a part of the Divine plan that from the very beginning of the Gospel preaching, properly so called, our Lord should have with Him some at least of those who were afterwards to be the first Christian preachers and missionaries, who might thus not only study His character and teaching in general, or, again, make themselves His disciples in all that regarded their own training in spiritual perfection, but also, in particular, observe Him in His method of teaching and instructing, in the rules on which His own Apostolical life was framed, in the arrangement of the time and the order in which He attended to the several duties of His Ministry, in His ways of dealing with sinners, or souls in doubt as to matters of doctrine, or those who were desirous of a state of perfection, or the many other various classes of men who came to Him for the benefit of their souls. St. Peter, after our Lord's Ascension, when another Apostle was to be added by the suffrages of the faithful in the place of the traitor Judas, laid it down as a necessary condition that he should be one of those who had 'companied' with the rest, 'all the time that our Lord Jesus came in and went out amongst us, beginning from the baptism of John;' and although we may see in the laying down of this condition a special reference to the one great and immediate duty of the Apostles at that time, namely, to be witnesses of our Lord's Resurrection, we cannot doubt that familiarity with our Lord in His Apostolical life was also required on account of the more general work of the Apostolate which was to be carried on, after His example, by the Twelve. This familiarity would secure, not only a perfect imitation of our Lord's method and conduct in the Apostles and in the never-ending line of teachers of successive generations who were to carry on the same work after them, but also that knowledge of the details of our Lord's Life, considered as the main subject of Evangelical teaching, which furnished, as we may say, the materials for the original unwritten 'Gospel' concerning Him, out of which the narratives of the four Evangelists ultimately sprang, when the time came for the separation of the Apostolic band and for the continuance of the work by hundreds of teachers who had never known our Lord personally.

The small band of followers whom our Lord had originally gathered round Him on the banks of the Jordan after His return from the mountainous desert which had been the scene of the Temptation, had, as has been said, accompanied Him to Galilee when He went to be present at the marriage-feast at Cana, and had then returned with Him southwards to Jerusalem for the feast of the Pasch, after which they had remained with Him in the territory of Judæa baptizing under His orders, until the short interval had passed which was to elapse before His return into Galilee through Samaria. They were probably with Him at the time of the healing of the nobleman's son who was sick at Capharnaum, but do not appear to have accompanied Him in that short visit to Nazareth, which issued in His humiliating rejection by His own townsfolk, and the savage attempt of the latter to put Him to death. Thus, when our Lord returned, after that Sabbath-day, to Capharnaum, He may have had no immediate companions with Him but His Blessed Mother and some of His cousins, who are known in the Gospel history as His brethren. But the future Apostles may have been perfectly aware that they might at any moment be called upon to join Him in some new enterprise for the glory of God and the benefit of souls. He had already spoken to them about the fields being white unto harvest, and about their own future mission as the harvesters in the Kingdom of God. They could not doubt that He was about to begin a new course of immense and laborious activity, and that they themselves would be called upon to bear their part in it. Meanwhile they fell back upon the ordinary duties of their callings and on their homes.

The manly industrious habits to which the Jews were trained are well known : every one had some handicraft or occupation, and we find St. Paul in the midst of his Apostolical preaching making a special point of supporting himself with the labour of his own hands. It was a part of the work of the Church in the world to elevate and to dignify labour, thus at once to cut at the root of the infinite miseries which flow from the luxurious idleness of large classes of men, and to guard society against the dissolving and disintegrating effects of the separation between wealth and industry, work and rank. The comparatively healthy state in this respect of the Jewish nation, scattered as it was over the world, was one of the elements of its condition which fitted it to be the leaven by means of which, in the hands of the Church, the whole mass of society was to be regenerated. The Christian system was to be, in a certain sense, eminently hierarchial and aristocratic, but the aristocracy, both ecclesiastical and social, was to be entirely open, or rather, the entire openness of the very highest grades of ecclesiastical dignity to men of every class and rank, was to work most beneficially, along with other kindred features in the Church system, by way of example as well as of direct influence, upon secular society as such. There is nothing in the history of our Lord's time to show us that the simple frugal artisan, peasant, fisherman, or carpenter, was looked down upon among the chosen people, though the Courts of the Herodian princes, apeing the traditions and customs of the Roman masters of the world, may to some extent have introduced a false standard, while, on the other hand, the want of regular training and sacerdotal learning in our Lord was objected to by His enemies as a ground for denying confidence to His teaching. This, again, does not imply that the mass of the people were ignorant of their religion and its obligations, but only that the peculiar learning which was considered necessary in a teacher of the Law was not to be acquired, in the ordinary way, save in the schools at Jerusalem. The ordinary religious and moral duties, the Commandments of God, the promises of the Law and the Prophets, were probably well possessed by Jews of all classes and ranks, and, as it was out of these that the Christian system of religious obligations and observances was to be developed by our Lord, there is nothing that need surprise us in the selection which He made in the case of the four Apostles, who are now to be specially mentioned as called by Him to be His companions and witnesses in the course of popular instruction and preaching on which He was now about to enter.

We are not told how long the interval had been which had passed since our Lord had taken leave for a time of His companions in order to pay the visit to Nazareth, of which so much has been said. It was probably immediately on His return to Capharnaum that He summoned them to His side in the simple and wonderful manner of which the Evangelists tell us. He was walking on the shore of the Sea of Galilee when 'He saw two brothers, Simon and Andrew,' now first mentioned by the two Evangelists who relate the incident, 'casting a net into the sea, for they were fishermen. And Jesus said to them, Come after Me, and I will make you to become fishers of men. And immediately, leaving their nets, they followed Him. And going on a little from them, He saw two other brothers, James the son of Zebedee and John his brother, and they also were arranging or repairing their nets in a boat, with Zebedee their father. And He called them straightway, and they at once left their father Zebedee in the boat with the servants, and followed Him.'[1]

The simple words in which our Lord called these four Apostles on this occasion are very general in their sense, and may imply a call, either permanent or temporary, to a companionship and following of our Lord of almost any degree of closeness. They are perhaps in themselves not so strong in meaning as the 'Follow Me,' which our Lord had already addressed to St. Philip on the very first occasion of their meeting, and which He afterwards used in inviting others to join Him, as St. Matthew himself and the rich young man who asked Him about perfection.[2] Yet the invitation to St. Philip does not seem to have implied at the time that unceasing and permanent following of our Lord to which the Apostles were not called until a much later date, and the same may be said of the call given to St. Matthew. The command here given was evidently for a special purpose, and when that purpose was satisfied, it is natural to suppose that the four disciples mentioned in the passage before us would return, as before, to their ordinary occupations, waiting for another call, whenever it pleased our Lord to give it to them. We may gather, with perfect security, from the place which the call of the four occupies in the two Gospels of St. Matthew and St. Mark, that they were now invited to join our Lord in the course of missionary preaching which He was about to begin.

---

[1] St. Matt. iv. 18—22; St. Mark i. 16—20.
[2] St. John i. 43; St. Matt. ix. 9; xix. 21.

This, indeed, is implied in, as it also explains, the use which our Lord made of the occupation in which He found them engaged. Not only were they fishermen by trade, owning, as it seems, more than one boat in partnership, and having several men under them in their employ, but they were actually at work with their nets, either casting them into the sea or preparing them for use. Their fishing, therefore, was going on when our Lord appeared on the shore, and now He was about to begin that fishery of souls, which was one great end of His Incarnation and Mission, and He bade them come after Him and learn to be fit workers in this great enterprise for the glory of His Father. He does not say at once that they are to fish for men, but that He will make them become fishers of men, by the example He was about to set them, and the grace and vocation which He would in His own good time bestow upon them. It was always His method to take the things that were before His eyes and use them as occasions of instruction, and as suggesting the imagery in which He would clothe what He wished to say, and so He now calls these four fishermen to witness and take a certain part in the spiritual work which was in many respects so well pictured by the humble occupations in which they had spent so much of their time.

Catholic writers have found many beautiful lines of thought in this comparison by our Lord of the spiritual work of the preacher among souls to the craft of the fisherman, just as the image of the shepherd and the sheep, as used in the same or nearly the same connection, has led to many devout and touching contemplations. The fisherman's business, in the first place, is one that is carried on amid much danger, or rather, it is always not far from danger, and sometimes and unexpectedly in the midst of it. It teaches, or ought to teach, that dependence on God and that sense of His nearness on every side which is one of the conditions of all Apostolical labour. One of the Psalms which are supposed to have reference to the deliverance of the people from the Babylonian captivity (cvi.), uses the danger of the sea as one of a series of parables in a way which has been used to illustrate this thought—

> They who go down to the sea in ships,
> And carry on works upon the mighty waters,
> These men have seen the works of the Lord,
> And His wonders in the abyss.
> He spake, and commissioned a strong wind,
> And it lifted on high His billows,
> They mounted up to the sky, they went adown the depths,
> Their soul in evil plight melted away.
> They reeled and staggered as a drunken man,
> And all their wisdom was swallowed up.
> And they cried unto the Lord when they were in trouble,
> And He brought them out of their distresses ;
> He stayed the storm into a soft breath,
> And their billows were quiet.
> Thus were they glad because they were in calm,
> And He brought them to their longed-for haven.[3]

Thus the work of Christian preaching is essentially a work which, if it is to be greatly successful, must be carried on, not, as it were, on a smooth and sunny sea, without any opposition or contradiction, but amid storms and tempests, such as of their own force and might are far more than enough to overwhelm those who hazard themselves in the undertaking. The passions of men, the ties and habits of sins, the maxims and unavowed principles of the world, self-love, ease, sensuality, whether of the grosser or more refined sort, are all in truth arrayed against the Christian preacher, and they are lashed up to furious hostility by the powers of evil, who are ever on the watch against the resolute and single-

---

[3] Psalm cvi. (cvii.) 23—30 (Kay's Translation).

hearted teacher of the Gospel. Their opposition is a sign of good because it shows that they are afraid of losing their prey, so much so that it may ordinarily be said that where there are few difficulties there may be but little fruit. St. Paul expresses this truth in the last chapter of his Epistle to the Ephesians, in the celebrated passage about the armour of God, which seems to be addressed in particular to the priests and other teachers of the Church. 'Our wrestling is not against flesh and blood, but against principalities and powers, against the rulers of the world of this darkness, against the spirits of wickedness in the high places.'[4] And the happy issue out of the storm depends not upon their own skill, prudence, or intelligence, so much as upon their prayer to God and their confidence in Him, and when they have been brought 'adown the depths,' as the Psalmist says, 'and all their wisdom swallowed up,' then God stays the storm, and they see His wonderful works, for in His strength they overcome cruel tyrants, they put a rein upon enemies, they melt the hard-hearted to tears, they bring the incontinent back to angelic purity, the fierce and savage to meekness and the proud to humility.[5]

To this entire dependence upon and constant recourse to God in the Christian preacher, another means of securing success must be added which has its parallel in the fisherman's art. He is obliged to be a careful observer and student of nature, of weather, wind, the changes of temperature, and the like: he must know the tides, he must be acquainted with the lie of the coast and the direction of the currents, the place where the fish are to be sought, the times when they are likely to be caught, and so on. All these particulars of weather wisdom and practical experience ought to have their

---

[4] Ephes. vi. 12, seq. [5] Sylveira, ad l. t. ii. l. 8, c. 8.

counterparts in that knowledge of men and of their dispositions, and of the times when they may be favourably addressed with the Word of God, with which the preacher of the Gospel must furnish himself, partly by study, but most of all by practice and familiarity with men of various classes and characters. He is to labour in gaining and using knowledge and skill of this kind, as if the whole success of his work depended upon himself, at the same time that he is trusting entirely to God, and looking to Him alone for the fruitfulness of the enterprise.

Again, the author of the commentary on St. Matthew which goes by the name of the *Opus Imperfectum*, and which has been wrongly attributed to St. Chrysostom, mentions another particular in which the image of which we are speaking has a fitness of its own. The hunter, he says, singles out his prey, a certain deer or other animal, and follows it on and on until he makes himself its master, but the fisherman casts his net as it were at random into the waters, not knowing what may be within his reach, and is content with whatever fish Providence may send into his way. The work of the Christian preacher is much of the same character, he does not aim at one person in particular, but at classes and masses of men, he scatters the Word of God broadcast, as the sower his seed, expecting that in many cases it will be wasted, or stifled, or only half fruitful, but that in some souls, he knows not who or which, it will light upon good soil. Here again is an occasion for dependence upon God, inasmuch as there may indeed be skill in preparing the net or the bait, and in casting them opportunely, but, as to the particular souls who are to be the prey of the Christian fisherman, he must rely entirely upon the merciful goodness of God. Nor, again, is it without its significance in the explanation of the parallel which our Lord's words suggest, that the fish are taken in the net perforce and against their will, or swallow the bait under the false idea of its innocence and pleasantness. Not that men can be in truth brought to God against their will, but that on the part of those whose duty it is to lead them to God they are to be approached as tenderly and even as craftily as if they might be expected to turn away from the Word of God, unless it be presented to them with all possible attractiveness and with nothing about it that can scare them.

Leaving aside other considerations which have been suggested by Christian writers as to the parallel between the labours of the Evangelical preacher and the industrious and simple fishermen whom our Lord called from their nets, we may dwell for a moment on the prompt and absolute obedience with which the Apostles met the call which was made upon them. This is particularly specified in the narrative of the Evangelists: indeed, it is the single feature on which they dwell. No one can suppose that the readiness with which the disciples obeyed our Lord had in it anything that was unreasonable or excessive, or that it came from enthusiasm and impulse rather than from a sense of duty. They had already seen enough of our Lord, their notions concerning Him were already high enough, even if they had not as yet risen to the perfect faith in His Divine Person which was afterwards required of them, for them to understand that His Word was to be law to them as representing to them the voice of God His Father. They had returned to their homes and to their ordinary occupations after the sojourn in Judæa and the journey through Samaria at His bidding, and because it was not as yet the will of God that they should enter in an altogether new course of life. Their duties were there unless He called them away for a special purpose, and when He did so, their duties were with Him. Nor, as we shall see, are we to suppose that He now called them away never to return to their homes, as if they were never again to occupy themselves as fishermen, or, in the case of the sons of Zebedee, never again to attend to their father, or in the case of Peter and perhaps Andrew, never again to live with their wives and families. The call was a call to a particular and determinate mission, and it was above all things to be characteristic of such calls in the Kingdom of God that they should be made by authority, received with prompt obedience, and obeyed with alacrity and perfect detachment from all human ties and claims. It may have been on this account that our Lord did not enforce the authority of His call by any miraculous display of power, as it would certainly have been an imperfect manner of obeying such a call if the disciples had hesitated, or reasoned, or asked questions, or pleaded excuses, however valid, for delay, or if it had been necessary to enforce the duty of obedience upon them by a miracle. Nothing can be the true foundation of such a special call as this but the direct will of God, brought home to the personal conscience of each one who is called in some one of those many ways which God uses in revealing to us what He desires of us at a particular time. Nothing can secure the blessing of God and the prosperous issue of the work to which men are in this manner invited to the same extent as prompt, immediate, unquestioning obedience, the obedience which puts everything aside, leaves everything undone, and does not stop to bid adieu, or turn to the right hand or to the left, the instant that the conscience recognizes the flash of Divine light or the sound of the voice

of Jesus Christ enjoining this or that as the service
which He immediately requires.

It must also be remembered, in estimating the
promptness and perfection of the obedience of the disciples, that there were many considerations which might
have held them back quite as forcibly as that attachment
to home and family, to the claims of father and mother,
or wife or children, which naturally suggests itself as the
chief motive for hesitation under such circumstances.
We need not doubt that these last-named motives would
have made themselves felt upon simple, affectionate
hearts, such as those of the four disciples ; and again,
although as yet there had been no very formidable
demonstrations of opposition against our Lord on the
part of the authorities, whether ecclesiastical or secular,
still the recent imprisonment of St. John Baptist, of
which the news must just have become public, may have
made it certain that our Lord Himself, and any who
might become His close followers, would be watched
with suspicion, and that no scruple would restrain such
a ruler as Herod Antipas from any act of violence which
he might deem expedient. But the ties of home affection
and the possible dangers of the new enterprise, could
hardly weigh so forcibly on the minds of Simon and his
companions as the humble sense of their own unfitness
to become the teachers of others, the associates of a
prophet such as our Lord. He called them not only to
hardships and labours and dangers, but to honour, to the
highest task that can be imposed upon man—a task
which He, indeed, might discharge without having need
of the usual training and learning, but for which the
disciples must have felt themselves to be manifestly and
even hopelessly disqualified. The higher their notions
of the Gospel and the new Kingdom, which was now
to be proclaimed, the more would they feel their own

insufficiency to be its ambassadors. The more perfect their understanding of the dignity of our Lord's Person, the less possible might it seem to them that they should be the men to take a part in His work, and be set as teachers over the multitudes whom they hoped to see become, like themselves, His disciples.

Thus their obedience was an act of the highest confidence in Him, as well of simple submission to His will, and it becomes the pattern of the obedience of those who, feeling most deeply their own utter incapacity for the more laborious and important duties in the Church, such as those of government, of preaching the Word of God to large multitudes, of conducting controversies with the heretics of the day, and the like, yet enter upon them in the simple serene trust that He Who calls them to a work so far above them will also supply them with the graces which are adequate to its perfect accomplishment. Diffidence, pusillanimity, timidity, to be content with low aims and paltry designs, when the glory of God is concerned, as if anything was really great or difficult to Him, or as if He could not work out the greatest results by means of the feeblest instruments—these and other defects of the same kind are rebuked by the simple and generous faith with which the four disciples put themselves at once at our Lord's disposal, even though He called them to an office of which they felt themselves so entirely unworthy. For many a soul which will not shrink from suffering and danger is still afraid of responsibility and the risks of a position of authority, to be ambitious of which is indeed a manifest proof of unfitness, while to shrink from it when it is put upon us by the clearly declared will of God, may be almost as inconsistent as ambition itself with perfect humility.

Holy writers have often insisted upon the one circumstance in these four disciples which is particularly mentioned by the Evangelist, and which certainly must be supposed to have had its influence in attracting our Lord's choice to them—the brotherly love which existed between Simon and Andrew, James and John, and the intimacy which seems also to have knit together the two pairs of brethren. We can imagine no other way in which our Lord could have more significantly shown that He required the closest charity and union of hearts and minds among those whom He called to His service, at the very time that He was showing by the call which He gave them that He insisted also on the renunciation of home and kinsfolk, and even of the most imperative duties of the natural order, when His service or His will demanded it. The holy brotherhood of the Apostolical band was not yet formed, and could not be formed until its members had lived and toiled together in the company of Him Whose ineffable and entrancing charity was to be its life. The tie between Simon and Andrew, and between the two sons of Zebedee, was in origin and principle only natural, but this our Lord could take as a beginning, He could refine and elevate it and spiritualize it, until nothing remained that was merely of earth, while every element of beauty and tenderness and union had been transformed into the pure gold of heavenly charity. Brotherly or sisterly love is in some respects the most perfect natural representation of the love that is to bind together the children of the Heavenly Father in His Kingdom, and, when our Lord chose His first followers, He showed His designs as to the one by letting His preference fall upon the other. And He did this, not so much at the first moment when He received any of His disciples, as at the time when He invited some few of His disciples to witness and share in the great work of the conversion of souls. For charity is not only the law of His Kingdom

in general, the condition of true life therein, and even
the outward badge by which the world is to know who
are His disciples. It is, still more, the essential condition
of all Evangelical success and fruitfulness in spiritual
enterprises, which can have no blessing upon them,
however ardent the zeal which prompts them, however
strong the faith in which they are carried on, if the
spirit of division is there to blight them, whether it be
that of the schism which separates whole bodies of
Christians from the centre of unity, or of the discord
which raises a cloud between workers who ought to
be perfectly united in heart and soul, in the aims and
the manner with which they carry on the work of God,
Who is charity.

CHAPTER III.

The Synagogue at Capharnaum.

St. Mark i. 21—34; St. Luke iv. 31—41 (comp. St. Matt. viii. 14—19);
Vita Vitæ Nostræ, § 30.

IT can hardly be by an accident that we have an
almost full account of one day, and, as far as we know,
of one day only, of the many weeks and months which
our Blessed Lord spent in His public preaching in
Galilee. At least, the account given us by St. Mark
and St. Luke, at the very opening of their general
narrative as to that preaching, of a Sabbath-day at
Capharnaum, which appears to have followed immediately on the call of the four disciples from their nets
to become our Lord's companions, seems as if it were
intended to give us a general idea of the manner in

which our Lord's days of teaching were spent. It is
remarkable also, that as St. Luke has placed it, it comes
so immediately after the history of so very different a
Sabbath-day at Nazareth, as to appear to be almost
intentionally contrasted with that. The Sabbath at
Nazareth had begun, indeed, brightly and hopefully.
The townsfolk of our Lord had assembled with joy in
the synagogue of the place, and He had expounded
to them, in the sweetest and most winning manner,
one of the most beautiful of the prophecies, even of
the Evangelical Prophet, concerning Himself and the
work of mercy, compassion, and grace which He was
sent to accomplish. But it was not the will of the
Father that He should conciliate the Nazarenes on
their own terms, but rather that He should begin
His public Galilæan teaching by a singular and marvellous humiliation which seemed to threaten even His
life. He was sent to preach and work miracles at
Capharnaum, not at Nazareth, and the only wonder
which He was to perform at the place where He had
lived for so many years in the practice of the most
sublime virtues, far more marvellous and precious in
the eyes of Heaven than external miracles of power,
was to be the saving of Himself from the hands of His
would-be murderers.

But the will of His Father now sent Him to Capharnaum, as Elias had been sent to Sarepta, and Eliseus
commissioned to heal Naaman, and at this chosen spot,
which for a time was to be exalted to Heaven by His
presence, teaching, and wonderful works, there was also
to be an outpouring of grace which was to prepare the
hearts of His hearers to listen to Him, and to work
together with His words to produce in them the
fruits of conversion and sanctification. We may fairly
consider, as has been said, that the incidents of this

Sabbath in Capharnaum were such as were continually happening there and in other places while He
was in the course of His preaching through the
country. This service in the synagogue seems to
have been in the morning, though the building was
used for private prayer at any hour of the day. The
building itself, as we learn from a later statement of
St. Luke, had been raised for the people by the munificence of a Gentile officer, one of those simple, upright,
and pious souls among the heathen whom a knowledge
of the Jewish law and customs had attracted to the
true religion, and who was afterwards to be the person
at whose prayer one of our Lord's most splendid
miracles was to be wrought. Synagogues were often built
just outside the towns, in order to avoid defilement,
and near some water, as here, perhaps, close to the shore
of the lake, on account of the habit of purificatory
ablutions which was a part of the ceremonial law. The
arrangements and administration were very simple, and
are interesting to us on their own account, and also as
having apparently suggested some of the details of the
system of the Christian Church.[1] On the occasion of
which we are now speaking, there would be many
in the synagogue who knew and were well disposed to
our Lord. There was the nobleman with his family,
who had become or were to become believers in our
Lord in consequence of the miracle of the cure of the
youth related in a former chapter. And we cannot doubt
that this wonderful cure had become widely known in
the town during the few days which had since passed,
and that many devout families were eager to see and
hear the Prophet Whose words had been so powerful
over disease, even at a distance. Our Blessed Lady
would be there, seated with the rest of the women

[1] See Sepp, *Leben Jesu*, p. 2, § 2, c. 13.

apart from the men, and there were the families of Peter and Andrew, James and John, and some others who had already become our Lord's disciples. The 'ruler of the synagogue,' to be mentioned later on as imploring our Lord's miraculous aid for his daughter, must have been in the audience, and it is difficult to suppose that the good publican, Matthew, was not present, especially as he selects so many of the incidents of this day for mention in that part of his Gospel in which he gives a chain of miracles of various kinds, as specimens of the wonderful works with which our Lord confirmed His teaching.

The freedom which seems to have been one of the customs of the Synagogue, and in consequence of which not our Lord alone, but His Apostles after Him, found no difficulty, at all events at first, in taking on them the office of public teachers, or expounders of the Law, is at first sight rather surprising to us. But it must be remembered that the liberty of teaching was extended to them in the character of Rabbis, and that these could not have been very numerous. It is, however, natural to suppose that in the synagogues, as in the Temple at Jerusalem, our Lord took upon Himself the authority of Teacher with that simple dignity and majesty which belonged to Him, and that there was something about His whole air and bearing which impressed all who came across Him with reverence, and made it impossible for them to question or resist Him. There is much in what we know of the indefinable influence of high sanctity—even in the degree in which it is found among those who fall immeasurably short of our Lord's holiness—which may account for the universal deference with which our Lord seems to have been received, even by officials and persons in authority, and this too, not only in the earlier stages of His career of preaching, when as yet there was no very decided or authorized opposition to Him, but when He transferred the scene of His labours from Galilee to Judæa, and so was more continually in the neighbourhood of the highest ecclesiastical authorities, who at that time had already made up their minds to His destruction. There is, no doubt, a spell and charm about sanctity which is felt by all those whose hearts are not entirely dead to good : such a spell was felt by Pilate at the time of the Passion, though not by the utterly frivolous and licentious Herod. In the case of our Lord's teaching in the synagogue and in the Temple, there was more than this, for He acted as Master and Lord in the house of His Father, and the majesty of His demeanour answered to the authority of His teaching. He never hesitated to act as possessing supreme power in all matters of religion, and we cannot doubt that this was among the features of His conduct which the Apostles observed and came to understand, as portions of the evidence on which was built up, by the silent teaching of the Father in His providence, their faith as to the Divine Person of His Incarnate Son. And it is not at all unnatural to suppose that the courtesy with which our Lord was always allowed to teach in the synagogues went in some degree beyond the usual deference which was shown to any Rabbi who might happen to come as a stranger into a Jewish town on the Sabbath-day, and that the dignity conferred upon His Sacred Humanity by its Hypostatic Union with the Ineffable Godhead of the Son made itself felt in imposing awe and reverence upon those who might otherwise have had the power of preventing much of His public teaching.

We must take into account the same wonderful influence of high sanctity, raised as it was in our Blessed Lord, even in His Human Nature, to the very loftiest conceivable pitch, in endeavouring to form an estimate of the effect of His preaching. We have it on record on the authority of the officials of the Temple, who on one occasion were sent by the authorities to seize Him, that 'never did man speak like this Man.'[2] The words may be understood as expressing a truth which those who uttered them did not dream of; for our Lord was more than man, and no man, not even the holiest, could speak as He spake. Here, again, we may form some idea, though inadequate, of our Lord's speaking, from what we know of the effect of the words of those who are nearest and most like to Him of all who have the office of speaking in His Name in the Church; we mean, the great Saints. The Church is continually adorned by her Divine Spouse both with holy doctors, whose office it is to hand on, to illustrate, and to unfold into new light the precious deposit of Catholic theology, in accordance with the needs and character of successive generations, and with famous preachers and missionaries, who have in its highest perfection the gift of sacred eloquence, cultivated by study and practice, and enforced by holy learning and the exercises of the spiritual life. In its largest sense, the ministry of the Word of God is almost the chiefest among the weapons of the Church, and Providence supplies her with a succession of men highly graced, both naturally and supernaturally, for the needs of this ministry, while, at the same time, a fruitfulness waits upon those who loyally and devotedly labour in this most difficult and even dangerous field, which cannot be accounted for save by the special outpouring of grace upon those to Whom the word is addressed. Experience shows that the highest flights of eloquence and the noblest gifts of persuasion are comparatively useless, when there is not holiness of life as well as

[2] St. John vii. 46.

orthodoxy of doctrine and due mission from authority to enforce the words of the speaker.

But over and beyond this, holiness has a power of its own which seems to dispense with any need of ordinary Christian eloquence of a very high rank. There are constantly instances in the Church of simple men of very mortified lives, who are very closely united to God and with their hearts on fire with love to Him, who are even deficient and halting in speech, who can hardly put two sentences together in perfect grammatical sequence, and whose words, if taken down and separated from the burning heart which breathes them forth, seem commonplace and inefficient indeed: and yet these are the men, a few words from whom melt the hard-hearted sinner to penitence, scatter the clouds of temptation, resolve the doubts of the hesitating, pour balm into the hearts of mourners, inspire the pusillanimous with the courage necessary for great spiritual enterprises, and even dissipate the prejudices and answer the objections of controversial cavillers. Such men bring the forces of the supernatural world to bear closely upon the hearts of all those whom they come across with a power which belongs to holiness alone. Their words are a sort of manifestation of God; but this is because they are their words, and in any mouths but theirs they would often, as has been said, seem even inadequate and poor as expressions of doctrine or as appeals to feeling. If such is the unquestionable prerogative of holiness, even when enshrined in the outwardly miserable garb of some poor country Curé or some simple friar of St. Francis, how much greater must have been the force of the words concerning the value of the soul and the duty of loving and serving God which came straight from the furnace of the Sacred Heart of our Lord Jesus Christ, when He was discharging the office for which He was specially set apart and sent—of giving 'light to those who sit in darkness and in the shadow of death, and of guiding their feet into the way of peace'?

We know, certainly, that all the words of our Divine Lord were 'the words of eternal life,' as St. Peter said, but we may perhaps see in the fact that so few of them in comparison have been preserved to us, and that of those few there are hardly any that can be called the words of a preacher as distinguished from the words of a Teacher, a witness to the truth of which we are now speaking. The words came forth from our Lord's lips with a power and a life which belonged to them because they were His, because they were first conceived in the Heart of ineffable Holiness and were the vehicles of the thoughts of the Soul which was the Soul of the Incarnate Son, and which, from the very first moment of its existence, had beheld the clear vision of God and had been inflamed with love for Him, and for man for His sake, in comparison with which the most rapturous affections of the highest Seraphim are as cold as ice. The whole energies of the Sacred Humanity were at that time bent to the great work of moving men to the love of His Father, and it is no wonder if the simplest, commonest words in His mouth had the might and efficacy which corresponded to the Person of Him Who spake them. Thus the Evangelists, with regard to all this course of preaching, in the simple sense of the term, content themselves with stating the fact that He preached, instead of telling us what He said. The records which they have handed down to us refer to special heads of doctrine which, as being peculiarly His own, were to be the foundations of all Christian teaching, doctrinal and moral, in the Church after Him.

The Evangelists, who do not tell us of the particulars of our Lord's teaching except in the cases just now mentioned, add in this place a feature as to the manner of His teaching which struck all His hearers, and which has continued ever since as a characteristic of His Church, which has inherited His work and represents Him in the world. 'They were astonished at his doctrine. For he was teaching them as one having power (or authority), and not as the Scribes.'[3] We have here an indication of the recognized presence in our Lord of something higher than influence, however great. To the influence of His wonderful sanctity was added the incommunicable and subduing force of evident inherent authority. He did not merely persuade, or convince, or win, or fascinate, but He commanded. His word was the word of a Lord, and whether in the domain of truth which was to be believed, or of duty and law to be acknowledged and obeyed, He spoke with authority which challenged faith and obedience as its correlatives. There are many ways in which the words of the Evangelists may be understood in which they are true in themselves, but do not quite rise to the full height of this meaning. It is true, for instance, that the teaching of the Scribes consisted mainly in the quoting the opinions of this or that great Rabbi, of past or present times, or in reasoning and drawing conclusions from the words of the Law. Even His prophets had spoken in the name of God, and not in their own. Our Lord did not quote authorities, and though He sometimes, especially in His disputations, referred His adversaries to the words of the Holy Scriptures, He spake as their

---

[3] St. Mark i. 22 ; St. Luke iv. 32. In both these places, as in the parallel passage in St. Matthew vii. 22, the Greek word used for power or authority is ἐξουσία. The proper English equivalent is 'authority' rather than power.

authentic interpreter, not merely as a doctor arguing from them. Again, our Lord's word was certainly confirmed and authenticated by His marvellous miracles, just as afterwards the witness of His Apostles was confirmed by the signs which our Lord had promised them. Again, it is true that our Lord spoke and taught and acted with the utmost independence and liberty, that, even though He would accept of hospitality, or allow of contributions for the sustenance of Himself and His disciples, He never did this so as to make Himself the servant of any man, or to be bound by the obligations under which He had placed Himself to spare reproof or admonition wherever it was needed. Again, His very humility and simplicity gave Him an unearthly power, and still further, His teaching was always enforced by His own example and conduct, inasmuch as He taught nothing which He did not first Himself practise.

All these are circumstances which, as we cannot doubt, enhanced the effect and the influence of our Lord's teaching; but, except that mentioned in the first place, they were features which might have been found in prophets and saints who had not the inherent authority which our Lord possessed. Indeed, other teachers, whose mission was only an ordinary mission, may also have shared that wonderful power over the hearts of men and of winning them grace to accomplish what they are taught which fulfils the words of the Evangelists in another sense also. All this, however, is not enough for their meaning as applied to our Lord; and we must consider that they are intended to point out a new manifestation of our Lord's character and office, arranged and decreed by the providence of His Father, and implying nothing less than that inherent sovereignty in the whole field of truth and duty, as being Himself the Way and the Truth and the Life, which we have already seen Him exercising in His private discourses with Nicodemus and the Samaritan woman, as well as in His early conversations with His future Apostles.

It must be remembered, both that the extraordinary messengers of God, who had been sent from time to time to the chosen people, had a right to speak authoritatively in His name, and also that the ordinary teachers and ecclesiastical rulers of the Jews had an official right to the obedience and respect of the people, inasmuch as, in our Lord's own words, they sat 'in the seat of Moses.' The notion of authoritative teaching was not therefore new to the Jews. They had always had teachers whose words came to them, on certain subjects, from God, and in this respect they were on a level which raised them indefinitely above the most enlightened of the heathen, whose philosophers could only argue and reason and conclude, their person and office adding no weight to the intrinsic power of their words. Still, between our Lord and the Scribes there was an immense difference in this respect, a difference which was evident on the face of His teaching, and which at once struck the people with wonder. For now had come about that of which the Apostle speaks to the Hebrews, that ' God, Who at sundry times and in divers manners spoke in times past unto the fathers by the prophets, last of all in these days hath spoken to us by His Son, Whom He hath appointed heir of all things, by Whom also He made the world.'[4] The same Apostle contrasts our Lord in point of authority even with Moses. ' Every house,' he says, ' is built by some man, but He that created all things is God. And Moses, indeed, was faithful in all his house as a servant, for a testimony of those things which were to be said. But Christ as the Son in His own house.'[5]

<hr>

[4] Hebrews i. 1, 2.　　　[5] Hebrews iii. 5, 6.

This is more than to hand on, even authoritatively, a tradition, or to teach faithfully the letter of a written law, though to the office of those whose duty it is to do this corresponds, on the part of those who are placed under their teaching, the duty of obeying them. But the Synagogue never undertook to decide all questions as they arose, and constantly left matters unsettled until a prophet should arise or until the Messias should come. When our Lord came, He at once taught with all the authority of the Lawgiver Himself, expounding this point or developing that, fulfilling, as He Himself said, the Law, in the amplest sense of the words, laying down maxims of perfection and rules of life which went far beyond anything that had been handed down from of old. And whereas the Scribes and Pharisees could go no further than to claim obedience for what they taught because so it was written or so it had been handed down by the traditions of the Synagogue, our Lord distinctly rested the duty of faith and obedience to what He declared and taught on the inherent authority of His own Person. Others taught with a derived and limited authority, He spoke as Himself, of right, the Teacher and Master and Lawgiver, the Truth and the Life. The authority and power with which His Sacred Humanity was invested were the authority and power of God, because they flowed from the dignity of His Divine Person. He could condescend to become Man like those whom He was to save and to teach, because so the condition of their nature required that, as the Prophet had said, 'their eyes should see their Teacher, and their ears should hear the voice of one admonishing them,'[6] that He should make Himself cognizable to their senses, address them in their own language, speak to them as one who was in everything like themselves—sin only

<hr>

[6] Isaias xxx. 20, 21.

excepted—and so could sympathize with as well as understand the feebleness of the created nature which was His as well as theirs. But He could not speak with less authority than belonged to Him, with hesitancy, or uncertainty, or ignorance, or fallibility, even if there had not been, in the wants of the nature which He came to heal and to elevate, a call on the mercy of God to grant it a Teacher Who could not err, nor deceive, nor be ignorant.

It need hardly be added that this doctrine does not contradict that of the perfect obedience of our Lord, or of that entire dependence, in all that He did and said in His Human Nature, on the will of the Eternal Father, of which He so often spoke to His Jewish enemies. Thus when He came to dispute with the ecclesiastics at Jerusalem about what He taught, He declared indeed that He did nothing but what the Father showed Him, that He spoke as He heard, that His words were not His, but His Father's. But in this He referred to His relation to His Eternal Father, Who, as He said, had 'sanctified Him and sent Him into the world,' and it belonged alike to the dignity of His Person and the conditions of His Mission that He should speak and teach in His own Name and on His own authority; nor did He ever for an instant put Himself on a level even with the prophets and lawgivers of old, much less with the ordinary teachers of the Synagogue, who were to be listened to and obeyed because they inherited to some extent the *magisterium* which had been confided to Moses.

It follows from this that in His teaching, as in the rest of His conduct, for example, in His miracles, our Lord appealed to and exacted the faith of His hearers in Himself. From the very beginning of His Ministry He taught and laid down the Law and interpreted the former revelations and declarations of God in a manner which appealed to and required faith. There were indeed His miracles, and the witness of St. John Baptist, and the witness of His Father, for Him to appeal to ; that is, there were ample reasons to justify that faith in His hearers which He required. But the great warrant for His words and His teaching lay in Himself. On the other hand, the blessings which were thus bestowed on conditions of faith were absolutely inestimable. St. Matthew applies, as we have seen, to the teaching of our Lord the expressions of the Prophet about the 'great light' which was to dawn upon the people that were sitting in darkness and in the shadow of death. And surely no image can more truly express the value of the new revelation concerning God and His ways, concerning the duties of man and the path which he has to follow in order to attain perfection, his relations to God as his Father, and the spiritual riches of the Kingdom of which he is made the heir. The same Evangelist places his remark, as to the wonder of the people at the authority with which our Lord taught, after the conclusion of his account of the Sermon on the Mount. That wonderful sermon is a specimen, then, of the treasures of spiritual doctrine which were poured forth for the benefit of the faithful by our Lord at this time, and which come to us, not only in all their intrinsic beauty and heavenly sublimity, as the speculations and theories of a philosopher of the highest wisdom, but stamped with the royal sanction of the Incarnate Son of God, legislating for the new Kingdom which He had been sent upon earth to found. There is the same mark of authority about the teaching of the Parables, and again, of the counsels of perfection, which are given by the same Evangelist in a later portion of his Gospel. Just as those altogether misunderstand the character and office of our Lord who consider Him only as the most perfect specimen of virtue and excellence of every kind, without comprehending the dignity of His Person, so should we lose in great part the blessing which has been provided for us in the teaching of our Lord, if we dwelt on its beauty and purity and unearthly sublimity, without at the same time understanding the authority which has enacted and sanctioned and promulgated it as the law of the New Covenant.

In the authority, then, of the Teacher, as well as in the substance of His heavenly teaching, we must place the fulfilment of that great prophecy of Isaias which has already been referred to, and which presented itself to the inspired mind of St. Matthew as the fitting description of the blessing, the first outburst of which he himself probably witnessed on that Sabbath-day in the synagogue at Capharnaum. To understand it fully we must go beyond the thoughts of the Scribes and Pharisees, with their halting, narrow, and captious interpretations of Scripture and tradition, and of the people who were under their guidance, with their stiff and carnal notions as to spiritual truths and the character of God. In comparison with other nations, the Jews were already basking in the light of day, as had been the case with their ancestors at the time of the great plague of Egypt. The Jews were to the Gentiles almost as the Christians to the Jews. We must try to form some idea of the 'darkness and shadow of death' in which the heathen world all around them lay, not only in those parts of it which were most cultivated and most prominent in the history of our race as it is now possessed by civilized nations, but in that large outer sphere, which we can only penetrate by conjecture, which lay beyond even the glimmering twilight, as it might seem by comparison, in which the Persian and Egyptian, the Greek and Roman walked.

The imagination falters at the attempt to measure the ignorance, the error, the delusion, the corruption, and the cruelty—the inseparable companion of corruption—which enslaved the world at the time when the light, of which Isaias and St. Zachary spoke, first blazed forth by the shores of the Lake of Gennesareth. It was to spread on all sides and throughout all the ages of the world's life, penetrating the thick and baleful darkness which lay over the face of the earth, flooding every corner and cranny where men are to be found, until, as the Psalmist says of the sun—

> There is nothing hidden from his heat.[7]

For the light of our Lord's doctrine is warmth as well as light, and nourishes and cherishes and unfolds life and growth, at the same time that it drives away darkness. And surely those who contemplate it under this aspect may well take up the next verses of the same Psalm, and apply to the moral and spiritual benefits of the Gospel light what is there said, even of the Old Law—

> The law of the Lord is perfect, restoring the soul !
> The testimony of the Lord is faithful, making wise the simple :
> The precepts of the Lord are right, gladdening the heart,
> The commandment of the Lord is pure, enlightening the eyes :
> The fear of the Lord is clean, enduring for ever,
> The judgments of the Lord are truth, they are righteous altogether.

But it would require many long meditations to draw out in full what the Psalmist has here sketched, the healing, restoring, elevating, gladdening, and illuminating power of the Christian doctrine, its eternal stability and its absolute and perfect justice. These qualities belong to it, because it is the teaching of Eternal Wisdom and Truth, and they could not avail us in it unless it rested on the authoritative word of a Divine Teacher.

[7] Psalm xviii. (xix.) 6 (Kay's Translation).

CHAPTER IV.

The Demoniac in the Synagogue.

St. Mark i. 23—26 ; St. Luke iv. 33—35 ; *Vita Vitæ Nostræ,* § 30.

AT the same time that the Evangelists tell us of the
beginning of our Lord's authoritative preaching in the
synagogues of Galilee, we learn from the same witnesses
that He began to confirm His Mission and teaching
by another marvellous display of power in casting out
devils from persons who were possessed by them.   The
language recorded by the Evangelists as used by those
who were present in the synagogue at Capharnaum on
the Sabbath-day, of which we have so full an account
given us by St. Mark and St. Luke, is such as to make
it appear likely that this was the first occasion on which
this power had been publicly exercised by our Blessed
Lord.   The people spoke as if it were a new and almost
unheard-of thing, just as afterwards the same astonish-
ment was shown when He stilled the tempest, or when
He gave sight to the man who had been born blind. And
at a later time, when He had sent out the seventy-two
disciples, St. Luke tells us that they came back to Him
with joy, and that what they spoke of above all was
that the very devils were subject to them in His Name.[1]
At the same time it must be remembered that there is
considerable evidence for the existence of exorcisms
among the Jews; nor, indeed, is it likely that in a
religious system instituted by God, which was for the

[1] St. Luke x. 17.

time the organ of His dealings with His chosen people,. and the depository of His truth and, to a certain extent, of His grace, there should have been no provision for the deliverance of possessed persons, no power accorded by God to the invocation of His Name against His enemies. Our Lord in one place argues with His adversaries from the practice of exorcism as known to them, and Josephus mentions the same practice. It is therefore natural to suppose that what was so new to the public on the occasion of which the Evangelists here speak, was the authority and intrinsic power which was shown in our Lord's manner, and the absolute sub-mission with which His simple command was received by the evil spirits. He used no rites, no exorcisms, He did not even order them in the name of His Father, but in His own, to depart from the persons whom they had possessed. It is in this sense, there-fore, that it must be understood that we have here the account of what was to the people at large, as well as to the disciples, the first manifestation of a power in our Lord which raised Him at once far above their ordinary teachers, and accredited His Mission and preaching in their minds as the direct work of God. Here was altogether a new head of miraculous evidence, which, like others of the marvellous endowments and prerogatives of His Sacred Humanity, was to remain afterwards in the Church. The incident, therefore, is most important in itself, and as marking a stage in that gradual teaching concerning our Lord which it was a part of His Father's providence to unfold in one magnificent page after another before the eyes of the people, and especially of the disciples.

The phenomena of diabolical possession, and of the power exercised both by our Lord and His disciples in casting out devils from persons who were affected in that particular way, belong to the class of facts which it suits the frivolous and unreasoning scepticism of the present day to deny, and even to ridicule. And in this, as in other matters of the same kind, the scepticism of unbelievers has been met more than half way by a foolish readiness on the part of many, who rank themselves among the defenders of Christian truth, to surrender whatever shocks the rationalistic and naturalistic spirit which largely pervades society—men who would be reluctant to be reckoned as fighting on the side of unbelief, though they do not sufficiently consider whether what they are willing to concede to the anti-Christian argument leaves them the power of logically and reasonably defending what they make it their boast to retain. It is not the object of the present work to follow out one by one the objections which have been urged against those parts of the Gospel narratives which relate to incidents such as that before us, as it is enough to set forth positively the truth as far as is required by Catholic doctrines on the one hand, and the direct statements of our Lord and His Evangelists on the other. It will be enough, therefore, here to say a few words on the general subject, before passing on to the particular incident before us, which is chiefly remarkable among others of the same class as having been the first in point of time, and also as having come about on so very important and striking a day as this first Sabbath of our Lord's public teaching at Capharnaum.

Diabolical possession comes before us in the history of the Life of our Lord, as well as in that of the Christian Church in all ages, chiefly in connection with that power over devils which is manifested in the deliverance of their victims from their influence, and which was certainly, both in our Lord's time and in the subsequent centuries, considered as an evidence of His Divine Mission and of the authority inherited from Him by the Christian Church. It is but a part of the great system according to which the Kingdom of God over His rational and free creatures in their state of probation is administered. This system must be considered as a whole, and not piece by piece—at least, it is unreasonable in the highest degree to question or to deny one part of it, while we admit without hesitation other parts with which the part which is questioned is in perfect harmony. The narratives which represent our Lord as dealing with certain persons as possessed by devils, as casting the devils out, as putting questions to them, and as according them a certain amount of liberty while He denies them more, do certainly bring home to us the truths that evil spirits exist, that they are allowed to tempt and to afflict mankind, and that they are still subject in every respect to the will and command of God their Creator, in a manner more striking and more palpable than any other. But the truths which have just been named would still exist, even if there had been no instance of diabolical possession and of our Lord's power in delivering persons therefrom in the Gospels. For they exist now as permanent elements of the condition of human nature in its present stage, even when the more visible and tangible instances of the license allowed to evil spirits are not usual. If, therefore, we were drawing up a formal argument against sceptics, we should have to begin by the inquiry, how far they are prepared to admit and how far to deny such truths as those of which the phenomena of possession are but the ulterior developments. It would obviously be unreasonable to enter on the question of possession with persons who are not prepared to admit the existence of evil spirits, and the license which is allowed them to attempt to seduce and destroy mankind.

And, on the other hand, if we had to deal with those who, admitting the general truths which have been named as to the spirits of evil and the liberty allowed them of using their natural gifts, under the strict control of God's providence, to seduce and afflict man, are still inclined, either to deny the possibility of the phenomena of possession, or to attempt to explain away the statements of the Evangelists as to those phenomena, we might fairly ask them to give their reasons for drawing what seems a simply arbitrary line between what they allow and what they disallow. It may even appear much more reasonable either to deny the existence of the devils altogether, or to deny that they are permitted in any way to assail and molest and seduce human beings in this their state of pilgrimage and trial, than to allow these two truths and yet to reject statements which are perfectly in harmony with them, unless it can be shown that it is impossible that evil spirits can be allowed to affect the bodies as well as the souls of men, or that God should permit them the other extremes of license which are involved in the circumstances of possession. The question then becomes a question of the justice of God, of the extent to which that moral liberty of man, which is essential to a state of trial and responsibility, is destroyed by possession, and the like, or again, as to the evidence on which the alleged facts rest, supposing them in the first instance to be admitted as possible.

The Christian account of the history of mankind begins with the assumption of the existence of other spiritual beings, creatures of God like man himself, who have been, like him, on their probation, and many of whom have chosen evil rather than good in that probation. It begins with the assumption that God the Creator of all has not destroyed these works of His hands on account of their rebellion against Him, that He still supports their natural existence, still allows them their natural powers and the use of those powers, even against Himself and His creatures, to a certain degree and measure which depend entirely upon His justice and free choice. It begins, in like manner, with the story of the temptation of the first human pair by the chief of these evil spirits, of his temporary triumph, of the fall of man and the consequent loss for the whole race of the preternatural and supernatural elevation which had been conferred upon him, and of the promise of the redemption and restoration of mankind by means of the Incarnation—a promise the very terms of which include a prophecy of the continual struggle of the evil spirits to mar and hinder, in every way in their power, the execution of the good counsel of God for the salvation of man. Moreover, in the Christian view, the history of the world is not intelligible unless very large allowance indeed is made for the permitted action of evil spirits in matters by which, in truth, the decision of the spiritual issues, on which the future of immortal souls depends, are not less closely touched than by the facts of diabolical possession. Indeed, to say this is to understate the case. Of the two ways in which the devils are allowed to exercise their powers to the injury of man, the way of seduction and deception, and the way of affliction and tyranny, the former is the more dangerous and deadly. But the phenomena of possession belong to the latter kind.

The unremitting warfare of evil against good has been allowed by God, partly judicially, as St. Paul tells us, and partly in order to the full probation of the faithful and of the saints, to extend to the almost complete obliteration in many races and for many generations of the true notion of God Himself, of the natural law which He has written in the heart, and of the primitive traditions which furnished the first fathers of mankind with a sufficient knowledge of His law and of the conditions under which help to keep it or mercy after having broken it might be secured. The evil spirits were allowed to place themselves in the seat of God, and to impose themselves on mankind as objects of the homage and worship due to Him alone, taking care to add all that further system of insult to Him and degradation and corruption to man, which was involved in the deification of the most shameful lusts and in the practice of every kind of moral impurity as a part of religion. A vast system of false worship, with its shrines and sacrifices and oracles and priests and false miracles, was permitted to place itself between God and man, to draw to itself much of the natural piety and reverence and instinctive yearning for God which were found among the best heathen, and to make itself the sanction of obedience to duty and even the guarantee of the hope of future reward at His hands. We have already had occasion to speak of the liberty permitted to the evil spirits in the way of afflicting and tempting the servants of God, and of seducing to further excesses those who had been disobedient or rebellious against Him, and it is only in harmony with all this that we should find that the devils were also permitted in a marvellous manner to make themselves the masters of the bodies and faculties of men from time to time, and to exercise over them all that dominion which is implied in the facts which are classed under the phenomena of possession. Further, it may surely seem, as has been said, that these phenomena are not

among the worst excesses permitted to the evil spirits,
though they have a terrific character of their own, in
that they are more visible and palpable, and seem to
represent to the eye and ear, in the most powerful
manner possible, the still more dreadful spiritual mis-
chiefs which the same hateful agents would work upon
the souls of men if they had their will.

It must be remembered that the term 'possession,'
which is commonly used as representing the extreme
limit to which the evil spirits are allowed to reach in
the exercise of the power which they acquire over
man, is not to be understood as implying that such
spirits can make themselves, in the full sense of the
term, the masters and owners of any human soul or
body.   No evil spirit can truly dwell in the soul as
its animating and directing principle, nor penetrate to
the centre of the personal will of man ; and as in
temptation, and in obsession—which is a stage of diabolical persecution far more mysterious than temptation
—so also in possession, the free-will of the possessed
person may remain altogether alien and adverse to the
use which the evil spirit may make of the power permitted to him.   Possession differs from obsession in
that in the latter case the sufferer is as it were besieged
by the evil one from without, though in a manner more
palpable, terrible, and unremitting than is the case in
ordinary temptations, while in possession the evil spirit
seems to dwell in the person possessed, and to use his
faculties and organs as instruments of his will.   He
speaks with his mouth, uttering horrible blasphemies,
or using words of languages which the person could
never have acquired, displaying a knowledge of things
at a distance, or of things far beyond the natural faculties
or acquirements of the person possessed, or again, he
uses the whole frame for the purposes of violence and

destruction which seem to require more than human strength. At the same time, the heart and mind and whole soul remain altogether beyond his power, so that the bodily frame in such cases seems to be animated by two different beings, though in truth the evil spirit is only an invader and a tyrant, and can never enter into the soul or make himself, in philosophical language, the form of the body over which he has been permitted to usurp so wonderful a power. This usurpation may go so far that, to all appearance, the evil spirit may be completely master, and the human personality be as it were entirely subjugated by him, but it is seldom that his reign is altogether either uninterrupted or completely established.

It follows from what has been said that, although possession may be in many instances, perhaps in the greater number, a permission accorded to the evil spirit as a punishment for the sin, either of the person possessed or of some one intimately connected with that person, still not only may it have other causes, but also it does not in itself constitute a state of sin, nor is it more incompatible with a state of grace, and even of high favour with God, than other temporal afflictions which do not appear to be of so spiritual a character, such, for instance, as grievous bodily sickness or common mental disorder. The purposes for which God may have permitted, before and at the time of the Incarnation, that the devils should so commonly have exercised this dreadful power over men, and those for which He may still at times permit the same, to a greater or less extent, may be many and various. The same end of His glory which is served by the permission of diabolical miracles, of the most violent temptations, of the terrible afflictions which the saints have sometimes endured at the hands of evil spirits, and of the

immense power of seduction which they have exerted
and still exert upon mankind, is equally served by the
permission of the phenomena of possession, which occasion a wonderful display of the dominion of God over the
proudest and most rebellious of His creatures, and in
which He is glorified, both as the author of the natural
powers which are so fearfully exercised as the restrainer
of their use to the exact limit of His will, and as con-
quering His enemies, not by any exercise of His own
irresistible might, but by the weakness of creatures whose
strength is absolutely infantine when compared with that
of those over whom they triumph in Him and through
His Church.

Again, just as many great Christian writers tell us
that it was the counsel of His providence that the great
remedy of the Incarnation should not be given to mankind at once, but in the fulness of time, and, as it were,
when men had learnt by their own miseries to long
for and so to value it, so it may have been a part
of the same counsel that the full tyrannical power of
the evil spirits should have made itself known to the
experience of mankind, in order to display more conspicuously the dignity and might of the great Deliverer,
before Whose presence and word the proudest and most
powerful of the enemies of the human race trembled
and became as nought. What is true of the time of
the Incarnation in this respect, is true also of the whole
period during which the life of the Catholic Church
is to last on earth. When the Catholic faith is carried
into parts of the world where it has never hitherto been
planted, or from which it has for a time been banished,
the Kingdom of our Lord is established by a conquest
of the powers of evil which corresponds in all essential
conditions to His own first Advent and the first propagation of His religion. And as it is the will of God

that the Church, even where she is firmly rooted, should never be without the witness of miraculous powers and the presence of the prophetical spirit, so also it may well be supposed that He will permit, at least occasionally, the phenomena of possession even in Christian and Catholic countries, in order, among other reasons, that the ever-living power of the Incarnate Son over the evil spirits may be manifested to each successive generation, and that it may be known in every age that in this respect also the authority which resides in Him is communicated freely to the Church and to the saints.

We know that one of the effects of the Incarnation has been to diminish the power permitted to the evil spirits over the bodies of men, who partake of that flesh and blood which has now been assumed and so, as it were, consecrated by a Divine Person. As the Church believes that all mankind, evil as well as good, will rise at the Last Day by virtue of our Lord's Resurrection, so it is not difficult to understand that, since our Lord has taken a body and soul and our whole nature to Himself, even the bodies of men are less under the power of His and our spiritual foes. It may also be remembered that Christian writers tell us that one of the reasons why the devils delighted in possessing themselves of men was the hatred which they especially bore to them on account of the Incarnation, which had been the occasion of their own revolt and ruin. If it seemed a special triumph of Hell that the evil spirits should be allowed to make themselves the masters of men's bodies, because possession implied a sort of invasion and conquest of that nature which the Son of God was to assume, it may well also have been one of the signs of the overthrow of their tyranny, that the Incarnation should debar them from a power which they had used in order specially to insult Him Who was to become Incarnate. But the full 'redemption of the body,' as St. Paul tells us, is yet to come, and will have, as its accompaniment or effect, the deliverance of the whole material creation from what he calls 'the servitude of corruption, into the liberty of the glory of the children of God;' and he adds, 'Even we ourselves, who have the first-fruits of His Spirit, groan within ourselves, waiting for the adoption of the sons of God, the redemption of our body.'[2] It is not, therefore, wonderful, either that cases of possession should be less frequent than of old, or that they should still occur, although, as we see in the modern developments of the mischievous and illusive power of the evil spirits which have of late become so common in some countries, God seems rather to permit them to produce other physical effects and appearances than those of actual possession.

In the same way, it becomes the majesty of God to use His enemies as the executioners of His justice and the ministers of His wrath, and this certainly is done in the most striking manner where He judicially allows them to possess themselves for the time of the persons of some who have incurred His displeasure. And He may also use the same evil agents in a similar manner to carry out His designs for the more perfect purification of His saints, or when He desires to see their faithfulness put to the test in a way of all others the most afflicting to them, save that it has been chosen for them by Him. But, whatever may be the reasons for which God permits these terrible manifestations of the natural powers and inveterate and deadly malice of the enemies of our salvation, whether it be in warning or in chastisement, or in proof of fidelity, or that we may know what the devils would do if they were not restrained, or for any other purposes of His own glory, it still

[2] Romans viii. 21—23.

remains true that possession always leaves the human will free, that Satan cannot enter into the soul in the sense in which the soul is open to God, and that the extreme limit of permission which is allowed to him does not prevent the person who is outwardly his victim from being even in the closest union with God, at the very time that the power of evil seems to have the complete mastery.

In the instance which is related to us by the Evangelists as having occurred on the Sabbath-day in the synagogue at Capharnaum, the person possessed by the evil or unclean spirit seems to have been in that state which permitted him to attend the ordinary religious services. He was liable to accesses of violence and occasional outbreaks, but when these were not upon him, the effect of the praises and prayers in the synagogue would probably have been soothing to him. It has been thought that the epithet 'unclean' as applied to this spirit signifies the particular character of depravity which infected him, as we read elsewhere of a spirit of lying, and the like. But the word unclean is so generally used of the devils in the New Testament, that it seems better to understand it of what characterizes all these fallen angels, an intense delight in impurity and obscenity, as most hateful to God, most contrary to the angelic purity from which they have fallen, and most pernicious, degrading, blinding, and hardening to the souls of men. The poor victim of possession may have been for a time free from any paroxysms of fury, and so able to enter the synagogue without remark, but now the presence of the Incarnate Son of God was felt by the demon who possessed him, and he at once broke out before all the assembled multitude in a loud, unearthly voice, which in itself seemed to indicate the nature of the being who spoke. 'There was in their synagogue a man who had an unclean spirit, and he cried out with a loud voice, saying, What is to me and to Thee, Jesus of Nazareth? Art Thou come to destroy us? I know Thee Who Thou art, the Holy One of God !'

The meaning of the words, 'What is to me and to Thee,' or what have I to do with Thee, has already been explained in a very different connection in the account of the marriage at Cana. There, as here, they imply something of deprecation of interference, as if the person addressed had influence or power over the person speaking which could not be gainsaid. But there the words are the loving confession of our Lord that His Mother's prayer could not go unanswered, even though it cost Him a miracle to satisfy her petition, whereas here they signify the acknowledgment of the miserable rebel angels that our Lord was their Master, that they could only hurt men as far and as long as He might permit, and, moreover, that His earthly mission had the especial purpose of curtailing their power, and hastening on the time of its final destruction and their rigid imprisonment in the place of torment prepared for them. Catholic theologians tell us that it is comparative liberty to the evil spirits to be allowed, as multitudes of them are from time to time allowed, in the just counsels of God, to leave their prison in Hell, though they carry with them always and everywhere the torments which belong to it, and to roam over the earth and through the air in their work of temptation and destruction, as far as it is permitted them, to the souls and bodies of men. They know, also, that the time is to come when this liberty will be no longer allowed to them, and the presence of our Lord, in Whom this evil spirit recognized at least something Divine, whether he knew or not that

He was the Incarnate Son of God, was to him the
presence of his Judge, and therefore the near presage
of that final condemnation and consignment to the place
of eternal torment which awaited him. Without love,
without hope, without repentance, he had yet the most
terrrible distinct conception of the unutterable misery
which he had chosen for himself, and the thought over-
mastered every other, that he was now about to meet
his full chastisement at 'the hands of the living God.'[3]

Fearful, indeed, is this cry, 'Art Thou come to destroy
us?' or, as it is found later on in the account of the legion
of devils in the land of the Gerasenes, 'Art Thou come
hither before the time to torment us?' For this is the
future to which alone those fallen spirits look forward,
this it is which answers in them to the blessed hope
of Heaven and everlasting life in the presence of God
which the Holy Ghost implants and fosters in the hearts
of the faithful. Eternity is ever present to them as
imminent, the thought of God is the thought of an
inexorable Judge, and everything that brings Him nearer
to them, or that implies any new action on His part
in their regard, is only the closer approach of the
terrible day when the sentence under which they already
writhe shall be solemnly pronounced and finally exe-
cuted. Jesus of Nazareth, the Son of God, in that
utmost humility to which He condescended for that
design of ineffable love and mercy which was to cost
Him all the sufferings of His Passion, when the very
name by which the evil spirit now hailed Him was to
be fastened over His Head on the Cross which was
to be the instrument of the salvation of the world,
is not to them a Saviour, nor are they to profit by
His humiliation and Passion, nor is the reconciliation
between God and sinners, which He is to work, to have

<hr>

[3] Hebrews x. 31.

F 2

any fruit of pardon for them, nor is His Blood to avail them, nor is grace to be won nor Heaven opened by Him for them. The most marvellous work that God has ever done or can do, the Incarnation with all its mighty issues, has only one character for them, the character of greater torment, and the Lamb of God that taketh away the sins of the world brings to them no love or mercy, but only wrath and judgment.

The next words of the evil spirit to our Lord have sometimes been understood as if they were uttered with the intention of moving Him to vainglory, or by way of flattery, or even of mockery. There are no doubt many instances on record in which the evil spirits have tried to overthrow the saints and servants of God by such means, knowing that if they can but be seduced to a deliberate act of self-complacency, their whole power will be taken from them, or at least their own ruin will follow, to compensate to the spiritual adversaries for any restraint that may have been put upon them by the exercise of such power. And in the far more ordinary case in which the ministers of God are engaged in delivering men from the yoke of Satan, from habitual sin, or an evil life, or the tyranny of false doctrine, or a state of rebellion against the Church, whether the deliverance be wrought by the administration of the sacraments, or the preaching the Word of God, or controversy, or in any other manner, nothing is more sure to render the efforts of such ministers inefficacious, or at least to bring upon themselves the spiritual ruin from which they are rescuing others, than the admission of the spirit of vanity and self-elation into their hearts. Thus, as we have said, some holy writers have supposed that this evil spirit, who may have been aware of the futile attempts made by Satan either to lead our Lord into sin, or to make Him discover Who He was, at the time of the Temptation, may have been carrying on the same kind of assault against Him now, by praising Him publicly and professing to acknowledge Him as the Holy One of God. No word that the devils say is to be believed, unless we know that it is uttered by them under compulsion put upon them by God to tell the truth, and therefore there is no reason why we should suppose that this evil spirit knew that our Lord was in truth the Incarnate Son of God merely because he said so. And the impudence and malice of these evil spirits is so great, that there is nothing, on the other hand, unreasonable in itself, in the supposition that these words were meant as a subtle temptation to our Lord, or that the devil, recognizing in Him a power which could deal with him as He choose, might have thought to fawn upon Him and flatter Him, if not in the hope of seducing Him to vainglory, at least in that of winning from Him some mitigation of the severe treatment which he dreaded.

But although all this be true, and although to recognize that this is possible enables us to understand better the utter mendaciousness as well as the shameless effrontery of the evil spirits, it seems more natural to suppose that this devil felt the power of the unseen Godhead in our Lord's presence, and that his words are simply those of abject terror. The title, 'the Holy One of God,' can scarcely mean less than the promised Son of God, holy not by participation, but by nature, and therefore the Incarnate Saviour Whose coming was to destroy the empire of the evil spirits. The terror felt by the devil is not inconsistent with the imprudent arrogance of the language used by him, on which some Catholic writers have dwelt. The cry against interference may be understood as a complaint, as if the evil spirit was in his right in possessing himself of the man, and claimed not to be disturbed, and the question, 'Art Thou come to destroy us?' as another lying complaint, as if the lawful time had not come, and the last words, 'I know Thee Who Thou art!' as a sort of mocking acknowledgment of our Lord's dignity—as if that were enough for Him to exact of His enemy.   And we may perhaps see in them also a perverse and malignant desire to thwart even yet, as far as was permitted him, the good and merciful purpose of our Lord in coming among men, enlightening them, and healing them by the saving doctrine which He was pouring forth to an audience which was hanging attentively on His words.   For it is always a thing nearest, if we may so speak, to the hearts of the enemies of God, to interrupt at any cost the teaching of the truths which our Lord came to reveal, and which He has commanded His Church to proclaim to the whole world till the end of time. When Catholic truth is thus powerfully and authoritatively taught, and especially when, as in the instance before us, the holiness of the Teacher adds a new and irresistible force to the innate might of the Word of God, and great streams of grace are poured out to soften and conciliate the hearts of the hearers, then the kingdom of Satan is overthrown and his power gone, unless he can raise some hindrance to the free course of the Word.   Again, the evil spirit, though crouching in miserable fear before the presence of his Judge, may still have noted that our Lord was hiding the majesty which belonged to Him under an appearance of humility and condescension, that He chose, for some purpose of His Father's glory and of the good of mankind, not to declare openly Who He was, and it is not unnatural to think that the subtle enemy of God and man may have thought to disturb this gracious purpose by proclaiming what it seemed our Lord's design not to proclaim.   And we find afterwards that when something of the same kind is related by the Evangelists as to the legion of devils in the country of the Gerasenes, on which occasion our Lord in His justice permitted the devils to proclaim not only Who He was, but further to enter into the herd of swine, the effect on the people of the country was rather to indispose them to receive our Lord as a Teacher, and that they came to Him beseeching Him to depart out of their coasts. And, once more, it was not, as it would seem, in accordance with the law of our Lord's Mission to accept the witness of the enemies of God as to the truths which related to His Sacred Person. That He cast out evil spirits indeed was a proof of His power to which He Himself more than once appealed, a proof which gave occasion to that malignant suggestion on the part of His enemies which so much grieved His Sacred Heart, the suggestion that He was in league with Satan, when in the finger of God He cast out the devils. In this way they might give unwilling witness to His Person; but their words were the words of liars and enemies, and they were not to be allowed to add their testimony as such to the witness of His Father, to the declaration of St. John Baptist, and to the marvellous evidence of our Lord's own miracles.

Thus we find that our Lord dealt with the evil spirit in this case as if His first object was to silence him rather than deliver his victim from him. 'And Jesus rebuked and threatened him, saying, Be silent, and go forth from him. And the evil spirit rending him, and casting him in the midst, and crying out with a loud voice, went forth from him, and did him no harm.'[4]

The malice and fury of the evil spirit were shown in his futile attempts at mischief, making the body of the man writhe and seem to be rent with pain, and throwing

---

[4] St. Mark i. 25, 26 ; St. Luke iv. 35.

him down in the midst of the people, at the same time using his voice for the last time in a loud shout. But, as is often the case in the violent contortions and writhings of possessed persons, no real harm was done, the deliverance was complete and immediate, the final struggles of the evil one only serving to enhance the impression of his indignant and impotent rage left upon the minds of the spectators. The calm which followed, the absolute peace after the tempest of unearthly violence which they had witnessed, the simple majesty of our Lord as He received the homage and thanks of the delivered person, produced an awe and reverential fear which sank into the heart more deeply than the hideous sights and sounds which had accompanied the display of diabolical malice. Anything that suddenly brings the unseen world near to man appals him and strikes him with terror, for he is accustomed only to the world of sense, and is startled and alarmed by what seems to reveal its comparative nothingness and emptiness. This is the case with anything that seems to transcend the world of sense; but when agents undoubtedly personal, such as the powers of evil, are allowed to make their malice and their terrible strength to some extent sensible, a new element of fearfulness is added, because they are felt to be enemies in all the vigour of spiritual life, burning with unquenchable hate against us, and the unseen world is thus brought home to men as full of powers capable of and bent on their destruction, the exercise of which, usually restrained, seems to be suddenly set free. But far beyond and above the terror inspired by what seems like the touch and grasp of the evil spirits thus fastening themselves upon man, is the awe which follows when the voice of the Master of the world, the Creator and Sovereign of all existences, whether material or spiritual, makes itself heard, commanding peace, and quelling in a moment the puny violence and impotent rage which have seemed to men terrible enough in themselves to destroy life and upset the course of the world.

Man is too feeble by nature, too much a creature of sense, he is too much haunted by the instinctive dread of God which is natural in a race not only weak but fallen, and which is a part of the penalty of sin, original and actual, not to cower and tremble in the presence of what is Divine, even when that presence has manifested itself in the exercise of power for the behests of mercy, in the deliverance of the souls and bodies of men from the most terrible slavery that can be witnessed on earth. And the awe which would follow upon the display of Divine power in the expulsion of evil spirits under any circumstances, for instance, when such a result might be witnessed after the solemn exorcisms of the Church or at the word of a great servant of God, would be much enhanced, as has been said, by the evident authority exercised by our Lord in His own Name and power without any appeal to His Father. Is it true that the great displays of God's power, especially in the spiritual order and in the dispensation of the Incarnation, are ordinarily in the way of mercy and beneficence, and such displays, awful as they are, can never be altogether and simply terrible to the men of good-will. And thus we may suppose that the fear of which the Evangelists tell us on this occasion, as possessing the minds of those who witnessed the expulsion of the evil spirit, was not unmixed with a loving joy and gratitude and confidence, such as might have helped them to listen with still greater eagerness to our Lord's teaching, and that thus the attempt of the devil to disturb the course of that teaching may have turned still more completely to his own defeat and discomfiture.

This is certainly the impression which follows most

naturally from the words of the Evangelists, in which mention is especially made of the confirmation which our Lord's teaching seems to have received in the minds of the people from this new manifestation of His authority. 'And all marvelled,' says St. Mark, and St. Luke adds, 'fear came upon all, so that they spoke and questioned among themselves, saying, What is this new teaching? what is this word? for in power and might He commands even the unclean spirits, and they obey Him and go forth.' Not only did He teach with authority, as a Lawgiver and King in His own Kingdom, but He showed moreover an absolutely unquestioned power and authority in dealing with unclean spirits, and this was a new confirmation of the authority of His teaching, as convincing and as cogent as the power of miracles itself. In each case a power which could only be that of God Himself was exercised by the new Teacher and exercised absolutely as His own. The devils, indeed, proclaimed him to be the Holy One of God, and He forbade them to speak. He did not deny what they said, but He would accept of no testimony from them. But He did far more than this, for He drove them out by a word, and showed Himself their Lord by the peremptoriness of His command and the resistless power of His word.

In a busy, thickly-populated country like Galilee, the news of marvels such as those which had been shown in the synagogue at Capharnaum flies from mouth to mouth, from place to place, without the aid of the modern appliances for the spread of intelligence of which we are so proud. If a miracle or a wonder of the sort of which we have been speaking were done in a temple in one of the teeming provinces of India or China at the present day, it would be known before many hours, or at least days, had passed, over the whole country. Much more would this be the case if the times were times of religious curiosity and excitement, when a universal expectation looked for the coming of some great Prophet, and when public attention had already been directed by other prodigies to the Person of Whom the new marvel was related. Thus we need not consider it an exaggeration on the part of the Evangelists that they tell us that our Lord's 'fame went forth at once over all the region of Galilee,' and the like. The news of what He had done, and how His teaching had been sanctioned by a great display of Divine power, flew from town to town, and village to village, as fast as if it had been carried by beacon-fires or the wires of the telegraph. Everywhere the people knew what it was for devils to take possession of men, and how difficult and uncertain were all ordinary processes, even by the official ministers of religion, for the deliverance of these miserable victims. And now a Teacher had come Whose simple word was a law which the evil spirits, howling and writhing in their malice, were obliged to obey. What was this new teaching? Wherever our Lord might go throughout all that wide and beautiful country He would find people ready to welcome Him and listen to Him, as One Who had shown that God was with Him by the exercise of the most unquestioned authority over the enemies of God and man alike. It was already known that nature had obeyed Him, that water had become wine at His word, and that diseases, in many of which the Jews saw the agency, more or less direct, of evil spirits, had fled away when He commanded them. But now the evil spirits had met Him, as it were, face to face, and had been forced to own Him as their Lord. The simple people reasoned better than the Pharisees afterwards, and saw in this an evidence more striking even than that of miracles, that the Kingdom of God had come.

NOTE I.

Instances of possession permitted as a trial.

It will hardly be necessary to prove at any length to Catholic readers that the phenomena of possession are sometimes permitted by God as a chastisement under which the possessed person may learn to amend his life, or again, rather as a trial to virtue than a chastisement, a trial which may be made the occasion of sanctification. The subject is treated at great length by Görres, in his *Mystik*, to which the reader may be referred. He gives an instance from the Life of St. Dominic, of a certain Sister Benedicta of Florence, 'who after having been for some time a slave to the world and its pleasures, was possessed by a devil, and so did penance for the worldly life which she had led. She lived near the Church of the Dominicans, and St. Dominic having come to the place, she was one of the first persons whom he induced to enter into herself and return to God. He was touched with compassion at her misfortune, and obtained by his prayers her deliverance from the devil. Instead of being tormented by him, as had before been the case nearly every day, she remained in peace more than a whole year. But as soon as her body was delivered, her soul became a prey to great temptations, and what had been to her a bodily remedy became a veritable malady to her soul. She became tepid in the service of God, and had to battle against the evil desires which had before besieged her. She complained of this to the man of God, who, remarking that the benefit which God had granted to her was perhaps given to her to her destruction, asked her if she desired to return to the state in which she had before been. She replied that she left herself to his discretion and to the will of God. "Well, my child," said the Saint, "I will pray to God that that may happen to you which is the best for your salvation." Some days after the devil again took possession of the body of this servant of our Lord, in order that her soul might be purified ; and thus that which had at first been a chastisement for her faults became to her a means of salvation and an abundant source of merit' (Görres, *Mystik*, l. vi. c. ii.).

One of the most striking instances of the sanctification of a soul under the terrible affliction of possession is contained in the chapter in Görres' work which immediately follows that from which the foregoing sentences are taken. This chapter contains the history of the Blessed Eustochia of Padua, a nun of the latter half of the fifteenth century, who was possessed from her very infancy, and was hardly ever altogether free from the molestations of the evil spirit till just before her death, which happened in her twenty-fifth year. This chosen soul was a child of adultery and sacrilege, and the possession to which she was handed over may be considered as a chastisement for the fault of her parents. She was persecuted by men as well as by the evil spirit, ill-treated in her father's house, ill-treated as a child in the convent where she was brought up, and again as a postulant, a novice, and a professed nun, by her religious sisters, and even by her confessor ; but her soul was from the very first drawn to a close union with God, and she endured all her sufferings with heroic patience and constancy.

CHAPTER V.

Miracles at Capharnaum.

St. Mark i. 29—34 ; St. Luke iv. 38—41 ; St. Matt. viii. 16, 17 ;
Vita Vitæ Nostræ, § 30.

OUR Lord's teaching in the synagogue at Capharnaum
had already impressed itself on the minds of His hearers
by the singular authority by which He spoke, as well
as by the astonishing power which He had exercised
over the evil spirit in the case of possession related in
the last chapter. It was, in the next place, to receive
another kind of confirmation, appealing to all the best
feelings of human nature, as well as to the near interests
of many who were among His hearers, by very singular
displays of miraculous power in favour of persons
afflicted in the more common way of sickness and
infirmity. It has already been remarked that it was
the will of God that the preaching of the New Law and
of the blessed tidings of salvation in His Gospel was
to be accompanied and authenticated by a very large
outpouring of benefits and blessings to the bodies of
the suffering, whose very maladies were, in their origin,
the penalties of original sin, and sometimes both the
fruit and the penalties of actual sin. The relief of these
by the merciful compassion of our Lord became thus
at once the evidence and the picture of the salvation
and restoration which He was bringing home to souls
diseased and weakened by the far more dangerous evils
of sin. A great number of miracles of this sort were

wrought by our Lord on this particular Sabbath-day of
which we have the account before us, or immediately
upon its close.

The first of these miracles seems to have taken place
in the middle of the day, and therefore on the legal
Sabbath itself. 'Immediately going out of the synagogue,'
says St. Mark, who must have had the account of an
incident so interesting to St. Peter from the Apostle
himself, 'they came into the house of Simon and Andrew
with James and John. Now the mother-in-law of Simon
was in bed with a fever'—'was seized with a great fever,'
says St. Luke, whose habit it is to notice accurately what
would strike a physician—'and forthwith they told Him
of her and besought Him for her. And going to her.
He raised her up, taking her by the hand, standing over
her, He commanded the fever, and it left her at once,
and she rose up straightway and ministered to them.' It
was the time of the daily meal, a meal which, on the
Sabbath, was usually made somewhat better and fuller
than on other days, and the mother-in-law of the Apostle
showed at once how perfect was her cure and how heartfelt and joyous her gratitude, by waiting upon our Lord
and the other guests.

Every particular of this simple scene has been made
the subject of devout contemplation and reflection by
Christian writers. It will be enough here to notice a
few of those reflections. Some authors remark on the
modest self-restraint of Simon Peter, who must have
known of the dangerous state of his mother-in-law before
the service in the synagogue began, but who would not
interrupt our Lord or molest Him with entreaties until
He had fully discharged the more important duties of
His public preaching. Again, St. Peter may have been
encouraged and fortified in his faith by our Lord's
display of wonderful authority in the case of the demo-

niac, and thus, as was often the case, one miracle may have led on to another. As our Blessed Lady and our Lord's brethren were now, as it seems, fixed at Capharnaum, our Lord's going to the house of Simon Peter must have been a matter of deliberate choice on His part, even if He had not been asked, for the sake of the poor sufferer whose son-in-law had just given himself more completely to his Master's service, and we have thus an instance, in this miracle, of the manner in which our Lord exercises a special providential care over, and shows exceptional favour to, the families of those who leave their homes at His call, to follow Him as His ministers or in the religious life. Peter and Andrew had not, indeed, as yet altogether abandoned their homes and their duties, for the call which our Lord had lately given them seems to have been a call to follow Him as His companions in the missionary circuit which was now to begin. But they had placed themselves at our Lord's disposal as far as He had asked it of them, and He now rewards them by entering the house of Simon as a guest and bringing with Him a great and miraculous blessing on his family. Other writers have dwelt on the intercession which was made for the fever-struck woman, inasmuch as our Lord sometimes worked His miracles unasked, when He had some special purpose for the glory of His Father in doing so, but at other times, and more ordinarily, He required the exercise of faith and prayer on the part either of the patients themselves or of those who might be said to represent them, that exercise of faith and prayer giving, in truth, as much glory to God and joy to the Sacred Heart as the benefit of the miracle itself. Again, it is noted that our Lord 'commanded' the fever, as the Master and Sovereign King of nature and of all natural causes, and yet that, at the same time, He gently took the sufferer by the hand and raised her up, thus to a certain extent veiling His own miracle, and, above all, carrying out the law of the dispensation of the Incarnation, in which it is the sensible touch of our Lord, the actual presence of the Sacred Humanity which has been made the Human Nature of a Divine Person, from which all benefits to the souls and bodies of men are to flow as from their source. And although one who had received from our Lord so wonderful a favour might naturally wish to spend some time in prayer, adoration, thanksgiving, praise, and the other holy affections of a grateful soul, still there is a more perfect simplicity in the manner in which the thankfulness of the person restored to health was shown on this occasion, in at once using her strength in waiting on our Lord and His disciples—as if to show in a parable, not indeed that we are to neglect the duty of thanksgiving and praise of God after the receiving of His benefits, but that to wait on our Lord and on those who belong to Him, the poor, the sick, children, or the ignorant and afflicted who are in need of instruction, guidance, help, and consolation, is the best and most immediate way of showing our deep gratitude.

The miracle which our Lord had wrought upon St. Peter's mother-in-law would become known at once to her neighbours, and in a short time it would spread over the whole of the little but crowded town. What had taken place in the synagogue, the majesty and authority of our Lord's teaching, and His peremptory command to the evil spirit to leave the possessed person, obeyed as it had been in a way which showed at once the irresistible power of His word and the impotent reluctance of the devil to abandon his prey, was already known in every household in the town, and there were probably few companies that afternoon in which the conversation was occupied with any other subject than our Lord. And now there came the further news of the miracle upon the fevered women. The Jews did not think it right to carry beds or pallets, with sick persons on them, through the streets while the Sabbath lasted, but it ended with sunset, and though the twilight in those countries is far shorter than in ours, there was still an interval between the setting of the sun and the absolute darkness of night which gave an opportunity to the eager zeal and devotion of the citizens who had seen and heard of doings so wonderful on the part of our Lord. 'Now when it was evening and when the sun had set, they brought to Him all those who were sick and who had devils, and all the city was gathered together at the door.' This is the picture given to us by St. Mark from the recollections of St. Peter.[1] St. Luke distinguishes between the sick and the demoniacs, and tells us that as to the first, our Lord laid His hands upon them one by one and healed them. The evil spirits He cast out by word, as we are told by St. Matthew. 'And evil spirits went forth from many, crying out and saying : Thou art the Son of God. And He rebuked them, and would not let them speak, because they knew that He was the Christ.'[2]

There has been much difference of opinion among

---

[1] St. Mark i. 32, 33. The description seems to be given in the words of one who was within the house at the time with our Lord. St. Luke writes more generally. 'All who had persons sick with various illnesses brought them to Him' (iv. 40). St. Matthew, who does not give the scene in the synagogue, nor speak at all of this Sabbath as the beginning of our Lord's preaching, mentions the healing of St. Peter's mother-in-law in a very few words, and then dwells particularly on the casting out of devils in the evening, rather than on the healing of the sick. 'He is giving a chain of miracles of various heads, and he has not before-mentioned any cure of demoniacs. Here he says, 'When evening was come, they brought to Him many that had devils, and He cast out the evil spirits with a word, and healed all that were sick' (viii. 16).

[2] St. Luke iv. 41.

Catholic Doctors as to the knowledge of our Lord
which is here attributed to the evil spirits. Some great
authorities think that although Satan himself did not
know who our Lord was at the time of the Temptation,
when as yet our Lord had worked no miracle and had
not taken upon Himself the office of Teacher, still the
miracles which He had wrought since that time, the
testimony of St. John, the manner in which He had
assumed authority in the purification of the Temple,
and the authoritative character of His teaching, had now
convinced them of the truth as to His Person. Others,
on the other hand, suppose that the devils merely con-
jectured that our Lord was the Christ, or even, as has
been said, that they uttered the words recorded by the
Evangelists in a spirit of flattery and adulation, hoping
thereby to seduce Him to self-complacency and vainglory. The words of St. Luke, however, are almost too
direct to be understood in any but the simplest way,
and it only remains to consider whether the knowledge
that He was the Christ necessarily implied that the devils
knew Him to be the Incarnate Son of God. We have
seen that the notions of the Jews were not clear as to
the Messias, whether He were to be indeed a Divine
Person or not : and although the natural powers of
the evil spirits so far transcend those of men as to
make it appear impossible that the devils can have mis-
understood the prophecies as to this point, it must be
remembered that their characteristic sin is pride, and
that pride has a blinding power even among men which
often seems absolutely miraculous. There is every reason
for thinking that the evil spirits were always on the
look out for the Incarnation, for reasons very different
indeed from those which made it the object of continual
longing and prayer to the holy men who were waiting
for the consolation of Israel. The Incarnation, if we

are to follow a common opinion among Christian theologians, was the Divine mystery, their refusal to accept
which had been originally the occasion of the fall of
the evil angels, and they knew also that it had been
promised to man after his fall as the means by which
his redemption was to be wrought, and the kingdom
of Hell destroyed. When they cried out to our Lord,
'Thou art the Son of God!' they uttered words which
reminded them of the cause of their own eternal misery,
because, if we follow the opinion alluded to above, it
was because they would not do homage to the Son of
God in a nature inferior to their own that they became
rebels and lost their thrones in Heaven.

These are reasons which favour the first of the two
opinions as to their knowledge of our Lord, namely,
that that knowledge was truly such. On the other
hand, it must be remembered that in the darkness and
confusion which their intense pride engendered, they
might be utterly unable to discern the fulfilments of
prophecy, or the other arguments for our Lord's Divine
character, which consisted in His miracles or in His
teaching. And again, as they had been unable to recognize
the mystery of the Incarnation on account of the
humiliation which it implied in the majesty of God,
even although that humiliation, as revealed to them,
did not go below His assumption of a created nature,
so now there might have been in the still further humiliation in which our Lord actually appeared, as a poor
man of the humblest rank, distinguished from others by
nothing except by His extreme meekness, poverty, and
condescension, abundant reasons which to minds like
theirs might seem to exclude the possibility that He
could be in truth the Son of God. And as it is
certain that many of the mysteries of the Incarnation
were purposely concealed from the knowledge of evil

spirits, it does not seem likely, at all events, that they can have had any perfectly clear and unwavering conviction as to the main truth itself, though they may have seen enough in our Lord to make them shrink before His presence as that of ineffable Purity and Holiness. Something has already been said as to what may have been our Lord's reasons for not allowing them to speak. They were not witnesses to whom His Father had given it in commission to proclaim Him, and He left the revelation of His Person and Divine Nature to the providence of His Father. We see this in His memorable words to St. Peter after his confession, in which He makes the blessing of the Apostle's faith to consist in this, that it is founded on the revelation made concerning Him by His Father Who is in Heaven. Our Lord even concealed His miracles, and forbade the person whom He had cured to speak of them. For He it was Who always left His exaltation entirely to His Father. He it is of Whom St. Paul tells us that, being in the form of God, He thought it not a thing to be clutched at to be equal with God, and if in the Incarnation itself He emptied Himself of His glory for the sake of humility, much more would He resent anything like a proclamation of the majesty of His Person from the mouths of His Father's enemies. And as the order of His manifestation was entirely in the hands of His Father, that order could only be disturbed and interrupted and marred—even if the malice of the evil spirits did not contemplate this—by their unauthorized and inopportune interference to make Him known, when it was not yet the will of His Father that all men should know Him.

The same Divine reasons which seem to have existed for concealing from the devils the mystery of the Incarnation, the manner in which it had been accomplished, and many particulars concerning it, may have had equal force against permitting them to make it known when they had guessed it, or come to feel, by experience of our Lord's power over them, Who He was. We are distinctly told by the Evangelists,[3] that after the great confession of St. Peter in our Lord's Divinity, He charged His disciples most strictly not to make Him known. For the proclamation of the full truth concerning His Divine Person was so to be brought about that, at the same time, neither the execution of the counsel of God concerning His Passion might be hindered, nor the people tempted to direct rejection of the truth above mentioned by the humiliation and apparent defeat which He was to suffer on the Cross. It is not wonderful, therefore, that, if even His own Apostles were to keep silence concerning Him until the Passion had been effected, the enemies of God and man should have been peremptorily forbidden from declaring Who He was.

St. Matthew takes occasion from the mention of the number of cures worked by our Lord on this Sabbath evening, to show how in this particular also what was done was in fulfilment of the ancient prophecies concerning the Messias. St. Matthew's reason for the quotation is obvious. He has, in this place of his Gospel, collected a certain number of instances of miraculous cures, the healing of the leper, of the centurion's servant, of Peter's mother-in-law, and those other miracles of healing wrought on the same day with the latter at Capharnaum. After thus showing how our Lord's teaching was confirmed by miracles of healing, he passes on to his chain of miraculous evidence, because the other links which he is going to add in the same plan are miracles of another kind, that is, of power over the winds and storms, and over the legion of devils, and adds another head to the series of illustrations from

[3] St. Matt. xvi. 20 ; St. Mark viii. 30 ; St. Luke ix. 21.

prophecy which ran through his Gospel by reminding his readers how these wonders of healing love had been predicted of the Messias. 'That it might be fulfilled which was spoken by the Prophet Isaias, saying, He took our infirmities and bare our diseases.'[4] We have here another trace of the argument from prophecy which was perhaps the most common weapon used by the Apostles in dealing with the Jews, while at the same time we may remember, as to this and other similar passages in St. Matthew, that an illustration from prophecy, the force of which might not at once be seen by a Jewish disputant, would still be full of instruction and consolation for the believers for whom the Gospels were written. The most distinct and pointed prophecy which fixed on miracles of healing as the attribute of the Messias, was perhaps another passage of Isaias, which our Lord Himself quoted, at a later date than the time of these miracles at Capharnaum, when St. John Baptist, hearing that He was now displaying what St. Matthew calls 'the works of the Christ,' the works prophesied of Him as such, sent his two disciples to put to Him the formal question, 'Art Thou He that art to come, or look we for another?' And our Lord replied to them by bidding them tell their master what they heard and saw, the blind seeing, the lame walking, the lepers cleansed, the deaf hearing, the dead raised to life; referring in the words which He used to a previous passage in this same prophecy of Isaias.[5] As this reference to prophecy on the part of our Lord is recorded by St. Matthew, it is clear that he had these passages of Isaias before his mind as he composed his Gospel, and it could not have been from any want of a distinct prediction as to the healing of bodily ailments by the Messias that he chose rather the passage in the

<hr>

[4] Isaias liii. 4.　　[5] Isaias xxxv. 5; St. Matt. xi. 5.

text, which is taken from the great prophecy concerning our Lord's Passion.

It is also remarkable that in this place as in many others in his Gospel, St. Matthew does not follow the Septuagint version of Isaias, but translates the words for himself in a different manner, which, however, has its foundation and authority in the original text. The words as he has translated them are generally understood by Catholic writers as containing a reference to the remedial power of the Sacrifice of our Lord on the Cross, and as referring to the deep truth that bodily infirmities and diseases of all kinds are at once the symbols and the consequences, direct or indirect, of sin, for which it was our Lord's office to make perfect atonement, and that thus, healing the root of all evil, moral and physical, by His own sufferings, He at the same time healed all the external manifestations of physical evil by the touch of that Sacred Humanity of His in which He was to be the Victim of propitiation on the Cross. No doubt, the power of God could heal diseases of the body without any necessity for the Sacrifice of Calvary, but our Blessed Lord, by the will of His Father, was to heal the source from which the evil flowed, and the exercise of His miraculous power in the healing of the body was the external manifestation of the power which He exercised as the Physician of the soul. When He healed this or that disease, it was by a partial application of His power: when He healed all moral disease and made a perfect atonement for all sin upon the Cross, He healed in principle and virtually all manifestations whatever of physical evil and suffering, at the same time that He renovated and elevated the whole nature of man, so as to raise it even above the weakness and feebleness, the liability to weariness and decay, the need of food and support, and the like, which are the conditions of its existence even apart from the maladies which are the legacy of sin. 'All that were sick, He healed,' says the Evangelist emphatically. His healing action went to the very utmost limit, healing root and branch, the fountain of sin in itself and in everything, internal and external, which has any connection therewith : and when He showed His power as Healer in the case of diseases of every kind, He showed it in relation to the most distant and indirect development, so to speak, of the evil which He came to cure. But, as this external exercise of His work of mercy and atonement had so close a connection with that more interior and deeper work by which He did away with sin, the Evangelist chooses to direct the attention of his readers to the great prediction of our Lord's Passion, from which He has taken and adapted these words.[6]

[6] It is right to add that there are several commentators who consider that the words of Isaias, as quoted by St. Matthew, refer to the direct removal of bodily diseases, and not merely to its removal, as it were, in its principle and origin by our Lord's suffering for sin. The Greek word βαστάζειν, which is rendered in the Vulgate by the Latin *portare*, ' ægrotationes nostras portavit,' has certainly a double sense, that of bearing, and of 'taking away.' St. Matthew uses it only twice, besides in the present place, iii. 11, xx. 12. In the last of these places it seems to mean simply to 'bear' (the burthen and heat of the day), and cannot mean to take away, to remove. In the first place, iii. 11, it *may* mean to 'remove.' The usual meaning in the New Testament seems to be, simply to bear ; but St. John uses the word at least twice where the meaning to 'take away' is the most easy, where he says that Judas was a thief, and ἐβάσταζεν what was put into the common purse and again when he makes St. Magdalene say to our Lord, thinking Him the gardener, 'Sir, if thou hast taken Him away, tell me'—ἐι σὺ ἐβάστασας αὐτόν. The learned commentator, Mazochi, contends strongly for this interpretation, which he confirms from the use of the Hebrew word *sabal*, which in this same chapter of Isaias (liii. 11) is translated by the Septuagint ἀνοίσει. (This, however, is translated by the Vulgate *portabit*, and it is the same verb which St. Peter uses, 1 Epist. ii. 24. 'Who His own self *bare* our sins in His Body upon the tree.) Mazochi's argument will be found in his *Spicilegium*, on St. Matt. viii. 17, but the greater number of his authorities are collected in his Dissertation on St. John xii. 6, on the meaning of the word βαστάζειν.

CHAPTER VI.

Preaching throughout Galilee.

St. Matt. iv. 23—25 ; St. Mark i. 35—39 ; St. Luke iv. 42—44 ;
Vita Vitæ Nostræ, § 30.

THE Evangelists do not tell us how late into the night of this eventful Sabbath-day the people of Capharnaum remained crowded round the door of the house in which our Lord had healed Simon Peter's mother-in-law. The summer may now have been well advanced, and if so, the night hours would be short, but it is probable that for our Lord they were made still shorter by the importunate devotion and enthusiasm of the multitude, who had listened to Him in the synagogue, and had witnessed or heard of the wonderful works of various kinds by which His teaching had been accredited. It is hard to think that any of those who had sick friends or relatives or persons possessed by devils to present to Him, went away before their wishes were in some sort satisfied ; and our Lord would do nothing in a hurry, and have a word of exhortation or instruction for each as He laid His hands upon them or commanded the evil spirits to leave them. Thus the crowd would diminish gradually, almost one by one, like the crowds around the confessionals at the time of some great Catholic Mission when the following day is a day of Communion. Late in the night our Lord would have retired to such rest as He allowed Himself, whether it were in the house of Simon Peter or in that which was now the home of His Mother and His 'brethren.'

But 'very early in the morning,' St. Mark tells us, 'He arose and went away into a desert-place and there prayed.' The dawn broke on Him on His knees communing with His Father, and when He was sought for in the house as soon as people began to stir, which would be at a very early hour, He was not to be found. The place to which He betook Himself need not be supposed at any great distance, but some retired spot away from the ordinary haunts of men, such as was Gethsemani, the Mount of Olives, not far from the walls and gates of Jerusalem. 'And Simon followed Him, and those that were with him, and when they had found Him, they said to Him, All are seeking Thee.' And St. Luke adds, as is his wont, another line to the picture, that the crowd followed in the footsteps of His disciples, and came up to our Lord after them, and were for detaining Him, that He might not depart from them. There was every readiness on their part to listen to His teaching, He had completely mastered their hearts for the moment, and it might have seemed a pity to abandon a field of labour where there was so much hope of profit for souls. But our Lord had a great work to accomplish, and the time which He could give to any one spot was necessarily short. He could make time for prayer which could never be omitted, but He could not defraud the other cities and villages to which He was sent for the benefit of Capharnaum. 'He said, To other cities also I have to preach the Kingdom of God, for therefore am I sent. Let us go'— this was said to Peter and the others whom He had called to accompany Him—'into the neighbouring villages and cities that I may preach there also: for to this purpose am I come.'

Capharnaum had had its day, a day of wonderful graces and of marvels of Divine power and mercy, and there were to be many more such days for that favoured city before the time was to come when our Lord would leave it for the last time. Now was the time for the other cities of Galilee. The very names of by far the larger number of them have vanished altogether from the memory of man, and the traveller who now visits the province must find it difficult indeed to strain his imagination so far as to picture it to himself as crowded with the populous homes of multitudes of men of which the Jewish historian tells us. And it seems that, in the short accounts of the Galilæan preaching of this first year of our Lord's Ministry which remain to us in the Gospels, we have not a single place named as the scene of any particular incident except Nazareth, Cana, and Capharnaum, while events which are connected with the two first-named places are rather prior to the beginning of our Lord's missionary course than parts of it. The healing of the leper,[1] indeed, seems to have taken place near some town the name of which is not given, and which may not have been Capharnaum, but with this exception the remark just made holds good. If the Sabbath-day at Capharnaum, the events of which have just been considered, was a fair specimen of what such days were in our Lord's course of teaching, there is no reason why we should be surprised at the silence of the Evangelists as to the details of the whole of that course. It would have been impossible, within the limits of any ordinary narrative, to relate the incidents of a number of successive days, each of them crowded perhaps with teachings, with miracles on the sick and on demoniacs, and with personal incidents of more or less interest. It has sometimes happened in the lives of great saints of

[1] St. Luke v. 12—14.

God who have had, either continuously or for a time, the commission to preach repentance from place to place, that some attempt has been made to take notes of their actions, sayings, and miracles; and the result has been that little more could be done than the giving of some general description, or the reduction of the account to something like a catalogue. So, no doubt, humanly speaking, it might have been with our Lord's preaching through Galilee, as afterwards with His preaching through Judæa itself, if it had been the purpose of God that the Gospel writers should attempt anything of the sort. But it does not appear that the Gospels were ever intended by their authors or by the Church to give a history of all that our Lord did or said, and there is great reason for supposing that they were originally compiled rather for purposes of instruction than as narratives.

All that we can know for certain, then, as to the places where, and the persons among whom, our Lord laboured during the summer of this His first year of teaching, must be gathered from the general statements of the Evangelists. These certainly lead us to infer that our Lord's activity at this time was very great indeed, and that it extended over a large tract of country. St. Mark tells us that ' He was preaching in their synagogues, and in all Galilee, and casting out devils.' This seems to imply that the synagogues were not the only places of His preaching, and that He even visited the villages in which there might be no synagogue. St. Matthew's account is still stronger in language. ' Jesus went round through the whole of Galilee, teaching in their synagogues, and preaching the Gospel of the Kingdom, and healing every sickness and every infirmity among the people. And His fame went abroad into the whole of Syria, and they brought to Him all that were sick, that

were seized with various diseases and torments, and
those that had devils, and lunatics, and paralytics, and
He healed them. And there followed Him great multitudes from Galilee, and from Decapolis, and from
Jerusalem, and from Judæa, and from beyond Jordan.'
He went then through the whole country, as far as it
was possible for Him to do so in the time which He
had before Him, and in so thorough a manner that the
Evangelists can affirm that He did this without any
qualification. He healed every kind of sickness and
disease, and He cast out devils everywhere. The universality of His preaching is testified by the distance to
which the fame of it spread. Galilee was but one
province, and yet the whole of Syria was full of Him.
From all parts, even where He had never set His foot,
people came bringing with them their sick friends, or
their friends who had devils, the lunatics, and the paralytics, who could not move themselves. And the stream
gathered as it rolled on. Not only from the towns and
cities in which He preached did great numbers join
themselves on to Him as followers, but people came to
listen to Him from parts of the country which lay
far outside the frontier of Galilee, from Decapolis on
the north and north-east, from Jerusalem and Judæa on
the south, and from the widespread region on the east
beyond the Jordan. It would then be no exaggeration
to say that the whole country was moved. The places
named by St. Matthew lay on all sides of Galilee, except
where it was bounded by the sea or by Samaria; and
their mention is proof that the influence of our Lord
was felt far more widely than had been that of His
Forerunner, St. John Baptist. The splendour of His
miracles, as well as the marvellous force and beauty of
His teaching, may have borne great part in producing so
widespread a movement, but it is hardly possible that

it can have been the result of occasional preaching here and there for a few weeks' time in all.

Personal incidents, anecdotes of what He said and did to this or that person, a miracle here and a dispossession there, how He answered this or that objection, how He called some persons to follow Him and rejected the offer to follow Him made by others—all these things would remain on the memories of men for a certain time, and would then pass away. The traces of His footsteps would be works of marvellous mercy, healings which lasted after He had gone, deliverances of the devil's victims, peace and reconciliation among families, and the like. But all the time He was not only converting souls, and working a marvel of mercy and power, not only setting an example to His future disciples and training them in the rules of the Christian Apostolate; He was also pouring forth the treasures of the New Law, the Evangelical precepts and counsels and maxims which were to become the heritage of the Church of all time and to be the principles of sanctity and beatitude to thousands of His chosen servants. These were to be preserved, though all else might pass away. They were kept at first in the hearts of the Apostles, and it was a part of the office of the Holy Ghost to bring them to their remembrance, and thus enable them to fulfil the most difficult part of the great commission which our Lord gave them before He ascended into Heaven, the part which bade them teach all nations whatsoever He had commanded them. From the Apostles they passed on to the teaching Church, one of whose greatest heirlooms was to consist in a treasury of heavenly doctrine substantially the same with the practical teaching of our Lord in His missionary life, and founded upon the principles and maxims which He taught in the synagogues in one town after another

of the crowded province in which this great light of
Christian truth was first displayed to the world. We
may feel reluctant to know that there are weeks and
months of our Lord's sojourn on earth, or rather of
that part of His sojourn on earth which seems particularly to belong to us, the three years of His Public
Life, as to the details of which we are left in ignorance
so complete, that we do not even know the names of
the places through which He passed about, 'doing
good, and healing all that were oppressed by the devil.'
For all the actions and all the words of our Lord were
full of heavenly grace and life, and our minds almost fail
us when we try to strain them to the thought of the
immeasurable blessings which were within the reach of
the multitudes among whom He moved so familiarly
and with so much condescension, day after day and
week after week. Such attempts help us to understand
the strong language of one who was from the very first
among our Lord's closest companions, that 'there are
also many other things which Jesus did, which, if they
were written every one, the world itself, I think, would
not be able to contain the books which should be
written.' But the providence of God has supplied us
in the Gospels, and particularly in the Sermon on the
Mount, with the chief points and fundamental principles
of our Lord's teaching, which come to us directly from
the Apostles who caught the words as they fell from
His mouth, and whose hearts were prepared by the grace
of God to receive them as seed into fertile and fruitful
ground. If Christians of any age in the history of the
Church are enabled by the same grace to receive the same
blessed seed, with fidelity like that of the Apostles, they
will have but little reason to envy the singular blessedness
of the dwellers in Galilee, for whose benefit these treasures
of holy doctrine were poured out for the first time.

We find in the writings and remains of Christian contemplatives the natural fruit of the workings of the imagination, trained and schooled in the habitual study of all that relates to our Lord's life and character, upon the slender but still deeply suggestive incidents which are preserved to us in the Gospel narratives. The habit of endeavouring to picture to ourselves the details of the scenes of which we have the slightest possible outlines in the accounts of our Lord's Life, is both natural and profitable in itself, and a great help to meditation and practical reflection, while it cannot be altogether without its happy influence on the affections and the whole character. It is but an extension of what every one must do for himself when he sets himself to contemplate the particular mysteries of our Lord's Life one by one, to try to fill up, from the general descriptions which relate to whole periods of that life, and from the characteristic features of the few scenes that are more specially dwelt upon in particular, the details of these larger pictures which must in the main have been very similar in composition to the others. It cannot be unlawful for the Christian imagination to use the liberty of the painter, who, when he has to represent a crowded scene like the marriage at Cana, or the entry into Jerusalem, or the 'Ecce Homo,' arranges his figures as he likes, gives to their countenances the expression which suits his conception of these characters, clothes them in the colours which his art requires, and fills up the background and other less prominent parts of the picture as he thinks best. The painter would sin against his art if he did not do this; but at the same time he is bound to observe the general law of truth in regard to the subject with which he is dealing, and this law is to be ascertained by a careful study of all the sources of information which are open to him in relation to that subject.

In the scenes of our Lord's preaching which are set
before us in the Gospels, we have so many details which
must have been more or less of general or frequent
occurrence, that they may be safely used in filling up
the picture of what has not been particularly described.
Thus the contemplative to whom reference has already
been made in this work, and whose recorded visions
deserve to be studied on account of their grace, simplicity, and apparent truthfulness, even apart from all
considerations of the marvellous manner in which they
may seem to have been communicated, traces our Lord's
footsteps, in that short part of His career which has
been dealt with in the foregoing pages, adding in a
number of details, which may certainly be considered as
simple imaginations in the place in the history which
they profess to supplement, but which are yet all more
or less repetitions or amplifications of incidents which
may have been ordinary to our Lord's Life, and which
on particular occasions are mentioned by the Evangelists.
Our Lord walks quietly on during the night after the
scene in the synagogue at Nazareth, He meets at dawn
some of His disciples, they travel on about the head
of the Lake of Genesareth.   There are some touching
scenes of lepers who come to Him and are cured, who
are forbidden to speak of what He has done, and are
told to go and show themselves to the priests.   In the
course of the few days which must elapse before the
Sabbath at Capharnaum, our Lord comes across the
Herodians and some caravans of pagan merchants who
are passing through Galilee from Damascus, He goes
and eats with one of the Pharisees, He cures a poor
afflicted sinner at the prayer of his mother, He is
watched by a select band of emissaries sent from Jerusalem and other places by the authorities, He teaches
in the synagogue on passages from Isaias which He

applies to Himself, He is besieged by crowds of sick persons who are in need of healing, and followed as He moves along by the demoniacs howling after Him and declaring who He is. We are reminded of St. John in his prison, and told how Herod summoned him to his presence and made him great offers if he would approve of his marriage, and how St. John rebuked him for his impurities, and bore witness to the true dignity of our Lord. Other ranges of society are then represented as being brought across the path of our Lord, such as a company of persons of good education and intellectual culture, whom He spends a day in teaching, and some schools for orphan girls and boys where He does the like. These details are indeed without any authority other than that of the holy woman from whose lips they were taken down. But, in the view in which we are regarding them, they are perfectly in harmony with what we know on the irrefragable authority of the appointed historians of the Life of our Lord, and, further, they are certainly a help to those who wish to be able to represent to themselves the daily incidents of that Life, like the simply imaginative parts of a great historical picture, of which the central figures and action alone are ascertained beyond doubt. And, if they do not directly increase our knowledge of our Lord, they at least repeat and reflect the rays of light which fall upon us from His image as drawn for us in the Gospels, and thus may not be without their fruit in enabling us to love Him better and serve Him more intelligently.

NOTE II.

On the arrangement of the Contemplations of Sister Anne Catharine Emmerich on the Life of our Lord.

The contemplative soul whose visions concerning our Lord's Life have been referred to in the last paragraph of the preceding chapter, as well as in other parts of this work, is the famous Anne Catharine Emmerich, whose Life[1] has lately been published in the series to which these volumes belong. These visions and contemplations are in part well known in England, on account of the popularity of the translation of her *Dolorous Passion*—the part of the whole which had the advantage of being arranged by the skilful hand of Clement Brentano. The remainder of the contemplations exist in German and in French, but have not as yet appeared in English, though selections from them have been promised in a companion work to the Life of the author already mentioned. The most attractive and popular of the French translations is that of M. Charles d'Ebeling, which has been arranged *selon l'ordre des facts*, by Père F. J. Duley, of the Dominican Order. For convenience' sake, it is to this last arrangement that reference has been made in the present work. But it must be remembered that the "order of facts" selected by Père Duley is his own—that which has seemed probable to himself. The visions were seen at different times by Sister Emmerich, and taken down from her lips by Brentano ; but neither the one nor the other is responsible for the arrangement as it appears in the pages of Père Duley.

These contemplations are, therefore, referred to in this work simply, as has been said above, as helps to the imagination as to what may have taken place. Our Lord's Public Life certainly extended for the three years and a half, more or less, which form the period commonly assigned to it, and every day and every hour was filled up. If we try to follow His footsteps day by day during a like space of time, we

[1] *The Life of Anne Catharine Emmerich.* By Helen Ram. Quarterly Series, 1874.

must of course betake ourselves to the use of the imagination, trained in careful contemplation of the scenes which are handed down to us by the authoritative historians. When Sister Emmerich's contemplations are carefully examined, it will be found that a very large part of them are, in this sense, based upon the Gospels. In the contemplations, as arranged by Père Duley, to which reference has been made in the preceding chapter, there is hardly an action or a saying of our Lord's which is not an echo or a development of something related in the New Testament. Indeed, this is so true, that a delicate criticism might object to them on that account. For example, the arrangement by Père Duley places in the space of time between the rejection of our Lord by the Nazarenes and the preaching through Galilee, such incidents as these—that our Lord defended Himself against the charge of healing on the Sabbath ; that He was already watched with great suspicion and hostility by the Pharisees ; that He used the argument from His miraculous power to prove His power to forgive sins, as afterwards in the case of the paralytic.[2] But these incidents, as far as we can judge, belong to a later stage of our Lord's preaching.

[2] St. Matt. ix.

CHAPTER VII.

Illustrations of our Lord's Preaching from the Lives of the Saints.

IT is one of the objects of this work to point out the
many features in our Lord's Life which were intended
to be perpetuated after Him in the life of the Church,
and thus to insist upon the identity of principle between
the two. The part of our Lord's Ministry on which we
are at present engaged was in some respects the very
central portion of the Divine plan for the redemption
of the world, for the great weapon which God intended
to use for the salvation of man was what St. Paul calls
'the foolishness of preaching' by the Church. Our
Lord was already engaged in gathering together the
stones out of which the Church was to be built, and
at the same time He was Himself using, practising, and
endowing with grace the methods and the weapons which
were to be so effectual in the hands of her ministers.
It is this which gives its immense importance to His
Public Life. Everything connected with His preaching
is of infinite value to the Church, and we may be
pardoned if we leave nothing untried which may illustrate, even in matters of lesser moment, a part of the
work which is so precious to us. It has already been
remarked, that the portion of His Public Life on which
we are now engaged is one as to which the Evangelists
speak in general terms rather than in detail. On the
other hand, we possess many details as to similar work
in the lives of the saints which it may be interesting

to notice shortly, in order thus, if possible, to learn from the reflected light which has illuminated them something more than we should otherwise know concerning Him Who is the Light itself. It is perhaps more true to say, not that we learn from the lives of the saints anything otherwise absolutely unknown as to our Lord's Ministry, but that we gather from the former what enables us better to understand the latter. The object of this present chapter is to do this with regard to some external circumstances which attended our Lord's preaching.

The interior resemblance between our Lord and His saints, which is the work of the Holy Ghost, can be fully perceived only by the eyes that read the soul. The practice in His saints of exterior virtues, especially of those winning virtues of humility, meekness, sweetness, condescension, and the like, which may be said to be our Lord's own in so peculiar a manner, and by which He drew men's hearts to Him with so irresistible a power, is something which the world can perceive and acknowledge, and we cannot take up the Life of any of the great Christian apostles without finding a thousand intimations of their resemblance to our Lord in this respect. It is only natural that the main outlines of their teaching should be identical with those of our Lord's, and this too is plain to those who will study what remains to us concerning them with an eye free from prejudice. Again, their practice of the virtues which seem particularly to belong to the Apostolical life, as they were laid down by our Lord in His charge to the Twelve and in His own example, is a point which stands out very clearly in their biographies. We are not about to insist on any of these points of resemblance, which may be incidentally noticed in future portions of this work. Our business at present is with two remarkable features in the preaching of our Lord which we find treated in the most summary manner possible by the Evangelists, while we happen to have full details on the same points in the lives of some of the great missionary saints, which details may help us to understand somewhat better what is implied in the comparatively short statements of the Gospel.

The points on which we are at present engaged are two : the immense multitude of miracles which appear to have accompanied the preaching of our Lord, and, in the second place, the manner in which He seems to have been followed from place to place by large bodies of disciples, who may be considered as distinct from the crowds which would naturally gather in one place after another to hear Him preach when He came into a town or city. Both these circumstances are not more than we should expect in the case of the Teacher Whose office it was to be the Light of the world. It was natural that His Mission should be confirmed by wonderful miracles, and that the hearts of large numbers of men should be drawn to Him by an irresistible enthusiasm. But both these circumstances are unusual, and rise far beyond the common experience of movements which may have their origin in a true desire to benefit mankind, and be carried on with energy and devotion. The magnificence of power, both miraculous and moral, with which our Lord and His saints have been adorned, is thus not easily conceived at ordinary times.

The strong statements of the Evangelists as to the multitude of our Lord's miracles seem to amount to this—that the working of miracles was so habitual to Him that it would be impossible to enumerate them, and that, in truth, the simple assertion that He healed everywhere every kind of disease and cast out devils everywhere is strictly accurate and involves no exaggeration. We have, of course, a great number of our Lord's miracles related to us in the Gospels. Sometimes, as seems the case in St. Matthew,[1] we have a string of cures of different kinds put together, as if by way of specimen; sometimes, and indeed more frequently, the miracles that are related are those which have an importance beyond themselves, as being connected with some particular doctrine, or as having led to some discussion, or as having to some extent influenced the action either of our Lord or of His adversaries. If all the miracles to which these last-named conditions apply were struck out of the Gospel history, we should have but few left which are related in detail, but we should still have a number of general statements as to the ubiquity and universality of our Lord's exercise of miraculous power. It is this last-mentioned class of miracles which we now propose to illustrate from the lives of the saints.

The lives of those whom we may call the missionary saints supply us here with an abundance of materials from which it is difficult to select. We shall take a few instances from the case of those whose mission as preachers was in this respect analogous to the preaching of our Lord, that they preached among populations who already had the faith. The preaching of our Lord was addressed to 'the lost sheep of the house of Israel,' though there can be little doubt that many Gentiles, whether proselytes or not, came within the range of His personal action. The Jews, then, to whom He addressed Himself, had not to be taught about God for the first time, or converted, like the Hindoos and Japanese, for example, to whom St. Francis Xavier was sent, from idolatry, or any other form of false religion, to the service of the true God. No doubt, the difference between the Jews and any Christian population among

---

[1] Chs. viii. ix.

whom the work of a missionary may lie is very great, but it is more natural to compare the latter to the Jews in the view which we are now taking of the evidence of miracles than to a simply pagan population. For this reason we prefer to illustrate the statements of the Evangelists from the lives of such saints as St. Bernard, St. Vincent Ferrer, St. Bernardine, and St. John Capistrano. These will be enough as instances: for the catalogue of saints and servants of God whose lives might be cited as witnesses is almost endless.

The first of these great saints was, as every one knows, a monk vowed to seclusion and prayer, and he only became an apostle, in the stricter sense of the term, on account of the exigences of the time, and for a particular purpose. That particular purpose was the preaching of the Crusade: a Crusade which, as is well known, after having been set on foot mainly by the influence of his preaching and the miracles by which that preaching was confirmed, ended in the salvation of many through outward defeat. Our present business is with the miracles which accompanied and accredited the preaching of St. Bernard in reference to the Crusade. It happens that we have what is, as far as it goes, a very minute account, giving the names of places and dates of a good part of the expedition which St. Bernard made into Germany for the purpose of seeing the Emperor Conrad and of persuading him and the people in general to take the Cross. This expedition lasted only a few months. It was late in the autumn of one year that St. Bernard left France, and he had returned to Clairvaux in the February of the next. We may imagine that some of our Lord's circuits of Galilee would have occupied Him nearly as long as this, and we have therefore a space of time in the life of the saint which may be considered as corresponding to one of these circuits.

The reports which remain to us of these weeks in the life of St. Bernard may be seen in the later editions of his works by Horstius and Mabillon, and have been reprinted with occasional notes by the Bollandists in their account of the Saint. They rest on the very highest authority, that of eye-witnesses, who in a number of cases give their names after the particular miracles which they attest. St. Bernard had with him, among other companions, one of his secretaries, Godefroy, who sent the community of Clairvaux the account of what he saw to console them for the absence of their beloved Father. The two first parts of what is called in Mabillon's edition the sixth book of the Life of St. Bernard, are founded upon these reports of Godefroy, and the third and last part is written by himself. If the contents of the book formed a narrative of banquets given to a prince in his tour through some country, addresses presented to and speeches made by him, diversified by accounts of his wonderful exploits among wild animals, his successful shots, and the like, they would be consi-dered as authentic and authoritative in the highest degree if they came to us on the same evidence as we have here for the miracles of the Saint. There can be absolutely no ground in reason for the denial of the miracles, except that of denying the possibility of miracles altogether and the utter rejection of all human testimony to their truth. The places in which the miracles took place stand in order in the book before us, as St. Bernard's path is traced through the diocese of Constance, through Kent-zigen, Herenheim, Lapenheim, Frienburg, Heyreresheim, Basle, Rinvel, Doningen, Schaffhausen, and at last Con-stance, a good many smaller places in its neighbourhood being also mentioned. A whole chapter is occupied with these. Then there is a long account of what took place at Spires, where the Saint met the Emperor Conrad, having already had a private interview with him at Frankfort. The famous scene at Spires is related, where St. Bernard, after celebrating Mass before the Emperor and his Court, turned round and spoke in such words of fire, speaking to Conrad not as a prince but as a man, and enumerating the blessings which God had showered upon him, that the Emperor interrupted him, declaring that he would no longer be ungrateful, but would take the Cross then and there, as he did with one of his sons and a number of princes and barons. The account of the miracles at Spires fills two long chapters. St. Bernard is then followed from Spires to Worms, where he had already been two months before, thence to Coblentz, thence to Cologne, Liege, Juliers, Aix-la-Chapelle, and Utrecht, Huy, Valenciennes, Cambray, and a number of other places on his way back towards his beloved home at Clairvaux, where also, and in many places in the neighbourhood, he performed a great many miracles. It is hardly possible to give an idea of the manner in which miracles seem to have been crowded together without long extracts, but we will try to give an account of a single chapter, relating to the latter part of this journey.

'Going out of Cologne,' say the narrators, 'we came to a place called Brunville, a monastery two miles from the city. The people followed the Saint, and brought him two deaf men, "whose ears God opened, when the blessed Father put his fingers into them, and breathed hearing into them from his sacred mouth." Then another witness, Eberhard, speaks. On the Tuesday morning, in the Church of St. Nicholas at Brunville, a blind boy was restored to sight before his altar. Scarcely had the shouts of the people subsided, when a deaf and dumb man received hearing and speech. Wolkmar adds that he was present when another deaf person was healed. And before that, says another eye-witness, we had seen another miracle on the road, the healing of a man whose arm and hand had been dried up. Gerard says that the day was full of miracles; the country was thronged with people as a city. The first miracle of all that day was on a man blind of one eye, who was cured. But the most wonderful was the cure of a grown-up girl, whom her mother brought, declaring that she had been deaf and dumb from her birth, a statement confirmed by many by-standers who knew her. St. Bernard laid his hands on her, and she spoke freely and heard perfectly at once. Godefroy adds that up to these miracles he had been in front before the crowd, but the chants of thanksgiving from the people made him turn back, and he carefully noted and proved the rest of the miracles of the day. A deaf and blind woman was restored to hearing and to sight, also three deaf men, one lame woman, and five blind, some of one eye, others of both. One blind boy was cured secretly, and St. Bernard stopped, and turning to him, made some one ask him whether he saw. " He had done the same," says another witness, "as to another blind man to whom he sent me to ask the question, and when I came back to say he had been enlightened, I felt it, said the Saint."

' In the evening, he adds, we came to Juliers, and the blessed Father, on entering the church, saw a lame woman lying before the altar, went up to her in great fervour of spirit, and raised her up " with as much ease as faith." He cured a blind man in the porch. The next morning, after Mass, says another eye-witness, a blind boy and a deaf man were cured. A young lady, niece of the Count of Juliers, one of whose eyes was blind and the other weak, was cured by the sign of the Cross. A gentleman who had been blind for twenty years was also cured. Many other things were done that day, and the people were often calling out, as was their wont after a miracle, "Christ uns genade!" But we have room only for a few cases. Eberhard tells us that on the road that day he remembers a deaf boy, a blind woman, and a lame woman, who were cured in the presence of all. Then the narrator comes to Aix-la-Chapelle, "a most famous and beautiful place, more fitted for the pleasures of the body than the health of the soul," as the writer says. There, in the royal chapel, at the altar of Blessed Mary, on the Thursday, a blind girl received her sight. Then a lame man was cured, and his stick hung up in the church for a testimony; then two women, whose hands had been withered up, "were cured in the self-same hour." The witness tells us how it was done. The holy Father stretched out the fingers of one of these women with his own hand, but the other was behind him, and complained that she could not get to touch him, so she was told to touch his robes, and got hold of his cowl, and as she tried to draw it to her, her fingers were stretched out, and she was healed. But there was never so great a throng anywhere as in that chapel, and so a great many things which happened were unknown. One witness says that five blind men received their sight.

'Then they came to Utrecht in the course of the next week. They slept the Wednesday night at our Lady's Church. On the next morning, after Mass, they took the blessed Father to a raised place, where he might heal the sick without being crushed by the people. The witness Wolkmar says he stood next to St. Bernard, and saw all that went on. Five blind men were healed, one deaf and one dumb man heard and spoke. Then another deaf man, and several maimed persons were cured. Gerard relates a scene which took place in the hospice that day. A deaf and dumb boy was brought to St. Bernard, and as he was making the sign of the Cross over him, a certain honourable youth, Conrad by name, a canon of Cologne, came to renounce the world, and to give himself to St. Bernard in religion. The Saint raised himself to receive Conrad, and as he did so, the boy began to speak and hear. The people were outside waiting, and then the boy was given to his parents speaking and hearing, and there followed great exultation. The cure became famous in that town, and others were at once brought, a lame woman, who was enabled to walk, and three blind men, who received their sight, and were led out to the people with joy and rejoicing.

'The last paragraph of this chapter may as well be given in the words of the witness, a monk named Philip. "When the holy man was going out of Utrecht, there was some reason for his turning aside to the Church of St. Servatius, for some business of Brother Norbert's, who was a canon of that church, but he at once renounced his canonry and the world. In the way thither a lame boy was raised up in our presence. In the Church of St. Servatius the people brought to our Father a lame man, asking him to lay his hand upon him. 'I know not,' he said, 'whether it will displease Blessed Servatius if we presume to do this in his house.' Then all cried out and said, 'My lord, it will not displease him,' and he said, 'In the name of our Lord Jesus Christ and of Blessed Servatius, arise and stand upon thy feet!' He rose up therefore without delay or hesitation, and there was great joy among the people. These things were done yesterday at Utrecht. To-day at Liege the whole clergy, which is very numerous in that city, had assembled, and they were awaiting the Father in the chamber of the Bishop, that he might preach to them. And behold, the Lord was beforehand with them in His word of power, and a certain lame cleric, who, from his middle downwards was so disabled that he could not stand at all on his feet, was brought to the man of God. And he, signing the disabled limbs with the Cross and feeling them, said, 'Walk, in the name of Jesus Christ!' And he was at once strengthened and began to walk, and the report went forth among the clergy, and they cried out, 'These are Thy works, O Christ, Who dost thus glorify Thy saints.' To Him be glory and power, now and for ever. Amen."'

The light that is thrown by this detailed account of some of the miracles of St. Bernard, or the Evangelical preaching of our Lord Himself, does not extend far beyond this, that it enables us to understand the words of the Gospels when they speak of the immense number of miracles by which that preaching was confirmed. St. Bernard's mission as a preacher was occasional and partial, that is, he was sent forth from his monastery on the occasion of some heretical teaching, some rising schism, or for the purpose of stirring up Christendom to a Crusade for the recovery of the Holy Sepulchre. He was not regularly a missionary saint, such as St. Vincent Ferrer or St. Bernardine of Siena. It is in the lives of these saints, and especially in that of the great Dominican preacher, that we must look for further illustrations which may help us to form a more perfect picture of our Lord's going through Galilee first and Judæa afterwards. Indeed, it is very difficult to compress into a small space all that is contained to this purpose in the life of St. Vincent alone. Everything about St. Vincent is marvellous and on a great scale. He came in the miserable period of the great schism of the latter end of the fourteenth century, and lived under the obedience of one of the Antipopes, Pedro de Luna, whose confessor and Master of the Sacred Palace he was. For, disastrous as the schism was, it was so far a merely personal or national quarrel that no one could be blamed for finding himself on the wrong side, and, as a matter of history, there were saints in each camp, so to speak, whose great object was to bring about the unity which was established at the Council of Constance. The times were deplorably bad, as is indeed shown by the fact that the schism was possible. St. Vincent himself left on record that he thought that there had never been in the world so much pomp and vanity, so much impurity, except in the times before the Deluge, and that the same was true of avarice and unjust usury, that simony reigned among ecclesiastics, envy and jealousy among religious, and gluttony in all classes, so that the fasts of the Church were never observed, while anger and vindictiveness caused innumerable murders, even among friends. This was the view, no doubt, of a preacher saint, of the evils of the time which he was sent to correct, but the mere fact of the providential mission of such a Saint in so marvellous a manner, and with such circumstances of magnificence, so to speak, to authenticate his mission, may incline us to think that there was no exaggeration in the estimate formed by St. Vincent. He was lying on what seemed likely to be his death-bed in mature age,[1] when our Lord appeared to him, told him that the schism was to end soon, as soon as the faults of men were ended, and that therefore, he was

---

[1] This seems to have been in 1396, though his preaching did not begin, on account of the reluctance of Pedro de Luna to let him go, till 1399. There is as much as seventeen years' difference in the dates variously assigned to his birth, and we cannot tell how old he was in 1396. The latest date given for his birth is 1357, and if this were certain, he would be nearly forty in 1396. The earliest is 1340, so that he would have been as old as fifty-six at the time of which we speak, and not far from sixty when his preaching began. This seems scarcely probable. There are two intermediate dates given, fixing his birth in 1346 and 1350.

to rise from his bed, and go forth to preach against vices, as He Himself had specially chosen him for that purpose. He was to bid sinners repent, because the Day of Judgment was near. It is said that at the same time our Lord told him three things: first, that He had confirmed him in grace, in order that he might be fit for His Apostolate; secondly, that he should have many persecutions, all of which he should overcome by the help of Divine grace, so that he should preach the Judgment over a great part of Europe with immense fruit to souls, and should then die on its extreme borders. And, in the third place, our Lord gave him instructions as to the method and rule which he was to follow in his preaching.

This is not the place to follow St. Vincent throughout his career of preaching, which lasted twenty years, during which he preached over France and Spain, the Low Countries, the north of Italy, as well as England and Scotland and Ireland. We cannot be quite certain how far he went eastwards into Germany, or whether he preached in Portugal. When he visited a country, he went throughout it in the most complete manner, going even into small towns and villages, and he returned over and over again to the same place. The space of time which he gave to different places seems to have depended on the fruit which he gathered. Sometimes he would remain only a few hours, sometimes for weeks or even months on one spot; and he would seem not to have taken the places of a country in their natural order one after another along a line of road, but to have gone now here and now there according to the needs of the people who called him. And he was frequently sent for by prelates or sovereigns to arrange urgent affairs in places under their rule.

We have a full account given by his biographers of the method observed by St. Vincent in his missions.

He had the fullest faculties from the Pope (as he was deemed), Benedict the Thirteenth (Pedro de Luna), as Apostolic Legate, and could absolve the most difficult cases; this power was confirmed to him by the Council of Constance and the lawfully elected Pope Martin the Fifth. At the same time he never entered a diocese or preached there without the leave and blessing of the Bishop. He ordinarily walked on foot with a staff in his hand, at the top of which was a small crucifix. In later years he had a wound in his leg, and was obliged to ride. He made a point of keeping his Rule exactly, and so never preached without the leave of his religious Superiors. He added certain austerities of his own to those which were prescribed him by his Rule. Every night he took a severe discipline, and when he was too weak to administer it himself, he made his companions give it him instead. When he entered any place, he knelt down, with tears in his eyes, and prayed for the people to whom he was to preach, and then rose up full of confidence, saying, *Non nobis Domine, non nobis, sed nomini tuo da gloriam.* Very often the clergy and magistrates of the place came out in procession to meet him, and conducted him to the church with great honour, as Apostolic Legate. Sometimes the crowd that came to meet him was so great, that he had to walk or ride with a portable fence carried by persons on each side of him, that he might not be crushed. After visiting the church, he dismissed his companions to the lodgings which he requested the people to give them, and went himself to a monastery either of his own Order or some other—very often a Benedictine abbey. He never relaxed his rule of fasting, and spent the night in prayer, in reading the Holy Scriptures, preparing the matter for his sermons, and in a short repose.

The next morning at dawn he went to confession,

recited his Hours on his knees, and then sang a solemn Mass in the church or cathedral. After Mass he mounted the pulpit and began to preach to the thousands of people who ordinarily came together when his arrival was known. His sermons often lasted two or three hours without fatigue either to himself or to his audience. After the sermon, he remained half an hour at the foot of the pulpit to cure the sick who were brought to him. Ordinarily he healed them all, and dispossessed many from devils. Then he and his companions heard confessions till mid-day, when he went to the monastery for his slender meal, after which he recreated himself by reading the Sacred Scriptures. In the afternoon there was another sermon, another healing of the sick, who were sometimes collected at the sound of a bell when the time came, and the rest of the day was spent in preaching to ecclesiastics, or to nuns in convents, or in hearing confessions, making peace between enemies, visiting and consoling the afflicted, and other like employments.

We must pass over with much regret the account which is given of the matter and manner of St. Vincent's preaching, which he varied very much according to the kind of persons to whom he was addressing himself, sometimes displaying great learning and profound thought, but ordinarily using the simplest and clearest language and supporting his arguments chiefly from Scripture, which he used very largely, the Old Testament as well as the New.[3] The concourse of people who thronged to

[3] The sermons of St. Vincent, as they have come down to us, do not seem to be more than notes put together by some of his hearers or secretaries. They throw a remarkable light on his history in this respect, that whereas he is said in a general way to have announced the immediate coming of the Day of Judgment, these sermons are expositions of the ordinary topics of Christian preachers, taken from the Gospels and Epistles for the Sundays. It would seem, then, that St. Vincent's preaching ranged over the common field of instruction, and was not directed to the excitement of terror or other exaggerated feelings in his audience.

hear him was enormous, frequently reaching the number of very many thousands; the universities closed their schools, the merchants and artisans left their shops and their work, when he appeared in a city. He had a voice which seemed to have the gift of suiting every kind of discourse and moving the most various sentiments, and it was heard by the standers on the outskirts of the immense crowds who listened to him, as easily as by those who were nearest to his pulpit. He had the gift which the Apostles and disciples received at Pentecost, of being understood by a number of persons of various nations at the same time, each one hearing the words in his own language, though St. Vincent only used his own native dialect. And, again, he had the corresponding gift of understanding people of any nation whatever when they came to him in confession. We have already spoken summarily of his daily exercise of the gift of miracles. It would be entering on an almost endless subject to attempt to specify those of which we have the record in particular.

Perhaps the most remarkable feature in the missionary labours of St. Vincent, considered as illustrating the points of our Lord's preaching with which we are engaged, consisted in the large companies of persons who used to follow him from place to place. These bands were regularly organized, and observed the most admirable discipline. At their head were a number of priests, who had enlisted themselves as his companions with the leave of their Superiors and of the Pope. They were his intimate friends, men after his own heart, learned, and remarkable for holiness, to such an extent that some of them had the gift of miracles.

Sometimes they had to preach instead of St. Vincent, if he was ill. But their chief work was that of secretaries, or catechists. Some had to bring about reconciliations, or to keep order among the multitudes. They sang in his High Mass, and taught the Christian doctrine to the ignorant. Others kept the alms that were offered, provided for the wants of the followers of the Saint, and distributed the rest among the poor.

The bands of followers, who were under the guidance of these priests, were very large and well managed, and it cannot be doubted that the effect produced upon the people at large by this multitude of fervent disciples was very great indeed. No one was admitted into these companies without a rigorous examination. The condition was, in the first place, that they should be free persons, that is, not bound in marriage, or to the care of children or of aged and needy parents, or to the service of creditors for debts unpaid. Married persons who had made provision for the care of their families, husbands and wives who agreed to separate and enter the bands of men and women respectively, were allowed to join. For these bands consisted both of men and women. Rich people were not admitted unless they sold and gave to the poor what they had. But they were to work, at the same time, for their livelihood, especially those who knew any useful art. Moreover, they were kept continually employed in teaching children of either sex, or in instructing converts. Lastly, it was required that they should be persons of good reputation, or that they should be determined to regain by a new life the reputation which they had lost. And on this condition people of all sorts and sects were admitted. Every evening there was a 'procession of penance,' formed of some of them, who went along taking the discipline. They were always present at the Mass and sermons of St. Vincent, and gave the best example of devotion and recollection at both. The rule was that they should go to Confession and Communion at least once a week.

The number of the members of these bands was usually as great as ten thousand: and it sometimes exceeded that limit. It was particularly remarkable that the greatest possible union and peace prevailed among them. There were among them men of every nation and rank, nobles and common peasants, learned men and artisans, ecclesiastics and seculars, Frenchmen, Spaniards, Italians, or others; there were converts from Judaism and Mahometanism, and persons reclaimed from lives of the greatest license and brutality, by the side of men who had never lost the innocence of their baptism. The progress of these bands through the country was like that of a peaceful army. The men marched separately, after a banner on which our crucified Lord was represented: the women were headed by a banner of our Lady. The ecclesiastics went in a separate band from the laity.

We may use a beautiful anecdote of St. Vincent Ferrer for the purpose of passing on to another great Apostolical preacher whose name has already been mentioned. St. Vincent was preaching in the north of Italy in 1408 with his usual wonderful success, and when at Alessandria, in Lombardy, he received the visit of a young Franciscan friar, who came to consult him about his desires of perfection. The next morning St. Vincent interrupted his sermon by an unexpected digression. He told his audience that there was present among them a certain religious of the Order of St. Francis, who was soon to become famous throughout all Italy, and to produce great fruit among Christians by his preaching. He himself, St. Vincent said, was old, and the friar of whom he spoke was young, and yet it was to happen hereafter that the latter was to be set before him in honour by the Church. This is understood as a prophecy that the young friar was to be canonized before

St. Vincent, as was actually the case. He exhorted them to be thankful to God, and to pray Him to accomplish what He had revealed, and then added, that as this was to happen, he himself would now return to France and Spain, and leave to the new preacher the care of evangelizing the parts of Italy which he had not as yet visited.

The young friar of whom St. Vincent spoke was St. Bernardine of Siena, who was then twenty-eight years of age, having been born in 1380, the year in which St. Catharine of Siena died. Three years before the visit of St. Vincent, Bernardine, soon after he had been ordained priest, broke out one day without preparation into an exhortation to some people whom he had gathered round him by bearing a heavy cross on his shoulders to a convent near Arezzo. The effect of his sudden preaching had been wonderful, and soon after the Minister-General of his Order appointed him a public preacher. His beginnings in this capacity were successful, but there was still doubt in his own mind and in the minds of others whether he was fitted for the office imposed on him. The story of his early years is one of graceful humility, intense purity, and great love of prayer and retirement. At the time of which we speak he was of delicate health, not likely to be able to bear the fatigue of long journeys on foot and the other labours of an active Apostolate. Moreover, he had some disease in his throat which made him hoarse and his utterance indistinct, nor could he make himself heard at any considerable distance. The doubt was settled by a miracle, for Bernardine betook himself to prayer, and begged that if he was to go on with his ministry God would be pleased at the intercession of His glorious Mother to remove the impediment. He seemed to himself to see a fiery globe descend from heaven and touch his throat, which was immediately healed.

The great successes of St. Bernardine as a preacher date, as it seems, from the time at which he had the interview with St. Vincent Ferrer which has been already mentioned. His ministry lasted till his death in 1444, no less than thirty-eight years. It was confined to Italy, mostly the northern provinces, and Tuscany, Umbria, and the March of Ancona. We do not read of any companies of followers, such as those of which mention is made in the account of St. Vincent, and, although St. Bernardine frequently worked miracles, he was not so wonderful a "thaumaturge" as the great Dominican. Like St. Vincent, he celebrated Mass in public every day before preaching, and generally on a portable altar erected in the piazza in which he was about to preach. It was remarked of him that he always took great pains to find out the prevalent vices and errors of the population to whom he was to address himself, and was generally very diligent in preparation. He is also said to have had a happy manner of introducing pleasantries into his sermons, which, like those of St. Vincent, often lasted two or three hours, without any weariness either in the preacher or in his audience. On festivals he is said to have strung together a number of different heads in his sermon, instead of keeping to one subject; and at the end of his sermons he was accustomed to hold up to the people a tablet, on which the holy name of Jesus was inscribed in letters of gold, that they might venerate it. The effect of his sermons was as wonderful as that of those of St. Vincent. The piazzas were crowded, sometimes with thousands of men and women, from early morning, on the days on which he was to preach. The children and babies were carried on their fathers' shoulders, or at their mothers' breasts, rather than that they should lose the opportunity of hearing and seeing him, and a general reform of manners followed, especially in the extinction of the feuds and enmities to which the Italian character is always prone, and which at that time were exceedingly rife.

Just as St. Vincent Ferrer may be said to have handed on the torch of Evangelical preaching to the young Franciscan friar who afterwards was known as St. Bernardine of Siena, so it may be said that the latter became the spiritual father of another great preacher of his own Order, the famous St. John of Capistrano. He was a few years younger than St. Bernardine. He began as a lawyer, in the employ of Ladislaus, King of Sicily, but some misfortunes into which he fell in those troubled times opened his eyes to the vanities of the world, and at the age of thirty he entered the Order of St. Francis, putting himself under the guidance and rule of St. Bernardine. His rapid progress in sanctity revealed the powerful influence of so great a master. He became, as a preacher, even more famous and influential than St. Bernardine himself, though the latter will always fill a larger space in the estimation of posterity, on account of the carefully arranged sermons which he has left behind him, which were put together at a late period of his missionary career. As sermons they are far too full of matter to be preached at once; they are skeleton treatises, each containing the matter for several sermons, such as sermons are now. Still it is possible that in the days of their author they may have been preached through at one sitting, if we may so speak; indeed, something of the sort must have been the case, as they are usually numbered according to the days of a Lent or an Advent.

St. John Capistrano's teaching had a most marvellous influence. His mere presence sometimes was enough to convert whole populations, and his historians relate a number of very stupendous miracles as wrought by him. During the forty years of his ministry he was almost always preaching, almost everywhere with the same immense crowds flocking to his feet which have been mentioned in the case of St. Vincent and St. Bernardine. Germany and Hungary were the scenes of his labours as well as Italy. Whole villages came out to greet him, as he passed, the clergy of the towns came in procession to receive him, and the masses of his audience were too great to meet anywhere but in the open air. When he was sixty years of age, and was sent into Germany at the request of the Emperor Frederic the Third, as Papal Legate, to put an end to the Hussite wars, his progress through Carinthia, Styria, and Austria to Vienna was one long triumph, and great miracles confirmed his preaching. At Vienna he is said to have preached in the open air to one hundred thousand persons: but the numbers may be supposed to be not accurately ascertained. He had great success in Bohemia. He passed into Moravia, Thuringia, Saxony, leaving behind him notable changes in the manners of many of the great towns; and he was then invited into Poland by King Casimir. The last year of St. John's life was among the most remarkable of all. The Turks took Constantinople in 1453, and filled Europe with panic. It was thought that they would soon be seen before the walls of Vienna and Rome. St. John, then nearly seventy years of age, was summoned to the councils of the Christian princes. He attended the Diet of Neustadt in 1455, sent by the Pope to encourage fainting hearts. In 1456 he met John Hunniades at Peterwardein, and was the life of the Christian host which gained the definitive victory under the walls of Belgrade. Both the Christian champions died in the same year. As to the miracles of St. John Capistrano, it will be enough to refer to a few lines from the

Chronicles of St. Francis, where, speaking of his preaching at Vienna, the writers say that the Saint had twelve companions with him, all of whom occupied themselves in noting down his miracles, but after having recorded seven hundred, they threw down their pens and gave up in despair.

It would be easy to multiply illustrations of this kind, from the lives of other saints, and especially of holy missionaries. The object of this chapter will have been attained if the numberless miracles of St. Bernard or St. John Capistrano enable us more easily to imagine what must have been the display of Divine power when the preacher was our Lord Himself, and when it was in the providence of God that His teaching should be confirmed by miracles of mercy far too numerous to be recorded. The crowds which flocked to the preaching of St. Vincent and St. Bernardine may make it easy for us to picture to ourselves the popular enthusiasm which waited on our Lord's footsteps as He passed from one thickly peopled part of Galilee to another. And the orderly bands of devout disciples, of both sexes, who marched from place to place in the train of the great Dominican preacher of the Judgment, may help us to understand that very large multitude which seems at an early period of His preaching to have followed our Lord from place to place. It was to a multitude of this sort, though perhaps not so perfectly regulated as that which followed St. Vincent, that the Sermon on the Mount was addressed, and we may perhaps suppose that it was for some such company that our Lord afterwards miraculously multiplied the loaves and fishes in the desert.

CHAPTER VIII.

The Sermon on the Mount.

St. Matt. v. 1 ; *Vita Vitæ Nostræ*, § 31.

IT has already been remarked that we have very few particular incidents preserved to us of the many months of extreme and varied activity which our Blessed Lord spent in the circuits of Galilee which are spoken of by the Evangelists. This dearth of distinct anecdotes, miracles, acts of authority over the devil, and the like, is amply compensated for by the abundant treasures of holy doctrine which have been preserved for us in that great monument of our Lord's teaching which is known as the Sermon on the Mount. It was certainly most natural that the attention of the Apostles should be particularly directed to the record of our Lord's teaching, which would come second only in importance to those acts of His in which the great mysteries of our salvation were wrought, and especially His Passion, and that, whenever a written Gospel came to be formed under their auspices and by one of themselves, it should be, in a very large measure, devoted to the preservation of that teaching. Such a Gospel we have, as has elsewhere been shown, in the Gospel of St. Matthew, and the manner in which this Evangelist hurries on in his story to the great collection of doctrine which is embodied in the Sermon on the Mount can hardly fail to strike any careful student of the New Testament.

St. Matthew seems to relate nothing before it except what was absolutely necessary, and he postpones to it those incidents of the Sabbath at Capharnaum which he selects later on in his Gospel, when he comes to weave, as it were, a chain of our Lord's miracles as specimens of His doings in that kind, incidents which nevertheless seem undoubtedly to have taken place at the very outset of our Lord's public teaching in Galilee, and of which the Evangelist may have been an eye-witness. Again, he contents himself, as we have seen, with the shortest possible description of our Lord's course of preaching, simply enumerating the wide circle of provinces to which the influence of that preaching reached, and then he dwells with loving fulness upon the Sermon on the Mount, which forms no inconsiderable part of his whole work, and is, we may venture to say, a record of our Lord's teaching perfectly unique in the whole New Testament.

The other Evangelists have added little of the same kind to these chapters of St. Matthew. St. Mark's object is to dwell on our Lord's wonderful display of Divine power, rather than on His direct teaching. St. Luke, always, like St. Paul, unwilling to 'build on another man's foundation,'[1] has marvellously contrived to give a complete Gospel, at the same time that he avoids, as far as is possible, the repetition of what others had said before him, for which he usually substitutes something similar. Thus he has given the far shorter Sermon on the Plain instead of this discourse recorded by St. Matthew. And the great mass of our Lord's teaching[2] which occurs in the central portion of St. Luke's Gospel, and which is peculiar to him, might be more fitly compared to the later teaching of our Lord in St. Matthew, where the Evangelist collects so

[1] Romans xv.   [2] St. Luke ix. 51; xviii. 29.

much which relates to what are called the counsels of perfection, than the Sermon on the Mount. The very large additions, on the other hand, to the remains of our Lord's teaching, which make up the greater part of the Gospel of St. John are chiefly disputations, a class of discourses almost entirely passed over by St. Matthew and the other Evangelists, or again, the outpouring of our Lord's most tender confidence to His intimate friends at the Last Supper. We are thus justified in considering the Sermon on the Mount as a document which has hardly any parallel in the rest of the Gospel records, as it is certainly a document which, more than any other, has furnished the principles of the moral teaching of the Christian Church in all ages.

St. Matthew introduces the Sermon on the Mount in direct connection with the multitude which followed our Lord, not only from Galilee, but from all the provinces of Palestine except Samaria. We may gather from this, what indeed might be considered evident enough from the substance of the Sermon itself—that it was delivered after the preaching of our Lord had been continued for some time, and His fame and influence carried far and wide. The course of a great preacher who goes about from town to town, marking his footsteps by works of wonder and beneficence, is like the onward flow of a mighty river, which swells in volume as it proceeds through the plain, gathering into itself the streams which drain the valleys which it passes in succession. Some of our Lord's hearers would follow Him for a time, and their places would be filled by others, but the multitude would gradually swell as He passed from place to place. The multitude would be in the main composed of persons to whom His teaching was becoming familiar, and who were being gradually raised thereby higher and higher in spiritual discernment and cultivation. The formation of something like a large body of such persons would be a great step towards the foundation of the Church. It would be the providing of the flock of which the Apostles were to be the first shepherds. Such persons would be like the good soil of which our Lord was afterwards to speak in the earliest of His parables, in which the seed was to be fruitful thirty-fold, or sixty-fold, or a hundred-fold. They may not, of course, have been as disciplined and as organized a body as the bands of which we read as following St. Vincent, but they may still have differed very greatly from a promiscuous multitude in the ordinary sense of the term.

It may also be remarked that the time was not yet come when it would be necessary or prudent for our Lord to wrap up His teaching in parables, which could only be understood by the intelligent, without becoming an occasion of spiritual injury to the ill-disposed, captious, or obstinate hearers. And if there were any such among the multitudes who would flock to our Lord's teaching out of curiosity in the towns, they would not be likely to put themselves to the trouble and inconvenience of following Him from spot to spot. Thus that sifting of His audience, if we may so speak, which our Lord afterwards practised when He came to speak in parables, would be attained in a different way if our Lord so arranged the places and occasions of His teaching as to leave behind Him the crowd of the less advanced hearers, to whom what St. Paul afterwards called 'the word of the beginning of Christ,'[3] was more fitly to be addressed, and gather round Him the other multitude of followers who had already been taught 'the foundation of penance from dead works, and of faith towards God,' and so might be led on to 'things more perfect.' That our Lord did actually proceed in this way on the

<hr>

[3] Hebrews vi. 1.

occasion of the Sermon on the Mount, seems to be implied by St. Matthew's language—'And seeing the multitude, He went up into the mountain, and when He was sat down, His disciples came to Him.' There would be no security against an utterly promiscuous multitude in the cities and towns, but when He withdrew to a comparatively lonely spot, He would still be followed by a crowd, but a crowd more or less composed of persons who were already His disciples.

When we come to examine closely the substance of the Sermon on the Mount in itself, we are at once struck with the preparation which it seems to require in the audience which was to receive it. This will be more naturally drawn out further on. But it may be well to dwell here on another remarkable characteristic of this Sermon. It is a wonderful close and compact body of doctrine, and, if it were merely recited or delivered as it lies before us in the volume of the New Testament, it would occupy a comparatively short time in such delivery. The most important and pregnant maxims and precepts are here set forth with the utmost brevity. The Sermon is in truth a perfect code and system of perfection. The Beatitudes and the Lord's Prayer, to speak of nothing else, contain a number of heads of doctrine which can only be developed by long meditation and explanation. We have certainly no right to say that our Lord could not, if it had so seemed good to Him, have put forward these precepts and maxims of heavenly wisdom in the short and almost proverbial form in which we now read them in the pages of St. Matthew; or that, if it had pleased Him, He might not have passed so rapidly from one subject to another, and compressed so many various heads of the most momentous doctrine into so short a time as would be required if we were to understand the Sermon, as a whole, to have contained nothing but what has been preserved to us. But the delivery of such a compact summary of doctrine in such a form in the course of ordinary teaching would seem at first sight improbable, and unlike our Lord's usual method of teaching, as far as we can gather it from the Gospels. It would certainly also be unlike the traditional manner of teaching in the Church, in which we are most familiar with the more gradual modes of instruction. The parables of our Lord, for instance, are usually devoted to the setting forth of one truth at a time concerning the method of God's government of the world, and the more didactic portions of the discourses in St. John's Gospel do not pass with great rapidity from one subject to another. Nor, indeed, as to any of our Lord's recorded discourses, whether private conversations such as those with Nicodemus or the Samaritan woman, or disputations such as those with the Jews at Jerusalem after the miracle on the Sabbath-day, or that in the synagogue at Capharnaum after the multiplication of the loaves, and others like them, or again, such as the long discourse with the eleven Apostles after the Last Supper, can we be certain that we have more recorded for us than the chief heads of the conversation, or argument, or discourse.

We are therefore left somewhat to conjecture, both in general as to the discourses of our Lord in the Gospels, and in particular as to the Sermon on the Mount, not indeed as to the perfect faithfulness of the report which remains to us, but as to its being a literal and exact record, word for word, of all that fell from our Lord. Nor is it forbidden us to suppose that He added explanations and developments of the doctrines which are summed up in the sentences of His Sermon, which developments have been omitted. Perhaps, however, when the occasion on which the Sermon on the Mount was delivered is considered, and its due importance in the series of the manifestations of our Lord is taken into account, it may seem more natural to think that it is not an ordinary discourse or instruction, one out of many, by way of specimen, which has here been preserved to us by St. Matthew. We may come to think that it had a character and authority of its own, as indeed might naturally be inferred from the unusual and very solemn circumstances of its delivery. It could not have been merely for convenience that our Lord 'went up into the mountain' on this occasion, as on one or two others, when He was about to take some very great step in the fulfilment of His Mission, such as the appointment of the Apostles or the manifestation of the glory of His Sacred Humanity in the Transfiguration. The delivery of this Sermon is an occasion of this kind, and we may thus arrive at a more accurate understanding of its authority as a kind of Code of the New Covenant, answering in many respects to the Law which was delivered on Mount Sinai in the Old Covenant. Many beautiful thoughts on this subject are to be found in the old Catholic writers, and it may perhaps be our best wisdom to look on them, not only as pious contemplations, but as resting on solid truths relating to the dispensation of the Incarnation, the office and mission of our Lord, and the manner in which they were gradually fulfilled, and, as it were, unfolded in His Public Life.

A careful study of St. Matthew's Gospel reveals the fact, which has been sufficiently dwelt on elsewhere in the present work, that he is not only careful to note all the fulfilments, and even illustrations, of the ancient prophecies as they come before him in the course of his narrative, but that his mind is so full of the correspondence between our Lord's Life and the types and

J 2

anticipations of the Old Testament, that he often seems to take it for granted that the resemblance will be obvious to his readers without any direct indication on his own part. We have seen how he appears, for instance, to refer to the history of Adam's temptation, in his own account of our Lord's temptation, and we may have hereafter to draw attention to other instances in his Gospel of the same tacit reference to the history of the Old Testament. Indeed, his habit of viewing our Lord and His history in the light of ancient type and prophecy is perhaps the true explanation of the manner in which he seems to accommodate to our Lord distinct predictions which were not always in the first instance directly applicable to Him.

The remark which has just been made as to St. Matthew's Gospel in general has its importance in a particular relation to the Sermon on the Mount. In a Gospel which is so mainly didactic, that is, so largely devoted to the preservation of the doctrine of our Lord as the ground and foundation of Christian teaching, it is natural that we should find our Lord Himself put before us in the especial character of a Lawgiver. The type in the Old Testament which would correspond to Him in this character would, of course, be that of Moses, and the giving of the Law on Mount Sinai by the Jewish lawgiver would naturally have some corresponding fulfilment in the promulgation of the Christian Law. When the circumstances and character of the Sermon on the Mount are compared with those of the giving of the Law on Mount Sinai, we find every reason for considering each as wonderfully characteristic of the two dispensations respectively, and the contrast as well as the resemblance comes out in very striking colours, as will be seen presently. Taking into consideration what has already been observed as to St. Matthew, it is not saying too much if we say that the contrast has been intended by him. But, again, we can hardly think that so important a parallel could have been drawn by him on his own authority, and simply in obedience to a favourite method of his own of regarding our Lord's actions as fulfilments of ancient anticipations. The correspondence and the contrast which he noted must have existed in truth, and if we find him, as the official historian of our Lord, thus placing the delivery of this wonderful Sermon in marked relation to the delivery of the Law on Mount Sinai, we have every reason for thinking that such was the intention of God's providence in arranging both the substance of the Sermon and the circumstances under which its laws were promulgated.

We may thus consider that the Sermon on the Mount marks another great step in the manifestation of our Lord by the providence of the Father. It is quite in keeping with this view that our Lord may already, either in great part or altogether, have delivered the several precepts, counsels, and maxims of which the Sermon is made up, in the course of His preaching through the towns and cities of Galilee, and that thus the future Apostles and the large band of those followers of our Lord who had followed Him from place to place may have been to a certain extent already prepared for the lofty teaching which is contained in this Sermon.

This, again, would explain the circumstances which have been noticed above, as at first sight making it appear that we cannot have the whole Sermon, as it was delivered, in the three chapters which it occupies in the Gospel of St. Matthew. The discourse as delivered on the Mount may have been a solemn repetition and recapitulation, a summing up in short and easily remembered precepts of a large mass of teaching which had been delivered in various places and at various times. It may have differed from our Lord's ordinary teaching in these respects, in being a summary and in bringing together in a small space a large range of doctrine. But it may also have differed from that teaching still more in the very great solemnity of the occasion, and in the majestic and authoritative manner in which the whole was delivered as the Law of the New Covenant. Our Lord at all times and in all places taught with authority, but He may not at all times and in all places have assumed to such an extent the character of the Lawgiver in the new Kingdom, as when He promulgated the Beatitudes in the place of the Decalogue, and corrected by His own teaching and interpretation the traditional meanings which had been attached to many commandments of the ancient code.

The scope of the Sermon on the Mount is to a great extent the same as that of the Decalogue: that is, it covers almost the whole of our duty to God and to man, though as to some parts of that large field the Old Law is left as it were in its integrity, without any additional explanation or more perfect direction. There are great additions, on the other hand, in the inculcation of our duty to God as our Father, that being the relation in which our Lord always regards Him, and would teach us to regard Him. And the chain of the Beatitudes contains a perfect philosophy of life, based on the maxims of faith and leading to the very highest perfection. But it is only necessary here to intimate the extent to which these two great legislations of the two Covenants correspond one to the other.

The difference between the two is, of course, far more striking. When we are once familiar with the thought of the general correspondence between them, and that our Lord on the Mount of the Beatitudes is fulfilling the type of Moses, or rather, repeating His own act in giving the Law to Moses on Mount Sinai, the contrast between the two Covenants manifests itself in every particular. The Lawgiver is in truth the same; but, instead of the terrible mountain, 'which if even a beast should touch it was to be stoned, and the burning fire, and whirlwind, and darkness, and storm, and the sound of a trumpet, and the voice of words which they that heard excused themselves that the word might not be spoken to them,'[4] we have our Lord in all His gracious condescension and sweetness seated on the slope of the gentle basin which is to be found at the top of the Mount of the Beatitudes, with hundreds and perhaps thousands of happy disciples pressing around Him, as eager not to lose one of the words of mercy and truth which flow from His lips, as the Israelites of old were eager to be delivered from the overwhelming terrors which the Word of God brought home to them. In each case the people to whom the Law was delivered had been prepared to receive it as authoritative by a number of prodigies of God's power. But the legislation on Mount Sinai had been preceded by the exhibition of a series of miracles of punishment and destruction unexampled, as such, in the history of the world—the plagues of Egypt and the submersion of Pharaoh and his host in the Red Sea. At the very time of the manifestation of God on Mount Sinai there was, as has been already said, a display of terrific prodigies. 'Thunders began to be heard, and lightning to flash, and a very thick cloud to cover the mount, and the noise of the trumpet sounded exceeding loud.'[5] But the lawgiving on the Mount of the Beatitudes had been heralded beforehand by a long course of miracles of mercy, of healing of the sick, deliverance of the possessed from the devils, and the like. The whole scenery of the

[4] Hebrews xii. 18—20.   [5] Exodus xix. 16.

respective legislations is characteristically different, for the wild howling wilderness is changed for the rich gentle beauty of the land of Genesareth. And if there is so great a contrast in the external circumstances and scenery of the different legislations, there is a corresponding but a far greater difference in their substance. The Old Law was a law of prohibitions and threats; the New Law is a series of blessings and promises; and whereas the only 'commandment with promise' which is to be found in the Decalogue is that which rewards filial dutifulness with length of days in this world, the very first of the Beatitudes promises nothing less than the Kingdom of Heaven to the poor in spirit. The very large use of promised rewards, the frequent urging of the motive of hope and the blessedness of resemblance to our Father Who is in Heaven, or of being rewarded by Him Who sees in secret, are characteristics of the New Law which has the Incarnate Son for its Lawgiver, and which is addressed to those to whom He has given power to become the sons of God, imparting to them, as far as it can be communicated to them, His own filial relation to the Father. This relationship is taken for granted throughout the whole Sermon on the Mount.

Moreover, the disciples to whom the Sermon is addressed are already considered as forming a body apart, even from the rest of the holy nation. They are the light of the world, the salt of the earth. They are to practice a kind of virtue different from and superior to the virtue of the Scribes and Pharisees, that is, of the ecclesiastical rulers and teachers of the Synagogue. The first year of our Lord's public teaching, in which this Sermon was undoubtedly delivered, may be considered with tolerable certainty to have passed without any very violent demonstrations of that opposition to Him and that spirit of persecution which were afterwards aroused. And yet even in this Sermon there are indications of the coming storm, and of this, not as a passing accident, but as an almost permanent condition of the body of the faithful who were to inherit these precious doctrines. There are to be false teachers, wolves in sheep's clothing; there are to be many who will call upon our Lord, and will be rejected by Him; there will be floods and rains beating upon the house, and showing whether it be built on sand or upon the rock. The passage at the close of the Sermon, where this image occurs, may be called the first picture of the Church in our Lord's teaching; and the very last of the great Beatitudes is that of the persecuted, while it is the only Beatitude on which our Lord enlarges as having a certain personal application to His own followers.

These features in the Sermon on the Mount correspond with the position which we assign to its delivery as marking a step in the gradual revelation of our Lord. He is speaking not only as a Teacher, but as a Lawgiver, not as a Master, but as a Founder. The teaching has made great progress from the exhortations to penance and faith, and the instructions given by St. John to various classes of persons to enable them to serve God faithfully in their several vocations. There is a distinct advance beyond the old standards of virtue, a distinct and authoritative correction of interpretations which had of old been fastened upon the Law of God. The recognized teachers of the people are set aside, as not rising, in their personal practice of virtue, to the high standard of the Gospel. The Beatitudes, the great principles of the New Kingdom, are followed by counsels of perfection and precepts of interior religion of the most sublime purity. At the same time, nothing is as yet said of the devotional, sacramental, and hierarchical system of the Church, while the doctrine of the Cross itself is enfolded in the Beatitudes, but not as yet openly displayed.

* * *

CHAPTER IX.

The Beatitudes.

St. Matt. v. 3—10; *Vita Vitæ Nostræ*, § 31.

It has already been remarked that the doctrines set forth with so much solemnity and authority in the Sermon on the Mount, containing as they do the most sublime Christian philosophy, are yet couched by our Lord in the simplest, shortest, and most pregnant language, like so many aphorisms or proverbs, and that, in this brevity and pregnancy, they remind us of the form in which so many great principles of the natural law of morality were summed up and promulgated in the code which was delivered on Mount Sinai. This remark applies especially to the Beatitudes, with which the Sermon on the Mount begins. There are other pregnant sayings and precepts in the Sermon on the Mount which are delivered by our Lord in the same royal tone of authority. But in many parts of the discourse before us it does not differ, so much as in the opening clauses, from other discourses which occur in the Gospels, in regard of the amount of development and expression which is given to the thoughts which are therein contained. Thus the Beatitudes have a character of their own, as compared with the rest of the Sermon, both as to their substance and as to the form in which they are delivered, and in this respect they may be compared to the Decalogue itself, as contrasted with the many other moral rules and precepts which occur in the Book of Exodus or of Deuteronomy. We can hardly be wrong in considering them in the light of this resemblance to the Decalogue as to the importance of their teaching, the position which they occupy in the legislation of the New Kingdom, and the particular form in which they are promulgated.

Some of the ancient writers have compared the words in which our Lord has laid down these great laws of His Kingdom, to the blessing spoken of in the first chapter of Genesis, when God saw what He had made, and that it was good, and blessed it, and they have seen in the solemn benedictions here pronounced by the Founder of the New Creation an indication of His identity with the God Who made the world. Thus, when our Lord blessed the virtues or habits which are crowned in the Beatitudes, He blessed the work of His own hands, a new creation of grace far more beautiful and noble than the natural man, which was to reflect in every line His own image and likeness, and to derive from Him its fruitfulness and power and felicity. The natural man grows and developes and operates and arrives at maturity by the silent working of the elements and vital principles of which his frame and substance are made up, under the blessing of his Creator: his relations with the universe around him, what he takes from it, what he gives to it, are the results of these conditions of his nature. The new creature who is formed and fashioned by the Holy Ghost after the image of Christ, has to take his own part, under the guidance of grace, in his own growth to maturity and perfection, and the development of the spiritual powers which are given him in his birth. And the laws and lines of his advance to the ripe fulness of strength and beauty which God designs for Him are traced in the Beatitudes.

They are no chance enumeration of blessed qualities which might be otherwise arranged or to which more might be added, nor are their rewards accidental or distributed at random, or the mere undeserved bounty bestowed by royal munificence on qualities which have no correspondence with the blessings which they receive. The grace which generates them is gratuitous, the glory which crowns them is their own by the laws of the Kingdom of God.

Thus it has been remarked that our Lord does not say that He will give the Kingdom of Heaven to the poor in spirit, or that He will make the meek possess the earth, or that He will show mercy unto the merciful, and so with the rest, though such language would certainly have been most true as well as most consoling; but He uses the form, that the Kingdom of Heaven is of the poor in spirit, and the like, in order that the reward may be understood to grow out of the virtue as the fruit out of the plant. Thus we may understand the remark of many Christian authors who have written on these Beatitudes, that the blessing which our Lord affirms and decrees is two-fold in each case, that is, that the virtue itself is blessed, and it is further blessed in that it has the reward and crown and fruit which He attaches to it. So that if by possibility, or for a time, the meek should not 'inherit (or possess) the land,' or the mourners not be comforted, or those who hunger and thirst after justice should not be satisfied, still they would be blessed because they are what they are. For each Beatitude, as distinct from the reward of which it is the condition and foundation, is an aspect of the perfect soul resting in its own pure tranquillity and peace in the arms of its Father and God, and as a wonderful gem, blazing with inherent brilliancy, may be different in hue or form as its different faces are looked on, and as the gem is what it is even though it have no rich setting, nor be worn in the crown of a king, so the perfect soul has always its own blessedness inherent in itself, or rather it is never shut out from the sight of Him to see Whom is to be blessed.

We find spiritual theologians, in accordance with this doctrine, assigning the highest place of all in the scale of states of the soul to these Beatitudes considered as such. The delicate system on which the arrangement is made need not be entered upon here in any fulness of detail, but it may be well shortly to allude to it. St. Bernardine of Siena[1] tells us that there are five degrees of grace by which the soul in the present life is led to the state of Beatitude. 'The first is sacramental grace, the second is virtue, the third the gifts of the Holy Ghost, the fourth the fruits of the same, and the fifth the Beatitudes.' Sacramental grace heals the soul. The sacraments are the medicines and remedies against vices, and thus their grace does away with sickness. The virtues give the faculties power to act well. He is looking upon all these five principles as causes of 'purgation,' and so he says that the virtues do away with the soul's weakness, giving it strength to operate. We have already mentioned that the virtues produce good acts of the ordinary kind and in the ordinary way, according to reason, natural or supernatural. The gifts of the Holy Ghost do away with all difficulty in working good, enabling the soul to work with facility and quickness: they also, as has been said before, are the principles of heroic acts of virtue, and of acts which might not be thought of or might not be prudent on ordinary grounds, but which are suggested and made possible and easy by the gifts of the Holy Ghost. The

---

[1] *Sermo de Christianâ perfectione Beatitudinum Evangelicarum,* art. 2, c. i.

fruits add the crown of joy and satisfaction to the good works of either kind, and in their ‘purgative’ character they do away with all weariness, fatigue, or sense of effort in such works.   Higher than all are the Beatitudes —‘the state and perfection of a soul already entirely purified.’   He gives the definition of ‘Beatitude’—‘A grace known to one who is truly wise, tending to produce sweetness of conscience, and already close on the borders of glory.’   It is a kind of grace, because it pre-supposes the habits of the virtues and the gifts informed by charity and grace, so as to make a man rightly and easily and joyfully undergo adversities, undertake difficult things, and work the works of perfection and supererogation. It is a kind of grace known to the truly wise, because it seems quite foreign to the opinions of human wisdom. All the Beatitudes, according to the opinion of the world, have misery as their companion or as their predecessor. He quotes St. Bernard, who says, ‘What is so hidden, as that poverty is blessed?’   And in St. Matthew our Lord says, ‘I confess to Thee, Father, Lord of Heaven and earth, because Thou hast hid these things from the wise and prudent,’[2] that is, of this world.   For these things cannot be perfectly known except one has had some experience and taste of God.   Then again, the definition speaks of ‘sweetness’ of conscience, because a Beatitude is the perfection of a soul already purified, and it preserves the mind from all remorse and reproach of conscience, and thus disposes it to a sweet and happy life.   And lastly, it is added, that the grace of the Beatitudes is already as it were on the borders of glory, for it is after all the blessedness of men still in their state of ‘pilgrimage,’ not yet arrived at their home and country, whom it makes blessed in hope, and in a certain sense actually blessed also, because it gives

2 St. Matt. xi. 25.

them a certain nearness and easiness of approach to God.'

This must suffice as to the perfection of the state of the soul in which the Beatitudes reside in their highest stage. It is at once obvious that the holy writers who speak of them in this almost technical manner have before their minds a generic condition of consummate sanctity, which might be conceived of other virtuous habits of the soul as well as of those particular excellences which are declared by our Lord to be blessed. Our present business is rather with the Beatitudes as principles of holiness, and lines, so to speak, of perfection, which may admit of many degrees between that stage of virtue which is obligatory on all under pain of sin and the high and beautiful serenity which belongs to the state of the soul on which we have been dwelling. Thus there are some acts of poverty of spirit or of purity of heart which are essential to the state of grace itself, and which may be produced by virtue of the sacraments. There may be other acts which require the habits of virtue, and others which are more extraordinary, and may be the result of the gifts of the Holy Ghost; others which may show the influence of His fruits, and others which may belong to the full and perfect Beatitude. When the Beatitudes are considered severally, it will be natural to inquire why these particular habits or virtues or states of the soul have been selected by our Lord rather than any others, why they have been arranged by Him in the order in which we have received them, and why He has connected with each one of them that particular reward or crown which He has assigned. For the present we consider them in general as the great principles and laws of the New Kingdom of which our Lord is King—a Kingdom, as He Himself said to Pilate, not of this world, but still in the world, and as truly a

Kingdom with its laws and character and spirit, its organization and variety of grades and ranks, its authorities and its subjects, as the Empire of Macedon or Rome or Persia or Assyria. When our Lord speaks of Beatitude in connection with this Kingdom and its subjects, He speaks of what sums up in itself the formal end for which that Kingdom has been created and exists. For the beatitude of man is the glory of God, and these two ends are substantially the same. The Kingdom of our Lord has for its end the glory of God by means of the beatitude of man, and the beatitude of man by means of his perfection, of which perfection He Himself is the normal type as well as the instrumental and meritorious cause.

This enables us to see the answer to the question how far the Beatitudes, being the laws of the New Kingdom, are obligatory on all its citizens. They are obligatory in so far as the perfection, which is the intention of God in founding it, is obligatory on its several members and on the whole body. Here, again, we are struck with the contrast between the new and the old legislation. We naturally speak of the precepts of the Decalogue, forgetting that they are almost exclusively in form only prohibitions. They set forth certain principles of the eternal law of morality by taking them, as it were, at the lowest possible point, at which their violation sinks to the level of direct grievous sin of the most obvious and unquestionable heinousness. The letter of the Law forbids, for instance, murder and adultery; and yet we instinctively feel that the principles of the natural law which are thus defended, as it were, on their remotest frontier, enact the custody of the thoughts and desires of the heart as well as the abstinence from outward sin, and that they are touched by any infringement of purity or charity of the most subtle kind. Thus the faithful Christian who passes his life in the strength of sacramental grace and of the indwelling of the Holy Ghost, free from any serious deliberate sin whatever, can find in the prohibitions of the Decalogue, as he is taught to understand them, an adequate code for his own continual self-examination. They appeal, in truth, to the motive of fear, and teach perfection by striking peremptorily upon the external acts by which the principles which they embody are violated. There are no particular punishments threatened for particular crimes, for the violation of the prohibitions involves the anger of God the Lawgiver in the first instance, and thus ensures the most terrible punishment.

But the legislation of the New Kingdom appeals to the motive of hope. The use of this motive, and of numberless particular promises to enforce it, is characteristic of our Blessed Lord. He is all bounty and munificence, His hands full of blessings, which He is yearning to bestow, and His promises, of which He is profuse, are the anticipations of the joy which will be when He actually bestows them, not in the way of mere bounty, but as rewards held out and won and then bestowed. Such a Legislator naturally puts forward the highest grade of the perfection which He desires and the noblest form of the recompense which He promises. There are certainly degrees in which the virtues of the Beatitudes are necessary to and obligatory upon all Christians. In some measure, poverty of spirit, meekness, mercifulness, purity of heart, are needful for salvation itself. The lofty teaching of the Christian code does not raise these degrees, nor abolish the compassionate mercy of God, according to which nothing but mortal sin can destroy the life of the soul. But the very form of the new commandments encourages men to press on very far beyond what must be observed under pain of sin, and these commandments enjoin an immense range of acts and habits which are, strictly speaking, and in general, matters of counsel rather than matter of obligation. And yet, high as is the sphere of the Beatitudes, they are still within the reach of all, in that they require no particular state of life or external vocation in those who may attain them even in their greatest perfection. The richest prince may be poor in spirit, the ruler of half the world, the more exalted in intellect or rank or influence, may be meek, the poorest labourer or the busiest merchant or lawyer may hunger and thirst after justice, and be clean of heart. There are in the Kingdom of God, in its present phase, differences of vocations and states, which require, and are supplied with, graces of a lower or a higher order for their due discharge; but these differences have no effect as to the attainment of the Beatitudes. Ecclesiastics and lay people, religious and seculars, spiritual rulers and the lowest of their subjects, are on a level as to the principles which are here embodied, which require perfection of the highest kind for their full possession, from which, nevertheless, no one is debarred. In the same way, the order of graces which are known by the name of *gratiæ gratis datæ*, miracles, prophecy, the power of healing, the discernment of spirits, and the like, are no passports to the Beatitudes, nor does their absence from any soul prevent the presence of the latter in all their fulness.

In thus rising beyond and above all the accidental and transient distinctions which divide the citizens of the Kingdom of Heaven in its present stage, however important those distinctions may be in themselves and in their possible consequences, the Beatitudes reveal their own essential, permanent, and fundamental relations to that future state of the children of God from which their name is derived, and of which they are, as has been said, in some sort an anticipation. They are the lineaments of that character of our Blessed Lord Himself, resemblance to which it is the work of the Holy Ghost to fashion the souls in which He dwells. They are the true 'pattern shown on the Mount'[3]— delivered as precepts on the Mount of the Beatitudes, exemplified in all the words and works of the Lawgiver Himself, and at last nailed to the Cross in His Person on Mount Calvary, where He finally won for those who would follow Him the blessings which He has attached to poverty of spirit, meekness and mourning, to hunger and thirst after justice, to mercifulness and purity of heart, where He was the great Peacemaker because He was the Son of God, and gained the Kingdom of Heaven because He was persecuted for the sake of justice.

In another respect also they seem to anticipate, not only the perfect blessedness of each several soul which will hereafter enjoy the vision of God, but that special feature of the felicity of Heaven of which we can at present feel that it will cause some of the tenderest and most exquisite of the joys which await us there, without being able as yet to understand their intensity. The happiness and perfection of a society must be greater in proportion to the capacity for union and mutual intimacy and affection between its members, and the time for Christians fully to know, perfectly to love and be united one to another, has not yet come. But the Beatitudes have a direct tendency to prepare the way for this perfect society hereafter, and even with regard to the present state of humanity they have an office of this character. There are sayings and passages in the New Testament which seem to speak in wonderful language of the Body of Christ and the mutual offices of its

---

[3] Hebrews viii. 5 ; Exodus xxv. 40.

K 2

members.   St. Paul, for instance, mentions our Lord as
the Head of the Body, unto Whom we are, as he says,
'to grow up;' 'from Whom the whole Body, being
compacted and fitly joined together, by what every joint
supplieth, according to the operation in the measure of
every part, maketh increase of the body unto the edifying
of itself in charity.'[4]   The Church is the fulfilment of
this description, both in the varied offices of the several
members, and in the spirit or life-blood of charity which
animates them all and is their bond of union.   But our
Blessed Lord, Who has founded the Church, has also
elevated and ennobled the natural society of which God
when He created man was the author and guardian—
and the laws which He has given in the Beatitudes are
the principles of that elevation and ennoblement.   For
the natural and the supernatural societies are identical in
their members as in their Author.   It cannot therefore
be, that any new and more powerful means of interior
and spiritual perfection which He vouchsafes to bestow
upon these members should not tend with marvellous
force to the good of the society, whether natural or
supernatural, which by His ordinance is composed of
them.   To raise men one by one higher in sanctity and
spiritual stature is to make them better for every end
for which their Creator intended them, and it belongs
to the nature of man, who is made for society, that whatever he gains morally or spiritually for himself he gains
for all around him.   If human society were an artificial
institution, arranged by mutual compact, and not enacted
by the Creator, the Beatitudes which come from Him
might come into collision with its principles.   As, on
the other hand, society is the creation of God, it cannot
but be made more perfect and more happy by the
working of these great laws.

[4] Ephes. iv. 16.

Thus the Beatitudes are, as has been said, the great principles of perfection in this New Kingdom of our Lord, founded upon that clear insight into the truth as to God, ourselves, His rights, and our duties and prospects, and the world around us, which is furnished by the gift of faith, which perfects reason, and is itself brought to perfection by the teaching of the Holy Ghost, in those souls which are obedient to His guidance, and in whom His gifts do not lie idle. They are promulgated by our Lord with sovereign authority—an authority which, as has been remarked, recalls the act of God in blessing the world which He had made. The very form in which these great principles are set forth reveals the condescending and beneficent character of the King of the New Kingdom; and we may now add that the Beatitudes are so couched as to be the laws of the Christian society as well as Christian souls one by one. They have a distinctly social character, and contain the blessing of the world at large, as well of those persons in whose souls they are made perfect. The order in which they are arranged, of which more may be said hereafter, is the order of the regeneration of society, and a sort of prophecy of the history of the Church. It is by means of the principles which are embodied in the Beatitudes that a Christian community was formed in the world, which, without altering the natural organization of society, penetrated it in every direction, breathing into it a new life and spirit, and thus healing the wounds and miseries which had so long afflicted mankind.

It is true that never as yet have the principles of the Beatitudes dominated the whole world: and that, when we speak of them as having regenerated society, we speak of their tendency and power rather than of their actual and historical effect. But the same may be said of any other manifestation of truth or communication of healing grace. The Sacrifice of the Cross is of infinite efficacy, and by virtue of it a new Creation has come into existence. But the actual results of what our Lord has done and suffered and purchased correspond rather to the disappointment which He allowed to cloud His Soul at the time of the Agony in the Garden, than to the intrinsic power of His work, or even to the glowing language in which the fruit of that work has been described by the Evangelical Prophet. The souls in which the grace which our Lord has left behind Him is allowed to accomplish all that it can accomplish, are few indeed; and what is true of single souls is true of that multitude and community of single souls of which the Church is made up, and of the teeming world around her, which she has the mission as well as the power to convert and transform and beautify, with all the glories of the creation of grace. She shows her Divine origin, her heavenly mission, her supernatural gifts, by what she does, because any one of her countless triumphs is the result of a power and a presence which are nothing short of Divine. If she had suffered greater losses and endured more relentless opposition and persecution than she has actually suffered, she would still have proved herself to be what she claims to be by evidence which no human reason could gainsay. But what is enough for testimony is not enough for complete success, and it is for a witness that the Gospel is to be preached to all nations. The gates of Hell have never yet prevailed, and never will prevail against her; but she is not until the end entirely to vanquish the gates of Hell. The Beatitudes contain a philosophy of Christian life which might long ago have regenerated society, and which can always, as far as it is allowed to work, elevate those whom it penetrates to a state of happy peace and security. They are fraught with the healing of the nations, and, as far as they have been allowed to work, the nations have been healed. Their power is not less now than when they were first uttered by our Lord upon the Mount. They can never grow old, for they are laws which came from the Heart of Jesus, Who is eternal, Who knows the needs of the creatures He has made, and has power to heal all their maladies. Over and over again Christian society may become diseased to the core, for the concupiscences of nature are fresh in every succeeding generation and in every child of Adam that comes into the world. But over and over again Christian society can be healed, for as the Wise Man says, God 'hath made the nations of the world for health,'[5] and that health is stored up for them in the undying legislation of the Beatitudes.

CHAPTER X.

The Beatitude of the Poor in Spirit.

St. Mark v. 3 ; *Vita Vitæ Nostræ*, § 31.

IT is now time to turn to the particular consideration of each of those great principles of the Kingdom of God which, as has been stated in general, are embodied in the Beatitudes. They are, as it were, the fundamental laws of the Gospel code, and the rest of the Sermon on the Mount either is in some degree a commentary on them, or at least assumes them as principles. It has already been said that the most reasonable supposition that can be made concerning the Sermon itself, is that which considers it as having been delivered as a solemn promulgation by our Lord, as King and Lawgiver, of the great heads of His teaching, the several parts of

[5] Wisdom i. 14.

which may have been already delivered by Him, more or less, in the course of His long preaching throughout Galilee, though they had not yet been summed up in so precise a form or proclaimed in so formal a manner in the presence of thousands of people. The descriptions which are given by travellers of what is called the Mount of the Beatitudes, the position of which is such as to agree very well with probability, as far as can be judged from the Gospel narrative, represent it as containing on its broad summit what appears like an extinct crater, a vast grassy amphitheatre, which would have held a very large number of hearers. If our Lord seated Himself, as is supposed, on one of the elevations on the inner edge of this natural basin, He might have had His more habitual followers around Him on either side, and before Him might have been spread the large but orderly multitude of those who, in a wider sense, had become His disciples. St. Matthew's account leads us to suppose that they were so much accustomed to follow Him that, when He went up into this low mountain, and it was known that He had there taken His seat, the multitude flocked after Him in the expectation of some great teaching. Thus the gentle cavity would be gradually filled before Him, the bands of pilgrims, as they may be called, falling into their places as they arrive in succession.

Little difficulty need be felt as to the possibility of so large a multitude hearing the Sermon which was to follow. There are many spots in the East as to which travellers tell us of what would seem to us the extraordinary facility with which the human voice is heard from mountain side to mountain side.[1] And, as we

---

[1] Stanley, *Sinai and Palestine*, p. 13, speaking of Mount Sinai, says, ' From the highest point of Râs Sufsafeh to its lowest peak, a distance of about sixty feet, the page of a book, distinctly but not loudly read, was perfectly audible, and every remark of the various groups of travellers descending from the heights of the same point rose clearly to

have seen, there are frequent instances in the lives of the great Christian missionaries, of a preternatural power imparted to the voice, so that it is heard at a great distance by the remotest member of a large audience. If such effects are occasionally produced in the providence of God in order that large multitudes of Christians may hear the Word from some saintly missionary, it is not difficult to suppose that, if there had been any need of a miracle in the case of our Lord, either when He uttered the Sermon on the Mount or at any other time, that miracle would not have been wanting. But there is no mention of it in the Gospels, and we may therefore conclude His voice reached the most distant hearers without any difficulty.

'And He opened His mouth, and taught them.' The simple Scriptural expression which St. Matthew uses does not of necessity signify more than that our Lord now began to teach them. But it seems that the Evangelist uses it of our Lord in no place but this, except when he quotes[2] the prophecy of the Psalmist,[3] which he applies to the teaching by parables. It is therefore fair to conclude that the words are here meant of some particularly solemn teaching of our Lord, and thus there is good ground for the manner in which they

those immediately above them. It was the belief of the Arabs who conducted Niebhur that they could make themselves heard across the Gulf of Akaba—a belief doubtless exaggerated, yet probably originated or fostered by the great distance to which in those regions the voice can actually be carried.' Of course at the Horns of Hattin, the traditional Mount of Beatitudes, there would not be the absence of verdure and water which exists in the desert of Sinai. Mr. Tristram, speaking of the amphitheatre at the bases of Ebal and Gerizim, says : ' From mountain to mountain could the chanted sentences easily be heard. The acoustic properties of that enclosed valley are very remarkable, and we have found it easy to carry on a conversation, and to distinguish every word from Gerizim to Ebal, in the still morning or evening air ' (*Scenes in the East,* p. 24).

[2] xiii. 35.   [3] lxxviii. 2.

have been understood by Christian writers, that our Lord, Who, as has already been shown, spoke of old by Prophet and Lawgiver, now spoke Himself, using no other word or tongue but His own, and that the greatness of the occasion on which He did this is meant to prepare us for the unexampled importance, splendour, and sublimity of the words which He was about to utter. For the first Christian teachers at Jerusalem, as we see from the speech of St. Stephen before the Sanhedrin, which is echoed by St. Paul in his Epistle to the Galatians,[4] took care to insist upon the truth that the Law had been given by Angels, and not spoken by the mouth of God Himself. We have thus the contrast between the Lawgiver on the mountain and the Law which was given on Mount Sinai, silently pointed to by the Evangelist. And he tells us, as has been said, that the people came to our Lord gladly, with confidence and joy, instead of flying in terror and begging that they may not hear the words which are to be spoken, as had been the case at Sinai. And our Lord opens His own mouth, to pour forth spiritual treasures and blessings, instead of using His creatures to utter the stern law of prohibitions with so many attendant circumstances of terror.

There is always, in any audience, a hush of silence when a much venerated teacher is about to speak, and curiosity frets itself in speculation as to what will be his first word, or the text which he will take. Our Lord, as we have seen, begins with blessing. Blessedness is the proper possession or quality of God Himself. He alone is the Blessed One, though, in His infinite goodness, He communicates His blessedness in various measures and degrees to the creatures whom He has made, according to their capacity of sharing it. Our

---

[4] See Acts vii. 53; Galat. iii. 19.

Lord's first words, therefore, promise a participation in the intrinsic blessedness of His own Godhead to those of whom He is about to speak. For the time has come for threats and prohibitions to pass away, for the new law of grace to be promulgated, the rewards of which are the blessedness now, and the glory hereafter, which corresponds to grace, as the fruit to the seed. But who are blessed? The promise of blessedness was not altogether new, because the same words are found before in several of the Psalms. 'Blessed the man who hath not walked in the counsel of the ungodly;' 'Blessed those whose iniquities are forgiven and whose sins are covered,' 'Blessed the man who understandeth concerning the poor and needy;' 'Blessed the undefiled;' and the like. All these are blessed in various ways, but our Lord is laying down the foundation of a new legislation and a new philosophy, and so He passes them all by, and says simply—'Blessed the poor in spirit! for theirs is the Kingdom of Heaven.'

There have been many Christian writers who, remembering that humility is the foundation of all virtues, that it was our Lord's great characteristic perfection, that He declared Himself meek and humble of heart, and other like considerations, have understood here that He meant in the first instance to declare that the humble are blessed. The words, 'poor in spirit,' may be understood in this sense, because humble persons consider that they have nothing of their own that is good—that all is the gift of God, and they truly understand, by the light of faith, the absolute poverty and nothingness of any created nature, and its entire dependence upon its Creator. But the word which is used by St. Matthew signifies poverty[5] and not humility, which is represented in the New Testament by a word altogether different. And when

---

[5] πτωχοὶ τῷ πνεύματι, not ταπεινοί.

our Lord repeated the Beatitudes, in a modified and shorter form, to a very different audience, as we are told by St. Luke,[6] He left out the qualification involved in the words 'poor in spirit,' and said simply, 'Blessed are ye poor, for yours is the Kingdom of God,' adding also, by way of contrast, 'Woe to you that are rich, for you have received your consolation.' It cannot therefore be doubted that this blessing of our Lord falls on poverty of spirit in its proper meaning. Poverty of spirit, then, is the first virtue or excellence which our Lord declares to be blessed, and which, by placing it where He does, He makes the foundation of, or the entrance to, the whole of that spiritual perfection on which His special blessing now descends.

The idea of poverty is one which can be understood by all. It is of two kinds, each of which may exist either with or without the other. Thus we have three states in which men may live and be called poor—the state of actual poverty, without the addition of poverty of spirit, the state of those who are both actually poor and poor in spirit, and the state of those who are poor in spirit and not actually poor. The first of these states misses the Beatitude, and when our Lord, in the Sermon on the Plain, declares the poor to be blessed, He speaks of the second state, that of those who are poor actually and also poor in spirit. The other two states fall under the Beatitude, but, as actual poverty does not earn it unless it be accompanied by poverty of spirit, it is the second, and not the first, to which His words conferring the blessing formally refer. The poor who are blessed are those whose actual poverty is animated and spiritualized and naturalized by poverty of spirit. On the other hand, there are many reasons why actual poverty when thus united to poverty of spirit makes the blessing

[6] St. Luke vi. 20—24.

more secure. Actual poverty stands almost in the same relation to poverty of spirit as humiliation to humility; in both cases the perfection of the interior excellence is made more easy of attainment by the practice of the external act to which it corresponds. We find our Lord, in consequence, insisting very much on the practice of poverty, at least in the case of those whom He called to a state of perfection. The instance of the rich young man occurs to the mind at once: 'If thou wilt be perfect, go sell what thou hast, and give to the poor.'[7] Again, a little later in the history, we find our Lord laying down the same doctrine, in effect, even to the multitudes, when He reminds them that men who have a tower to build sit down and calculate whether they have money enough to pay for it, and that a king going to war takes account of his forces, to see whether he has soldiers enough to meet the foe with, and then He adds, 'So also, every one of you who doth not renounce all that he hath, cannot be My disciple.'[8] He compares therefore poverty, at least of spirit, the renouncing of all that a man has, to the revenues which are necessary for the building of a tower, or to the soldiers who are required to form an army. In each case the comparison implies the fundamental necessity of poverty, at least in spirit, though it was to actual poverty that the rich young man was invited, and our Lord's words in the last-quoted passage ought perhaps to be understood of the same actual poverty.

The relation of poverty of spirit to humility is also easily discovered. Humility has been said by some of the saints to be truth; that is, it is the recognition by faith of the truth concerning ourselves, our origin, our

---

[7] St. Matt. xix. 21 ; St. Mark x. 21 ; St. Luke xviii. 22. The importance of the lesson is evidenced by the fact that these three Evangelists repeat it.

[8] St. Luke xiv. 33.

relation to God, our natural powers, the use we have made of them. In the same way, poverty of spirit is truth. It is the recognition, by the light of faith, of the truth as to all external things that in any way can be spoken of as riches, goods, and the like, our position with respect to them, and the use which God intended us to make of them. And it may be easily understood that, in order to grasp the full truth as to external things, we must first have grasped it as to ourselves, or rather, that the first truth is the foundation of the second. It is equally easy to see how poverty of spirit is connected with humility, how, either when united with actual poverty, or when disjoined from it, it is the means at once by which humility may be gained and by which it may be preserved. The one virtue is the perfect and practical acknowledgment that we are nothing, and the other is the same acknowledgment that we have and possess nothing. The first fully and practically recognizes God as the source of everything. The other recognizes God as the owner of everything. Humility extinguishes in us, in consequence, all esteem of ourselves for anything that we are, or seem to be, or seem to be capable of being, and thus it is in its perfection in those who have been raised to the very highest places in God's creation, as our Lord in His Human Nature, our Blessed Lady, the saints and angels. They have received more from God than any others, and the measure of their gifts is the measure of their humility and sense of their own utter nothingness. Poverty of spirit extinguishes in us all ownership in anything that we have, or seem to have, or seem capable of having, and thus this too is the virtue of heaven and of all Heavenly states, for the angels have nothing of their own, in Paradise there was and would have been no property, and in the first beautiful days of the Church at Jerusalem

the renunciation of property and community of goods
sprang into existence, as if by virtue of the natural
Christian instinct as to this Beatitude. And the same
holy principles have been enshrined in the institutions of
the religious life, which is the ever-living representation
in the Church of the laws of perfection as laid down by
our Lord.

The range of subjects to which this spirit of poverty
is to apply is of course co-extensive with that of the
good things, of whatever kind, which man can possess or
be without. The first and most obvious class of these
good things contains wealth, money, lands, houses,
property of whatever sort. Under the same name we
may place rank, position, birth, reputation, influence,
abilities and gifts, bodily and intellectual, family, friends,
connections, prosperity, while the same principle of
detachment may be extended also to spiritual gifts, inasmuch as with regard to all these things, from the lowest
to the highest, we are not to have our hearts wedded
to them, if we have them, or to covet them, if we have
them not, unless it be God's will that we should have
them. And thus we are to imitate our Lord, Who
willingly made Himself poor, as St. Paul says, for our
sakes, and we are not, when we have them, to use them
as our own, but in entire dependence upon God. And
of all the poor our Lord affirms the blessing, which He
bestows by affirming it, whether the poor in outward
condition if they bear their poverty in intelligent faith
and are detached in spirit as well as in act, or those
who practise poverty by choice, whether in religion or in
a secular state, whether as consecrated by vow or not,
or again, those who by the will of God remain in the
possession of riches and other good things of the world,
from which they are detached in heart, and so are truly
poor in spirit.

It is thus that in this, the first act, as it were, of
His legislation, we see how wonderfully our Lord has
provided that the precepts which He lays down and
the blessing which He pronounces should be within
the reach of all classes of His subjects. The Gospel
Kingdom is indeed principally for the poor, whom, as
St. James tells us, 'God hath chosen, rich in faith, and
heirs of the Kingdom which He hath promised to them
that love Him.'[9] But it would be to destroy the whole
order of the world as God has arranged it, to promise
such a blessing as that which is here held out to any
particular class, and it is our Lord's own doctrine in one
of His most solemn parables, that even the highest
vocations do not of themselves secure the highest
crowns.[10] The advantage of actual poverty, and the

[9] St. James ii. 5.

[10] This is the teaching of the Parable of the Labourers in the Vineyard (St. Matt. xx. 1—16). As the circumstances under which this
work is published make it likely that some time may elapse before the
writer reaches that part of the book in which this parable may be fully
illustrated, he may be allowed for the present to refer to a short paper
on the Parables, published a few years ago. 'God, Who is just and
bountiful to all, yet chooses whom He wills for the higher callings in
His Kingdom. He is the Father of all, the Lover of all souls ; but
there are those whom He calls to higher privileges and more glorious
states in this world and the next than others. But yet the masterful
freedom of God in His choice and in the distribution of His gifts goes
still further yet. The rewards of the next world do not necessarily
correspond to the outward callings in this. There are first who are last,
there are last who are first. Those who are called to states of perfection,
or, again, to conspicuous positions in the visible Church, or to Apostolical labours and duties, are not of necessity either the only chosen
ones of God, or His dearest souls. Notwithstanding the pre-eminence
of such states, the really highest places in Heaven are for the saints,
those who are truly nearest to God in this world and in the next ; and
the saints are to be found in all vocations and states of life—married or
single, secular or religious, princes, warriors, as well as priests, rich as
well as poor, young as well as old, not according to the quality of their
outward state, but according to the intensity and richness of their
inward grace and the faithfulness of their co-operation with it ' (*The
Theology of the Parables*, pp. 40, 41).

extent to which it facilitates the acquirement of the graces of poverty of spirit and humility, have been already spoken of. But it is not the rule of our Lord's Kingdom that all are to become actually poor, any more than it is the rule that all are to keep virginity, or to leave the world for the state of religion. The Beatitudes, therefore, are put within the reach of all, the rewards are held out to all, to the monarch on his throne and the noble in his palace, as well as to the peasant in his cottage and the religious in his cell. And, again, as the crown of this and of the other Beatitudes is within the reach of all, so also do all lie under the obligation of the principle of the Beatitudes. For, as has been before said, all, rich as well as poor, noble as well as simple, young and old, laymen and ecclesiastics alike, are bound to poverty in spirit in that degree which is requisite to avoid sin, and the Beatitude is thus far not a counsel, but a precept.

What has already been said as to the truth on which this principle of our Lord's is grounded, will help us to see to some extent the Divine wisdom of the enactment, and the exceeding tenderness of the love which has made it a law, as far as it is a law, for our sakes. The poor in spirit are indeed, as St. James has said, rich in faith. A great number of the truths which God has revealed to us combine to show the reasonableness and necessity of the spirit of poverty. These truths include the sovereign dominion of God as the Creator and Lord of all things, and as the end of man's existence. The doctrine which St. Ignatius has laid down so strongly as to the use of creatures, the end for which they all are made and set around and within the reach of man, bears directly upon this poverty, for it cuts at the root of all affection for them in themselves, and teaches that they are only to be used so far as they help us to attain the end for which we are made. Again, that loving trust with which our faith teaches us to rest upon God's care for us, and again, the idea of Him which it presents to us as so infinitely wise and merciful in the distribution of His gifts and in the providence with which He rules us, assist the mind and heart to rise to this detachment. Much more, in proportion as the thought of what our Lord calls the 'true riches' takes possession of the mind, as it opens to the intelligence of the ineffable value of grace and the splendours of the spiritual world, and learns by experience to set store by all that frees it from the ties and cares and false attractions of earth, will it come to shrink from temporal riches and all that can be classed under the same head, not only as worthless in themselves, but as dangerous to the soul by distracting it and occupying its attention, and coming as a cloud between it and the true objects of its affection.

Again, the relation in which we are placed by our Christian privileges to God as our Father, and which is so much dwelt upon by our Blessed Lord in this Sermon, and in other parts of His moral teaching, has its actual fruit in that detachment from earthly goods and earthly cares which is the mark of His children. Our Lord sets before us a little further on the example of the birds of the air, who do not reap or gather into barns, and of the lilies of the field which He clothes with beauty and glory to which the royal magnificence of Solomon could not be compared, and He adds that 'your Father knoweth that you have need of all these things.' Poverty of spirit naturally engenders all the virtues which belong to this filial relation to God; an entire dependence on His will, as that of a most loving and careful Father, and an absolute resignation to all that He may dispose concerning us, as having a right to arrange His children's lot, and as loving them far too well to make that lot press on them severely. The filial spirit pours itself out in prayer and ready communion with God, it asks and receives, as our Lord said, that its joy may be full, it makes its necessities and desires known to the Father with tender confidence, that there may be the fulness of joy in the love which asks and then receives, and the love which is entreated and then given. It receives all things lovingly from His hand with immense thankfulness. The Kingdom of God is the realm of prayer, and poverty of spirit is one of the foundations of the spirit of prayer. The words in which our Lord describes it may almost be said to convey the same double idea as our word 'beggar.' For when men are rich in faith, and detached from all earthly desires save of what is necessary, their minds and hearts are all the more open to spiritual needs, and as their life is one of faith and hope and love of God, they will ask boldly and with the greatest confidence, having no earthly attachments to keep down their soul in its flight to God, and feeling that kind of simple confidence in having kept nothing back from Him which made Peter say so boldly, 'Behold we have left all, and followed Thee. What therefore shall we have?'[11] Such men have, moreover, far greater experience than others of the rich and fatherly providence of God in supplying abundantly all their needs, whether of body or soul.

Again, poverty of spirit is the characteristic of the children of God in the large-heartedness and magnificence with which they dispense the external goods which He so often places in their hands, and with which they devote themselves to great labours and enterprises for the sake of their neighbours. It has been a characteristic of Christian times and Christian communities in which this spirit has taken deep root, that there has

[11] St. Matt. xix. 27.

L 2

been great munificence, and even profusion, in public works of charity, in buildings to the honour and worship of God and for the good of others, the advancement of knowledge, and other ends of the same character, while the dwellings and habits of the people who have been thus distinguished for public spirit in the Christian sense of the words, have been simple and humble. Poverty of spirit, as embodied with other kindred instincts in the religious state, has been the agent in reclaiming the desert, in bringing countries into cultivation, in felling the forest and draining the morass. It raised all over Europe the most noble churches and cathedrals that have ever been seen, it founded colleges and hospitals and almshouses, while at the same time it stored up the remains of ancient literature, and was the main depository of theological treasures and the science of the saints. All the great achievements of Christian industry and Christian intelligence have been the fruits of poverty of spirit, which sets men free from self-love and low thoughts and aims, and enables them to conceive great designs and undertake what seems impossible, labouring, as the Wise Man says, 'not for themselves only, but for all that seek out the truth.'[12]

Again, although it may be fairly questioned whether the poverty of spirit of which our Lord speaks can ever become deeply characteristic of a community, unless it be witnessed to by the practice of actual poverty in religious institutions, which bring the principle of our Lord's teaching home to the eyes and hearts of the people at large, it still belongs to this part of the subject to point out other social blessings beyond what have been already enumerated, which the diffusion of this holy instinct is sure to produce. One of the greatest

[12] Ecclus. xxiv. 47.

of these blessings, besides the material benefits conferred on society and civilization by men who are poor in spirit and detached from the love of earthly things, is the honour in which poverty is held as a state which witnesses to the truths of faith, and which has been consecrated and ennobled by our Lord Himself and thousands of saints after His example. The pagan view of poverty, which looks upon it as a misery, a disgrace, and even as a crime, has a direct tendency to separate class from class, and to create heartburning, discontent, and envy in those who are involuntarily and hopelessly poor. It sets the seal of habitual and public opinion to the doctrine that money is to be sought as the one great good, it discredits labour and industry, and favours the accumulation of enormous wealth in the hands of a few, and luxury of every kind. A community in which labour and poverty are in honour is simple, frugal, happy, and united. It will be blessed with a comparative immunity from crime and discord, because one of the chief incentives to such evils is covetousness. It will be the sort of commonwealth in which, as the poet says, the property of private persons will be small, but that of the State great.[13] There will be few great palaces and enormous estates, but the buildings and institutions in which the public service is carried on, and works of beneficence, piety, or charity are housed, will be large and splendid. The people will be capable of great enterprises and heroic sacrifices for the good of the commonwealth, and while it will present fewer temptations than others to the rapacity of the spoiler, it will appeal without any fear of an ungenerous response to the devotion of its children if it should need defence. The blessing of the faith, in this instance, will penetrate the whole public and private life of such a community,

---

[13] Privatus illis census erat brevis, Commune magnum.

and an aggregate of nations built up in this way upon Christian principles would make a Christendom, from which in no long series of centuries the conversion of the kingdoms of the world unto the Empire of Jesus Christ might be expected with confidence.

The social and political fruits of this blessed spirit are, of course, only the external indications of the richness of virtue and fertility of grace, to which it gives birth in the soul itself. We have already spoken of the close alliance between poverty of spirit and humility, an alliance insisted on by the masters of the spiritual life, and in humility we reach what is the root of all the virtues, the quality which enables God to endow the soul with a profusion and multiplicity of grace. It is also evident that true poverty of spirit cannot be consistent with any uncontrolled passion. Cupidity of some kind or other is the mainspring of every passion, every vice, every injustice, all selfishness, hardness of heart, disregard of our neighbour's interest, wrong judgments, enmities, and the like. Poverty of spirit is the destruction of cupidity, and in this sense also it is the parent of all virtue; of that 'justice, and peace, and joy in the Holy Ghost' in which St. Paul says that the Kingdom of God consists.[14] Justice, that is, in the full practice of Christian virtue, peace in all that regards our neighbour as well as the serene happiness of a good conscience towards God, and the orderly tranquillity of our own interior, and, as founded upon this peace, the ineffable joy which the Holy Ghost creates in simple and guileless souls. It seems as if there were a special gift of joy for those who have made themselves actually poor for the sake of God, as we see in the lives of saints like St. Francis, and as, indeed, the daily experience of many religious persons witnesses: and this joy could not be theirs

[14] Romans xiv. 17.

unless their external sacrifice came from that true poverty of spirit of which we are speaking.

It is thus not difficult to see how the other virtues and excellences which are included in the wonderful chain of the Beatitudes are connected with poverty of spirit as their root or source. For if it directly leads to humility, and if it implies a strong practice of self-restraint and the taming of the passions, it must be closely connected with meekness. Its keen perception of the nothingness of the world and of all worldly objects, and again, of the rights of God, allies it with mourning, while its detachment from the desire of all lower and transient goods prepares those in whom it reigns for hunger and thirst after the true and lasting goods, and those goods, in this life, are the acts and practices of justice in the largest sense of the word. Again, it is certain that poverty of spirit has a distinct relationship to mercifulness, one large part of which is the employment of temporal goods, of time, and labour, and all other things in our power, in the compassionate relief of all the wants of our neighbours, according to the saying of the Apostle, ‘As poor and yet enriching many.’ The whole world is full of the monuments of the munificence and devotion of men who have been poor of spirit, and if the fruits which the eye can see, and which history records, have been so abundant, we may be sure that the interior and spiritual works of mercifulness and compassion have not been less abundant. Purity of heart, again, which in one sense has the highest blessing of all, that of seeing God, begins in poverty of spirit, by which it detaches itself from all earthly things, not simply in the way of a negative withdrawal from them—which might imply nothing more than an absolute insensibility, as a blind man denies himself the pleasures of sight, or a deaf man the delights of music—but an emptying of the heart of all such attachment, in order that it may be open to receive the full streams of Divine illumination, the gifts of faith and hope and charity. And lastly, the work of the peace-maker naturally requires poverty of spirit, which secures entire disinterestedness in those to whom such works are committed, and so gives them a force and authority and attractiveness which are usually denied to others. And the grace of being persecuted for the sake of justice, with the wonderful reward promised to it, is naturally allotted to those who have no earthly attachments, and who having begun by leaving the world in affection are already, in the sense of St. Paul, crucified to it.

In the last place, it cannot be forgotten by Christians that our Lord's own Life began and continued and ended in poverty. All the Beatitudes are, indeed, the outlines of the character of our Lord, and they reflect the circumstances and condition of His Life, but poverty was so pointedly chosen by Him from the very outset, that it can hardly be that the desire to follow Him and to be like Him should not at once generate in the soul which it enters the thought of imitation in this respect, or if actual imitation be not within the reach of all, at least the thought of gaining the spirit of poverty in order to follow Him as closely as possible. The Christian view, moreover, of the poverty of our Blessed Lord is not simply that it was chosen by Him out of humility or detachment, but that He had distinctly in view the healing of the miseries which had flooded the world because of the contrary love of riches, and the expiation of the evils by which God had been offended in consequence of the passion of avarice and the pride and hardness of heart to which it had given birth. The poverty of Christians after the pattern of our Lord, has a share in the same character of healing and expiation, because He has touched and, as it were, consecrated poverty to that effect. It is a part, therefore, of its present blessedness that in all these respects it brings men near our Lord, and makes them share the condition which He chose for Himself, as well as the work of restoration and atonement which is peculiarly His own.

CHAPTER XI.

Poverty and the Kingdom of Heaven.

St. Matt. v. 5 ; *Vita Vitæ Nostræ*, § 31.

THE reward of the poor in spirit is the Kingdom of Heaven, and the reward of the persecuted, which closes the series of crowns which are promised by our Lord in the Beatitudes, is the same in terms with that which is assigned by our Lord to poverty of spirit. We are thus at once led to the consideration of its meaning, which seems somewhat different in the two cases. For the 'Kingdom of Heaven,' the favourite phrase of our Blessed Lord, which is echoed again and again in this Gospel of St. Matthew, represents a large and complex idea, and the particular meaning in which it is used in each place must be gathered from the context. Thus, in the passage before us, it is clear that the rewards of which our Lord speaks correspond, in a sort of contrast, to the several virtues to which they are respectively assigned. This is evident from the reward which is given to the mourners, to the merciful, and others. It seems as if the reward in each case was some heavenly compensation for what has been sacrificed or endured for the sake of God—a compensation more or less in the same kind, as is but natural in a Kingdom in which glories correspond to graces, and crowns to merits. Again, many holy writers have insisted on the truth that the ' Kingdom of Heaven,' which, as a specific reward, is assigned in the first Beatitude and in the last, is also the general and universal reward in all the Beatitudes. And, as the Kingdom of Heaven, in its fulness, is the possession of God in eternal felicity, and, as far as it may be had now, is the same possession of God according to our capacity, it is clear that there can be no reward which is not included in that Kingdom. We are therefore led to see that even the ' possession of the land,' or the being filled with justice, or the being made the objects of mercy, which are rewards which appear most of all to belong to the present state of the Church and of human life, are to be included in the general notion which we may form to ourselves of the Kingdom of Heaven, which our Lord in more than one place speaks of as already come, or again, as immediately at hand, while at the same time He bids us, in the daily prayer which is to be offered in His Church until the end of time, implore of God that His Kingdom may come, as if that coming were something altogether future.

There is nothing to surprise us in this complexity in the notion of the Kingdom of Heaven. Even the kingdoms of the earth may be looked upon from many sides and present many aspects. The word kingdom sometimes represents the royal dignity and power of the sovereign of the State, sometimes the State or Empire itself, or its administration or government, or the people who are its subjects, or the territories which are embraced within its borders, or the forces which it commands, or the laws by which it is ruled, or the form of its polity, or the material resources and wealth which it possesses, or the character which distinguishes it in history. This or that prominent and characteristic feature in any particular subject-matter may be attributed to it as furuishing a general designation. If the idea of an earthly kingdom is so multiform and various, how much more natural is it that many ideas and conceptions of excellence and happiness of various kinds must be heaped together in order to convey anything like an adequate notion, as far as such notion can be conveyed in human language, of that combination and accumulation of goods of every kind which belongs to the Kingdom of God, which is most perfect in every respect, in respect of its King, its people, its form, its dominion, it resources, its extent, its method of propagation, its manner of dealing with its enemies, and the internal occupations, riches, and blessedness of its subjects!

We have at present only to deal with the Kingdom of Heaven, as it is specially assigned by our Lord as the reward in the first Beatitude. And St. Bernardine remarks, that it is only in these two cases in which the Kingdom of Heaven is put as the reward, that our Lord speaks in the present tense. The rewards in all the other Beatitudes are future: as to these two it is, 'theirs is the Kingdom of Heaven.' They already possess what is promised to the others. 'Poverty and temporal persecution,' he says, 'are sisters, and to them the keys of Heaven are granted, not only in promise, but even in possession. For,' he goes on, 'Evangelical poverty has nothing in this world, and persecution can take away from a man all that he has in the world, and the world itself. But our most provident Creator and Governor will let no one of His creatures be without a home, and as poverty of spirit and the persecuted have no home on earth, He gives them the possession of the Kingdom of Heaven.' St. Bernardine has already spoken of the heavenly character of poverty of spirit in that it makes

men like the angels in possessing nothing of their own
and caring for nothing but God, as also in that it makes
them so closely to imitate and follow our Divine Lord.
And now he goes on to compare the effects of poverty
on the soul to the qualities of the blessed in Heaven,
whose four gifts of impassibilty, agility, subtilty, and
brightness, are in some sort figured by the indifference
which poverty of spirit engenders as to any temporal
losses, the easiness with which it enables men to follow
our Lord and to enter Paradise, and the richness of
graces with which the soul is endowed by it. Further
on in the same sermon,[1] he compares the fruit of the
spirit of poverty in the soul to the state of beatitude
as to four points, namely, liberty, security, healthiness,
and satiety of all desires.

These and other contemplations of the saints and
holy doctors may assist us to understand how it is that
poverty of spirit has for its crown the possession of the
Kingdom of Heaven. The two principal notions which
are contained in the idea of a kingdom are those of riches
and power. If we follow the rule which has already
been laid down, as to the various meanings which are
to be attached to the term 'the Kingdom of Heaven' in
the several passages in which it occurs, we shall naturally
look, when it is to be understood of that which is to
be the crown of poverty of spirit, for that meaning which
conveys the notion of riches. The poor in spirit, then,
are put in possession already of the Kingdom of Heaven,
in that the treasures of God are open to them in return
for their abandonment of and detachment from the
good things of earth. We have seen that a great variety
of goods, natural and intellectual, may be included
under the general term riches, and we must therefore
conclude that all corresponding goods of the Kingdom

---

[1] *Advent: De Christiana Vita*, Serm. v. art. 3, c. 3.

of Heaven are at the disposal of the poor in spirit. Theirs is the treasure of graces and virtues, the strong vivid faith which can move mountains, the hope that firmly grasps the promises of God, the charity which fastens upon God as its one object and unites them to Him now and in eternity. In them is fulfilled that wonderful promise made to the father of all the faithful, the Saint of the Old Testament who gave up his home and country at the bidding of God, that God Himself would be his exceeding great reward. God gives Himself to them in a large and general donation, in return for the sacrifice which they have made of all things for Him. The powers of the spiritual life are theirs in virtue of this gift of the Holy Ghost, with all His gifts and fruits, and for them the ordinary channels of grace, the sacraments of the Church, the Word of God, prayer, penance, and the like, are full of rich fertility and abundance, which cannot find room in souls which are attached to the good things of this world. Not the powers alone, but the delights and joys of the Heavenly Kingdom are theirs, familiarity with God and His angels, the thoughts and contemplations, the measures of judgment, all the aspirations and desires and interests which belong to the sons of God, the peace and contentment which no earthly chances or vicissitudes can touch, the ineffable bounding delight of absolute repose in the providence of the Father.

It may also help us to understand the blessing of the poor in spirit, if they are compared to the other citizens of the Heavenly Kingdom, who also have a certain work and a certain life upon earth. If the veil which hides us from the invisible world were withdrawn, we should be like the servant of the Prophet whose eyes were opened, and beheld 'the mountain full of horses and

chariots of fire round about the man of God.'[2] For
the angels of God are all around us, in every place
and at all times; and they have all their missions, of
mercy or protection or chastisement, to the children
of men. They are always active and vigilant, and the
silent work which they do according to God's providence
in this world cannot be counted up. But they pass
through the world as the citizens of another kingdom.
The riches and treasures, the palaces and cities, the
works of art and precious stones, all that is valuable
and beautiful in the eyes of men, has no more charm
for them than the dust of the streets, and they are
indifferent whether the guardianship entrusted to them
takes them to the hovel or the dungeon, to the halls
of the kings or to the council-chambers of nations.
All things around them have but one aspect in their eyes,
that in which they are to regard them with reference
to the service of God on which they are intent. Such,
in kind, at least, is the detachment of the poor in
spirit. Like the angels, they are citizens of the Kingdom
of Heaven, its many mansions and places of rare delight,
its treasuries filled with richer gems than gold or silver
or diamond or ruby, are their inheritance and at their
disposal, and they regard earthly goods of whatever
kind simply as to be used or left alone, according to
the degree in which they may serve or may hinder the
advancement of God's glory.

In another sense too, the Kingdom of Heaven is theirs,
for to them is committed its advancement and propagation upon earth. Their poverty is the fruitful teeming
field from which springs up the harvest of noble works
and lofty achievements of grace, sufferings, and humili-
ations which conquer the world and destroy the work
of Satan. Those to whom His Kingdom belongs as

<hr>

[2] 4 Kings vi. 17.

a right have a power to impart it, and the prayer of the poor in spirit wins the graces of conversion and perseverance for many souls besides their own. And as in this sense they have some share of the royal power and Mission of our Lord Himself, so in the end they are to share the judicial power of His Kingdom when all enemies have been conquered, and the world, His witness against which they have carried on, is gathered at last before the throne of His Majesty.[3]

CHAPTER XII.

The Beatitude of the Meek.

St. Matt. v. 4; *Vita Vitæ Nostræ*, § 31.

IN the first Beatitude our Lord may be said to have laid down a principle, which may rectify all false judgments and inordinate desires with regard to what men commonly consider the good things of this life. The blessing which He has there pronounced falls upon the mortification and extinction of the great concupiscence which reaches forth to external goods, of which riches are the chief, because they are the means by which all others may be obtained. Our Lord does not simply bless the extinction of the concupiscence and nothing more, but the virtue which is founded upon faith and fostered by grace, which begins in the acknowledgment of the supreme dominion of God over all the things which can be the objects of desire, which makes them,

---

[3] The 'judiciary' prerogative of the poor belongs more properly to a later passage in our Lord's Life. See Alv. de Paz, t. ii. l. v. cc. 12, 13.

as it were, all over to Him in affection and spirit, and so, emptying itself of all ownership in these fleeting goods, is fit to receive in abundance from His bountiful hands the true treasures of His Kingdom. There is another concupiscence or principle of selfishness in us, which is seated even nearer to the centre of our hearts than the love of riches, and that is the love of ourselves, our own honour, our rights, reputation, consideration, independence, self-will, and liberty. A man may be utterly poor as to the good things of the world, and yet full of pride, impatience, anger, ready to resent any slight as an injury, to assume an arrogant position in relation to others, and incapable of obedience either of mind or action. Though poverty of spirit, as being so nearly akin to humility, is allied in consequence to that other offspring of humility which we call meekness, still it is not uncommon to find the concupiscence which is opposed to meekness raging furiously in those who have laid what might be the foundation of the Beatitudes in the practice of actual poverty. As poverty of spirit is humility and truth, in reference to external goods, so meekness is humility and truth in reference to our own independence, honour, and all that touches them to wound them, or that can be sought for as a means of pampering them. Thus it is natural that the great Healer of our concupiscences should proceed from the remedy of avarice to the remedy of pride and anger, and that meekness should follow poverty of spirit in the chain of His Beatitudes. Here again we shall find that He builds on faith and truth, that the virtue which He crowns consists in a due appreciation of the rights of God, that it is in itself more blessed as purifying and perfecting the soul, making it capable of great gifts and favours from God, that it has a blessing for society and the Church as well as for the particular soul in which it dwells, and that it has a claim which may be called natural, according to the nature of the spiritual kingdom, to the special reward which is assigned to it by our Lord.

Meekness, as has already been said, is the virtue which keeps down all the inordinate impulses of self-love in the direction of pride, liberty, ambition, anger, impatience, resentment, envy, revenge, and the like. In our present condition, in consequence of the miseries of life and the presence of selfish passions all around us, meekness has more frequently to manifest itself on what we may call its passive side, in patience, resignation, obedience, and gentleness under injury. But the sphere of the virtue of meekness is not confined to its influence in making the soul bear peaceably and religiously the many evils and burthens to which our condition is liable. It also tames the desire and ambition of honour and consideration of every kind, being founded on the truth, which faith enforces upon the mind, of the utter absence of any claim or right on the part of any creature to esteem or deference of any sort as due to itself, and of the unapproachable and incommunicable right of God to all honour and rule of every kind and degree. Thus meekness, like poverty of spirit and humility, is a virtue not of earth only and of this mortal life, but of Heaven and of eternity, though in the next world there will be no trials to patience, nothing that can provoke to anger, or arouse envy or resentment. Yet, as there is poverty of spirit, utter detachment from all ownership, and as there is humility, in Heaven, so also is there meekness; and the virtue as it is practised here, and as it is pronounced by our Lord to be blessed, regulates and keeps in place all the movements of the irascible part of the soul, whether they are excited by the desire of honour and esteem or ruffled by the denial of these when they seem to our self-love to be due.

It appears from this that the virtue of meekness, of which our Lord speaks, is no mere softness, or gentleness, or want of spirit, or insensibility. It is ordinary with the Christian virtues that there should be certain natural qualities, which exist in a greater or less degree in men of various characters, and which resemble the respective virtues and may be made their foundation, but which are very far from being identical with them. Thus, in the present case, there is in some men a sort of sluggishness and apathy of constitution which nothing can rouse, or there is a natural gentleness and mildness which seems to take nothing amiss, or, again, there is a timidity of character which shrinks from conflict and resistance, and so yields everything to an aggressor. But these only resemble Christian meekness, and are not the same as that virtue. They are not founded upon faith and grace, nor do they recognize in the dignity of God the adequate motive for their acts. They are often, indeed, partial and inconsistent. They fail when there is a severe trial of patience, they give way to certain persons and not to others, and under certain circumstances, and not under others. They have not been gained or matured by self-discipline, they are not rooted in self-conquest.

It has been the case with many of the saints of God who have been famous for the virtue which is ennobled in this Beatitude, that their natural dispositions have been strikingly contrary to the false or imperfect meekness of which we are speaking. Instead of being naturally apathetic, they have been quick and fiery, more inclined to harshness than to gentleness, aggressive rather than yielding, men of strong will, independent character, decided judgment, to whom docility, obedience, submission, silence when thwarted or opposed, have been qualities of particular difficulty. Yet these are the men in which the virtue of meekness has been so conspicuous, that persons who have not known their natural character have thought them apathetic and phlegmatic. Injuries and contumely seem to have no effect upon them. But it is in truth the work of a special and long-cultivated grace which keeps them from breaking out into anger, or even from feeling its movements in their soul. It has been the work of prayer and long self-discipline, fostered by consideration of the wonderful gentleness of God in dealing with His enemies, of the example of our Lord's meekness in His Passion, and of the many benefits which imitation of Him in this respect secures for the soul, and by practice of the acts of this and the kindred virtues, with the powerful assistance of grace, that has made them so tranquil, serene, and unruffled, not only externally, but also in the very depths of their heart, and enabled them to go on still further than mere calm endurance, to speak sweetly and lovingly to those who insult them, to turn to them the other cheek, to do them kindnesses and pray for them, and to forget their conduct entirely, except so far as it is a reason for showing them a special charity. These are the acts of true meekness, which is therefore the virtue of a manly, brave, and enduring character, requiring the greatest courage and self-control, and often rising to a height at which natural courage fails entirely, as, for instance, in the refusal of opportunities of revenge and in the gentle bearing of an insult at which the blood naturally boils. Heroic acts of this virtue under such trying circumstances have often been rewarded by God with great gifts of grace, high vocations, or splendid miracles. It is far harder to bear shame and ridicule, and to disregard the false maxims of the world in obedience to the principles of the Gospel, than to endure great sufferings and pain, and to risk life itself in defence of what is considered honour.

It is also to be remembered as to the virtue of meekness, that it is not only quite consistent with the most heroic firmness and constancy in what is good, but it is also an essential condition of true Christian firmness. Those in whom force of character is merely a natural quality, are likely to be strong and even overbearing in matters which are of little importance, and yet to fail and yield deplorably when principles are at stake. On the other hand, Christian strength of character, so to call it, is founded upon the most absolute meekness and lowliness of heart, which yields in all that is not of importance out of reverence to God, and then, when the trial of principle comes, and some holy truth of faith or rule of the Church has to be maintained against clamour and obloquy and intimidation of every sort, it stands firm as a rock, out of the very same reverence to God which has been the cause of its gentleness on other points. Thus the most heroic of God's servants in the Old Testament, such as Moses and David, are noted in Sacred Scripture for their remarkable meekness, and the great victories of the Christian martyrs, simple children, or women or men whose lives have never been ruffled by any storm of passion, have been the victories of meekness. The same gentle submissiveness and pliancy of character runs through the whole generation of the saints, and lies at the foundation of their indomitable fortitude and irresistible courage.

It is the will of God that obedience should be the law of His Kingdom both in Heaven and on earth, the law of the human society which He has ordained, as well as that of the supernatural system of which the members of the human society are members by grace. Obedience and subordination, the guidance of inferiors by superiors, who are in their turn illuminated from above, is the law of the heavenly hierarchies, as well as of the Church and men here below. But obedience and authority equally require meekness in those on whom they are respectively imposed. The ruler, natural and supernatural, lay and ecclesiastic, religious or secular, the sovereign, the husband, the parent, the master in whatever society, spiritual, social, domestic, or voluntary, must rule in meekness and gentleness, as having in himself no claim to authority and so to obedience, but only as having received it as his commission from God for which he must give an account. And on the other hand, the subject and inferior in all the various forms of society of which we have been speaking requires meekness, docility, control over his self-will and natural love of independence, readiness to put aside his own judgment and distrust his own forces and his own lights, in order that his obedience may have the blessing of God and become prosperous and fruitful. This holds good in every department of the action of intelligent creatures, in the region of faith and speculation, in the spiritual life, as in intellectual pursuits, in the administration of the Church or of religious communities as well as in the government of the home or of the State. And thus meekness becomes the bond which knits together the whole of the various societies of which God is the author. Pride, independence, self-will, self-confidence, are as destructive of peace and happiness and prosperity as uncontrolled anger or unrestrained lust.

It is plain that a virtue of this universal importance and operation can be no natural gift, and can be founded upon nothing short of that knowledge of God's supreme dignity and that entire sacrifice of self-will before it to which it has been traced. This is confirmed in a marvellous manner by what has been observed by some holy writers, that when St. Paul comes to describe charity itself he uses hardly any other colours than those which paint meekness : 'Charity is patient, is kind, it envieth not, it doth not deal perversely, it is not puffed up, it is not ambitious, seeketh not her own, is not provoked to anger, thinketh no evil, rejoiceth not in iniquity, but rejoiceth in the truth, beareth all things, believeth all things, hopeth all things, endureth all things.'[1] Almost all these points on which the Apostle insists are characteristic of charity exercising itself in the acts of meekness. It is meekness that gives patience under adversity, that is the parent of the kindliness and benignity which never repays an injury. It is meekness that excludes envy at the happiness of another, and that secures against remorse of conscience, because it does no evil. It is meekness that is not puffed up, because it acknowledges its own unworthiness of all honour, that seeks no pre-eminence because it has no ambition, and escapes the narrowing influence of cupidity, because it seeks not its own. It is not provoked to anger, because it counts nothing as an injury, it is no prey to evil suspicions, because it thinketh no evil, it has no joy in the misfortunes of others, because it rejoiceth not in iniquity, it is free from delusion and error, because it rejoices in the truth. It bears up bravely under trial and persecution, because it beareth all things, it hopeth all things from God, and so is safe from despair, it endureth all things, and so can never be broken down.

[1] 1 Cor. xiii. 4—7.

CHAPTER XIII.

The Meek possessing the Land.

THE idea of meekness which is thus to be gained from considering its true foundation and exercise and character is certainly very different from that of the natural mildness and softness which are sometimes mistaken for it, but which differ from it altogether both in the root from which they spring and in the weakness which they exhibit under any severe pressure. In the same way, the blessing which our Lord allots to the meek has at first sight that same character of unexpectedness and paradox which marks also the reward of the poor in spirit, and, as we shall see, the other rewards also which are to follow in the rest of the Beatitudes. The poor in spirit are rewarded by that to which they seem especially to give up their claim, that is, by wealth, but it is the wealth of the Kingdom of God, not the riches of the world. In the same way, the meek appear especially to renounce the world as far as it is a thing to be possessed as a matter of right, for it is the characteristic of meekness to yield its right to others, not to strive to contend, even for what is lawful, to give way in everything, and so to be a prey to the violence and aggressiveness of others. Worldly possessions, high position, honour, consideration, and the like, are the ordinary objects of ambition and competition, and their loss is resented with anger, pride, passion, and the desire of revenge. All these passions have no place in the conduct of the meek, whose hearts are subdued and kept down by the vivid faith with which they see their own nothingness, and that they have no right or claim to anything as their own. They therefore neither seek all these objects of earthly desire, nor consider them their own when they have them, nor resist when they are taken from them. It seems therefore a strange thing that our Lord should allot to them just that very reward which they seem to have renounced, or, at least, to have no taste for, when He says, 'Blessed are the meek, for they shall possess (inherit) the land.' The blessing which is here pronounced by our Lord has sometimes caused a difficulty, even to Catholic expositors, and, as is often the case, the very difficulty itself, when it is more clearly examined, yields its own fruit of instruction and doctrine.

It may be observed, in the first place, that there certainly seems to be a sort of antithesis intended in the expressions used by our Lord, as if the land which the meek are to inherit was put in contrast to the Kingdom of Heaven which is assigned to the poor in spirit, as well as to that surrender of all earthly considerations and yielding of their own interests which are characteristics of the meek. It is almost as if our Lord had meant to say, If you are poor in spirit, you have already the Kingdom of Heaven, and if you are in addition meek, you shall have the inheritance of the earth likewise. Again, we must remember that the word which the Vulgate translates *possidebunt,* 'shall possess,' is, strictly speaking, to be rendered by the English word 'inherit'— which implies that the meek shall receive the 'land' which is promised them not so much as a gift, or as an acquisition, or a conquest, but by right of inheritance from their Father to Whom it belongs. The meek, then, are here declared to be those to whom the inheritance of the land shall fall. Again, it is important to remember that our Lord is here, and here alone in the whole chain of the Beatitudes, using the words of Sacred Scripture and quoting one of the Psalms of David. It is natural, therefore, to turn to the Psalm which is quoted for light to help us to understand our Lord's meaning, as He could not but have intended to refer to the whole passage from which the words which He adopted were taken.

The Psalm in which the passage quoted by our Lord occurs may be said to have for its burthen the exhortation to meekness and patience under trial, especially the trial of what seems the unjust exaltation and prosperity of the wicked. It is that which begins: *Noli æmulari in malignantibus*—'Chafe not thyself because of evil-doers'[1]—and the phrase 'inherit the land' is repeated over and over again like the few notes of music in a long piece which recall and embody the 'motive' of the whole. It is a Psalm that may embody the thoughts with which David encouraged himself to that patient expectation for the promise which had been made him, which was one of his great merits. He left his cause to God when he was persecuted and banished, and would never avenge himself or lift up his hand against Saul, whom he had more than once in his power. God had promised him the kingdom, he had been anointed by Samuel, but he would do nothing to take it to himself, meekly leaving to God to bring about the fulfilment of His promises in His own time. In the Psalm before us, whether or not it belong to this period of David's life, the thought of the quiet practice of good by waiting on the Lord, and refraining from

[1] Psalm xxxvi. (xxxvii.)

all indulgence of the indignation and anger, which are naturally roused by injustice and the prosperity of the wicked, occurs over and over again. 'Trust in the Lord and do good, and dwell in the land, and thou shalt be fed with its riches.' 'Cease from anger, and leave rage, have no emulation to do evil. For evil-doers shall be cut off, but they that wait upon the Lord, they shall inherit the land. For yet a little while, and the wicked shall not be, and thou shalt seek his place, and shall not find it. But the meek shall inherit the land, and shall delight in abundance of peace.' 'The Lord knoweth the days of the undefiled, and their inheritance shall be for ever. They shall not be confounded in the evil time, and in the days of famine they shall be filled.' 'Such as bless Him shall inherit the land, but such as curse Him shall perish.' 'The unjust shall be punished, and the seed of the wicked shall perish. But the just shall inherit the land, and shall dwell therein for evermore.' 'Expect the Lord, and keep His way, and He will exalt thee to inherit the land, when the sinners shall perish thou shalt see. I have seen the wicked highly exalted, and lifted up like the cedars of Libanus. And I passed by, and lo he was not, and I sought him, and his place was not found.'

We are thus able to gather up the general teaching of this beautiful Psalm, and to see how our Lord's words may be understood as a promise that the meek shall have that blessing and protection from God's providence which is so constantly mentioned in its successive verses. God will take care that they shall have the inheritance that is theirs, which they abandon to His protection, contenting themselves with the quiet observance of His law, without any attempt to vindicate themselves, to claim their right, or oppose the wicked and the oppressor with their own weapons. What belongs to them by virtue of God's promise will come to them by His providence, though they do not strike a blow for it. David himself is the great historical example of the fulfilment of his own words, for the kingdom became his though he would use no violence to win it. The meek are of all others the persons to act in this way, and the promise therefore specially falls to them. In this sense we may understand our Lord's words as referring to a law of God's providence, which is carried out even as to temporal goods in the case of the meek, unless there be some higher law to operate in particular cases, the working of which puts them in a better and loftier position than the allotment of temporal goods. There are some such laws mentioned in Holy Scripture, as for instance that which promises long life to those who are dutiful to their parents, or to that which St. Peter quotes from the Psalms: 'He that will love life and see good days, let him refrain his tongue from evil, and his lips that they speak no guile,'[2] and the rest, or again the promise of special deliverance in the evil day to the man 'that understandeth concerning the needy and the poor.'[3] These blessings are rules of God's government of the world, and though the temporal benefits which they promise may often be superseded by spiritual favours which are far more precious, it may still remain the method of God's action to bless the dutiful, or those who guard their tongue, or those who are merciful to the poor and afflicted of every kind, in the face of the whole world, in order to make known His regard for the virtues which are thus practised, while on the other hand He constantly visits the undutiful, or the unmerciful, or men of a bad tongue, with temporal punishment as well as with eternal.

---

[2] 1 St. Peter iii. 10, 11, from Psalm xxxiii. 13.   [3] Psalm xl. (xli.)

We find that this interpretation of our Lord's words is adopted, with his characteristic simplicity and directness, by the great St. Chrysostom, who illustrates it by the example of Abraham, who was so meek that he would bear no contention between his own herdsmen and those of Lot, to whom accordingly he gave the choice in which part of the land of Canaan he would dwell. And then when Abraham had made this sacrifice for the sake of peace, we are told that God bade him lift up his eyes and look from the place whereon he then was, to the north and to the south and to the east and to the west: 'All the land that thou seest, I will give to thee and to thy seed for ever.'[4] Thus what he gave up by meekness he received as an inheritance as a reward of his meekness. This then is a general law, as our Lord implies, in the Kingdom of God, and the meek are blessed, because it secures them abundantly, fully, permanently, and from God Himself, what they are not willing to contend for among men. The principle is expressed in the Psalm, from which our Lord takes His words, with reference to the temporal possession of the Promised Land, exactly as if the case of Abraham had been in the mind of David, and because such was the language which befitted the time of the Old Covenant. But the promise of God and the enforcement of that principle of His government to which allusion is here made, cannot be limited in operation to temporal benefits alone. Or rather, perhaps, it should be said, that promise and that principle, as far as they regard temporal possessions and the inheritance of the earth, rest upon features in God's character as it is revealed to us, which have far higher and more spiritual effects in His dealings with His creatures. Our Blessed Lady dwells upon this among other numerous characteristics of

<hr>

[4] Genesis xiii. 14, 15.

God, in the *Magnificat*, when she says, ' He hath put down the mighty from their seat, and hath exalted the humble.' He requires meekness, submissiveness, humility, in those to whom He grants the possession of the infinite treasures of different orders which He has thrown open to His creatures. He has from the very beginning given the inheritance to the meek, and will do so until the end. The fallen angels fell through pride, the angels who were confirmed in grace and made heirs and possessors of Heaven, won their crowns through meekness. So it has been in the history of man, in the election and rejection of nations for empire, in the choice God has made of those whom He has specially favoured or reprobated in whatever order. The proud are always cast down, the meek receive the inheritance.

Before passing on to the more spiritual instance of the working of the Law, which have suggested the interpretation put on these words of our Lord by the majority of commentators, it may be well to consider how large is the range of meaning in which they may be taken almost literally. The earth is given by God to man as his inheritance, and this may well be understood of all that is so given, life, and all its circumstances and conditions, fraught with a number of blessings and benefits which address themselves to his various needs and to the different parts of his nature, physical, intellectual, moral, and spiritual. It may be said that those alone inherit this life, who enjoy it, understand it, profit by it, gather from it the instruction and help and blessings of various kinds which the great Father of all intends for His children. There are, for instance, savage nations in occupation of some of the fairest and wealthiest regions of the earth, who may be said to dwell in them without inheriting them. The civilized traveller from a country less blessed by nature can see and understand the resources of the land, which are unknown to its occupants. The soil is fertile and rich, there are streams to turn a thousand mills, pastures on which flocks without number may be fed, plains which may yield exhaustless crops of corn and maize, the climate is so fostering and genial that the vine, the olive, the palm, the fig may flourish there, along with the richest spices and most delicious fruits of the most favoured islands of the East. The mountains are full of metallic treasures, and forests and quarries are there to supply all the wants of architecture and commerce, while the coast is rich in natural harbours, and the land lies in such a position on the face of the globe with reference to other countries as to ensure to its inhabitants prosperity, importance, and even empire, if its resources were developed, which the few ignorant tribes which range over its face are utterly unable to unlock. Such a people may be said to occupy, but not to possess or inherit the home which God has given them, because they have not the intelligence to know what the gift is, or the energy to turn it to account.

If this be true as to the natural blessings which are on every side of us, in regard to the use which may be made of them for the purpose of our natural life and social or political well-being, it is surely true also of the world and condition in which God has placed us, the circumstances around us, the opportunities we have of improvement, instruction, and the practice of virtue, with regard to the higher ends of our being. Men of the most cultivated intellect, and who study most industriously even the physical world in all its wonderful arrangement and harmony, may yet, as is shown by example every day, altogether miss the lesson which God has written therein for man to learn, and be deaf and blind to its eloquent witness to Himself, His goodness, power, and majesty. The reason why they do not hear what is ringing in their ears and do not see what is held up before their eyes, is the want of meekness of intellect. Meanwhile, men of simple humble minds read all these lessons without effort, and thus seeing God as He means them to see Him in the works of His hands, they inherit the earth with a possession of which others are deprived.

Again, to take another instance, men of strong passions, untamed ambition, reckless lust, who indulge their natural greed for power or pleasure, or who strain themselves in the continual pursuit of wealth or the honour of this world, may be rich in lands and possessions, and have all the means of temporal enjoyment at their command and yet after all they do not enjoy life or their own possessions. They can no more enter into their inheritance in all these matters, than an idiot can inherit intellectual treasures of literature or art which his fathers have accumulated for him, and this, not for lack of the act of possession, but for lack of the faculty of possessing anything in a rational manner. The defect in the idiot is the absence of intelligence; the defect in the men who are the slaves of passion or ambition or avarice or the disquiet of worldly cares or the restlessness of an evil conscience, is the lack of meekness of mind and heart.

To those who have this meekness, the whole world is a possession and a home, they enjoy even the riches and treasures of others, whatever has delight and joy and profit to give yields them to the meek, and they inherit it as the children of Him Who gave the earth to man, not by the law of human inheritance which allots what is called property in this world, but by the right of the Creator of all things, Who has made all things to be used, and given to men of humble hearts the title and the power to use them.

Again, a great part of the natural inheritance which is intended for God's children in this world is the teaching concerning Himself which is contained in the course of history, His providence in the government of mankind, of the Church, of single souls, which, to those whose eyes are enlightened by Him, is full of sweetness and beauty and tenderness, as well as of justice and holiness. But for the understanding of all this, meekness is necessary; for 'He will guide the mild in judgment, and He will teach the meek His ways.'[5] The reverent faith which recognizes Him as the Ruler of all things in His providence, which sees His hand in all that comes about, adores His judgments and waits patiently on His will, is rewarded by the gifts of intelligence and wisdom, while the contrary spirit of pride and self-will and independence grovels in darkness, and in its ignorance is tempted to find fault with and rebel against what it cannot understand. Thus meekness is necessary in order to use the gifts of God, natural as well as spiritual, aright, to understand them and see His action in them and take home the lessons and instructions they are meant to convey. The same may be said even of their enjoyment. For they are not truly gifts to, nor are they truly enjoyed by, those who use them as their own or as the instruments of pride or of sin, and so, though in this sense they may occupy the land, they do not possess it or inherit it. To the meek they are the works of God, the gifts of their Father, all that is good and beautiful and profitable in them is a quality which reflects Him in His beauty and goodness, and the quiet, tranquil thankfulness of a childlike spirit enables them to use them as they

[5] Psalm xxiv. 9.

are meant to be used, and to recognize and rejoice in their loveliness with a simple depth of discernment and intensity of delight which can have no place in the soul disturbed by passion. It may be said that even the common beauties of nature are sealed books to the proud and passionate, because they require in those who are to enjoy them something in harmony with their own peace and obedience and dependence on their Creator and Lord, Whose ineffable repose and beauty and might they reflect in their several degrees. Thus it is that the gentle heart inherits all that is soothing and elevating in what human genius has produced, such as the restful music of poetry or art, in which the soul pours out her longings for higher and nobler things than she as yet possesses. The contact of nature, even in her simpler scenes, and of whatever bears on it the stamp of natural piety in human works, has a soothing influence for them, of which sensuality, dissipation, frivolity, or the sterner tempests of ambition, envy, or hatred, deprive the souls in which they reign.

These are considerations, then, which suggest that, when we enlarge our ideas of what our Lord may have meant by the earth or land which the meek are to inherit, we may find that there is no difficulty in understanding the words in their plain literal sense. And it is only an extension of the same interpretation to understand that our Lord means to teach us that meekness is the condition on which alone any gifts of God to man can be truly enjoyed and used as they ought to be by His children, that it is the key which unlocks His treasures, which opens the secrets of Scripture or of doctrine to the student, secures the guidance of the Holy Spirit to those who have to rule or teach, and enables men to profit by all holy inspirations and means of grace of whatever kind that are provided for them in the Church. It is in an especial manner true that meekness is necessary for the discernment of the manifold action of God upon the soul, for He speaks ordinarily when there is calm and peace, and in the same way the soul that would converse with God in prayer must be quiet and docile. And this is the account to be given of the inability of many Christians to pray and meditate : there is some inordinate passion in the soul which has not been conquered, some end of self-love which has not been abandoned, and there is in consequence an absence of that docility and tranquillity which prayer requires. If, then, we consider that in the 'inheritance of the earth' may be included the intelligent and profitable use of all that God has given to His children as their possession in this life, whether spiritual, moral, intellectual, or material. 'Whatsoever things are true, whatsoever things are honest, whatsoever things are pure, whatsoever things are lovely, whatsoever things are of good report'[6]—it may be said that meekness is the one disposition and virtue which enables man to use and enjoy and possess all these things according to the intention of his Creator.

It must be remembered that there are also other senses which have been adopted by Christian interpreters of the text, which convey deep truths, and may also be combined with what has already been said. In the first place, some holy writers say that the meek possess the land on which they tread, the land which they carry with them, and the land which they seek.[7] The land which they carry with them is their own body, and it is a matter of daily experience that those who subdue the passions of anger, envy, revenge, self-will, and the like, are rewarded by

[6] Philipp. iv. 8.

[7] *Terram quam terunt, terram quam gerunt, terram quam quærunt* (St. Bernardine).

God by the empire over their own body, the subjugation of the more carnal part of their nature, while on the other hand, pride, anger, and the other kindred passions, where they are allowed to rule, are ordinarily accompanied by or tend to the indulgence of even the filthiest lusts. This is so true that even intellectual pride and the pride which leads men into heresy, the subjects of which are usually men of cultivation and even of religious profession, are nevertheless frequently chastised by the rebellion of the lower appetites. The pattern of all purity, on the other hand, is our Blessed Lady, the humblest and the meekest of the daughters of Eve, she to whom the Church sings—

> Virgo singularis,
> Inter omnes mitis,
> Nos culpis solutos,
> Mites fac et castos.

It cannot be too much insisted upon, that any indulgence of anger, pride, irritability, a domineering temper, or again, of vanity, conceit, and the other faults which have so great a tendency to blind men to their own defects, is nearly connected with the rebellion of the lower appetites, and that it may be in vain to chastise the flesh and to endeavour to keep down the more carnal passions by mortification, as long as those others are left unchecked. For as Cassian writes, 'As much as a man advances in gentleness and patience of heart, so much will he advance also in purity of body. And so much the further as he has driven back the passion of anger, so much the more firmly will he grasp the virtue of chastity. For no one will avoid the fiery heat of the body, but he who has first repressed the movements of the mind. And this is most openly declared by that Beatitude which is praised by our Lord's own mouth, when He says, "Blessed are the meek, for they shall possess the land." In no other way, therefore, shall we possess the land, that is, in no other way shall the rebellious earth of this our body be subjected to us, but by the firm foundation of our mind, in the first instance, on the gentleness of patience : nor will any one be able to keep down the rising battles of lust in his own flesh, unless he be first armed with the weapon of meekness. For "the meek shall possess the land, and shall dwell therein for ever." '

Again, there is another sense in which this promise has been understood, according to which the meek are promised the empire of the hearts of all those with whom they have to deal. The benignity and loving condescension of God are the attributes which are especially dwelt upon by St. Paul when he speaks of the Incarnation, which is itself the expression of those virtues. Meekness was above all other things the characteristic of our Lord, the one virtue which He invited us all to study in Him when He said, ' Learn of Me, for I am meek and lowly of heart,' and then He promised rest to the soul as the reward of docility in this respect. Meekness then is the characteristic virtue of the economy adopted by God for the salvation of the world, and it is so on account of its attractive and subduing powers over mankind. Thus we see it especially in great rulers, such as Moses and David, who had rather to lead the people to something new, than merely carry on institutions already in possession —and in the Christian ages it has been the peculiar badge of Apostolical men, even of those who have had to act strongly and severely in vindication of the rights of the Church, the law of God, or the integrity of the faith. The happy charity and easy freedom which reigned in good Christian families, or in religious communities, or among the faithful generally in Catholic times, and which still are found in countries as yet unspoilt by the modern spirit, have their root in the diffusion of Christian meekness through all ranks and classes, and it is not wonderful that this meekness should be blessed with the power of making its way at once to the heart and winning love and influence. ' My son,' says the Scripture, 'do thy works in meekness, and thou shalt be beloved above the glory of men ;'[8] as if all Christian actions of whatever kind were to have this colouring of meekness shed over them to clothe them with graciousness and beauty, and as if the love which is thus won by the meek were far more wonderful than all that is glorious among men.[9]   There are many virtues the acts of which in themselves are not conciliating to others besides those who perform them, as acts of authority or justice, the reproving what is amiss, resisting aggression, and the like.   These acts are all lawful and honourable in themselves, and may be, in any particular instances, absolutely necessary duties.   But they are all to have the gilding of meekness to adorn them, and even where it is a Christian's duty to be angry or to contend or to reprove or to command unwilling obedience, he is still to be meek and gentle while he is firm and even peremptory, as our Lord was not wanting in meekness when He drove the buyers and sellers out of the Temple, or reproved the Scribes or Pharisees. And works done in meekness have the blessing of our Lord's promise in this sense, that they have a special power of gaining men's hearts and of ruling them.

---

[8] Ecclus. iii. 19.

[9] The Greek version has $\delta\iota\epsilon\xi\acute{\alpha}\gamma\alpha\gamma\epsilon$ and the Latin *perfice* for the word ' do ' (thy works in meekness). These renderings seem to imply that meekness is to be the beginning, middle, and ending of all good works, and that it gives all our actions their due perfection. They are to be good in themselves, and well done in their kind, and then made perfect by the gentleness and meekness in which they are done by us.

The other common interpretation, which understands the words of our Lord as of the 'land of the living,' that is, of Heaven, hardly needs more than a simple statement. The empire which the meek exercise over their own passions, which enables them to rule their own souls and bodies in peace, and to win the love and obedience of all with whom they have to do, is to be perfected and crowned by the possession of God Himself in His Heavenly Kingdom, which is essentially the realm of peace. And thus we have in this Beatitude the fulfilment of those other words of the Psalmist, which follow those which our Lord has quoted: 'The meek shall inherit the land, and shall delight in the multitude of peace.' For meekness is peace in itself, as pride and anger are war and disturbance, and in this way a meek and quiet heart is a sort of image of the ineffable peace of God Himself. And as it rules in perfect tranquillity its own movements, and the body in which it is encased, and the world in which its lot is cast, and the men across whom it is brought in its path of action, so also will it hereafter secure the possession and inheritance of the children of God in the intense and unchangeable joys of the Kingdom in which they are to reign with Him.

CHAPTER XIV.

The Beatitude of the Mourners.

St. Matt. v. 5 ; *Vita Vitæ Nostræ,* § 31.

In the first two Beatitudes our Lord certainly declared
principles which sound as strange paradoxes in the ears
of the world, while at the same time He showed a royal
authority and magnificence in the rewards which He
assigned to virtues so unknown or so despised as poverty
of spirit and meekness. And yet, as we have seen, the
apparent paradox was in each case founded on the truth.
It is no extravagance or exaggeration for man or for
any creature, whether fallen or not, whether in Heaven
or on earth, now or hereafter, to acknowledge his own
utter poverty in the universe which God has made, his
own entire want of any right to possess, or to use, or
to have anything in whatever order of good as his own.
Nor is it to go beyond the truth, or to sink to a level
which is too low for the deserts and rights of any
creature, to recognize, in the same way, that he has no
title of his own or claim to honour, respect, consideration, or esteem, and that, in consequence, he has no
right to resent what appear to be insults, injuries,
disrespect, and the like. The lowest and poorest place
that a creature can take is that which most truly belongs
to him, for he has and is nothing of himself. These
first two Beatitudes may be said, in this sense, to belong
to Heaven as well as to earth, and they might have held

their place among the first principles of the Kingdom of God if man had never fallen, and if the condition of the world had never in consequence been changed. The next Beatitude is, like all the others, a virtue or habit founded upon truth and faith. As the first is the recognition of the truth as to what we have or can have, and the second the recognition of the truth as to what we are in ourselves, so the third is the recognition of the truth as to the condition of things around us, the state of the world in which we live, which is what it is, in so far as it is different from what it might have been, in consequence of the action of the free-will of creatures as well as of the ordinance of God's providence. The gift of an intelligent nature enables us to understand this, take it in, and assume towards it a certain attitude of mind and heart and conduct. And the difference between those who live by faith and those who live by sense, those who follow the teaching of the world and those who are the disciples of our Lord, is based on the difference of view with which they regard the history and actual condition of man and all things around him, the import and value and effect of the present and the past, the things which are the objects of sense or thought or desire among which his lot is cast, his way of dealing with them, and his future prospects as affected thereby.

It is this which makes the third Beatitude a point, as it may be regarded, at which the apparent paradox, but real truth, which our Lord's teaching embodies, arouses the most active resentment of the world. The other Beatitudes do not seem to touch it to the quick— indeed, it has its meed of admiration and applause for poverty of spirit, meekness, mercifulness, peaceableness, purity of heart, and the like, as being at least beautiful with a heavenly beauty, and in a great measure beneficial to mankind. But the blessing which falls on the mourners pierces the hollowness of the world, and reveals its emptiness and falsehood. For the world is a lie, and this Beatitude is the touchstone which puts it to the proof in a way which the others do not. The philosophy of the world consists in two things, a practical falsehood as to man's responsibility and his future as depending on the present, and a line of conduct, based on this falsehood, in which the good things and enjoyment of life are pursued as the true ends of his existence. This philosophy is summed up in the maxim which St. Paul quotes, 'Let us eat and drink, for to-morrow we die.'[1] The classical passage in Holy Scripture, so to speak, in which the false doctrine of the world is put forth is in the Book of Wisdom, where the thoughts of worldlings are drawn out almost as they might be met with in the strains of some heathen poet, the slave of lust. 'The time of our life is short and tedious, and in the end of a man there is no remedy, and no man hath been known to have returned from Hell. For we are born of nothing, and after this we shall be as if we had not been. For the breath in our nostrils is smoke, and speech a spark to move our heart. Which being put out, our body shall be ashes, and our spirit shall be poured abroad as soft air, and our life shall pass away as the trace of a cloud, and shall be dispersed as a mist which is driven away by the beams of the sun and overpowered with the heat thereof. And our name shall be forgotten, and no man shall have any remembrance of our works. For our time is as the passing of a shadow, and there is no going back of our end, for it is fast sealed, and no man returneth. Come, therefore, and let us enjoy the good things that are present, and let us speedily use the creatures as in youth. Let us

---

[1] 1 Cor. xv. 32, from Isaias xxii. 13.

fill ourselves with costly wine and ointments, and let not the flowers of the time pass by us. Let us crown ourselves with roses before they be withered, let no meadow escape our riot. Let none of us go without his part in luxury. Let us everywhere leave tokens of joy, for this is our portion and this our lot.'[2]

There is a certain strain of sadness and complaint about this chant of the worldlings in the pages of Scripture, which represents perfectly the misery which underlies every human view of the conditions of life which is not the view of faith. But the world's great effort is to forget this misery, to hide it, if possible to disbelieve it, and the resentment with which thoroughly worldly people turn upon any person or any doctrine which reminds them of it, is the proof of the failure, even in them, of the attempt to banish from their minds the hated truth to which everything around them bears a witness which is echoed by their own conscience. They cannot help acknowledging how little it is, after all, that they can do to escape the doom which is so soon to fall on their short-lived pleasure, but they have no resources but to do what they can, and thus to imitate the Egyptian king of whom Herodotus speaks,[3] who, having been told that he was to live only six full years more, endeavoured to make the period twice as long by turning night into day and spending his whole time in revelry and debauchery. There are others, again, who are not exactly worldlings, but men of thought and reflection, and even sometimes of genius, who speculate on the condition of human life without the aid of faith, and, indeed, with a resolute will set against all belief in religion, and these men, instead of giving themselves up to wanton revelry, turn upon Nature, as they call it, for

[2] Wisdom ii. 1—9.
[3] Mycerinus. See Herod. ii. 153.

they do not know God, and revile her as the cruellest
and most inhuman of mothers, as ruling the world, as
they deem it, in such a way as to afflict and torture
mankind, and indeed all creatures that are capable of
feeling and suffering, in the most barbarous manner,
proving thereby that if there be a Ruler of the world,
He cannot be good if He is omnipotent, nor omnipotent
if He is good.   These, then, are the two views, it may
almost be said the two lines of action, which the condition of human life elicits from men who have no faith.
They either seek to drown their knowledge of the truth
in dissipation or debauchery, or they set themselves to
rail against their Creator and His laws.[4]

[4] The thoughts which are expressed in the following passage from
Mr. Mill's *Essay on Nature*, are probably familiar to many minds
which have not the miserable courage to utter them.   We quote them
both as showing to what an extent of unreasonableness an infidel
thinker of the highest intellectual gifts may be led, and also how dark
the whole world practically is to those who have not the faith : ' Killing,
the most criminal act recognized by human laws, Nature does once
to every being that lives ; and in a large proportion of cases, after protracted tortures such as only the greatest monsters whom we read of
ever purposely inflicted on their fellow-creatures. . . . . Nature impales
men, breaks them as if on the wheel, casts them to be devoured by wild
beasts, burns them to death, crushes them with stones like the first
Christian martyr, starves them with hunger, freezes them with cold,
poisons them by the quick or slow venom of her exhalations, and has
hundreds of other hideous deaths in reserve, such as the ingenious
cruelty of a Nabis or a Domitian never surpassed. All this, Nature
does with the most supercilious disregard both of mercy and justice,
emptying her shafts upon the best and noblest indifferently with the
meanest and worst ; upon those who are engaged in the highest and
worthiest enterprises ; and often as the direct consequence of the noblest
acts, and it might almost be imagined, as a punishment for them. She
mows down those on whose existence hangs the well-being of a whole
people, perhaps the prospects of the human race for generations to
come, with as little compunction as those whose death is a relief to
themselves, or a blessing to those under their noxious influence.   Such
are Nature's dealings with life.   Even when she does not intend to
kill, she inflicts the same tortures in apparent wantonness.   In the
clumsy provision which she has made for the perpetual renewal of
animal life, rendered necessary by the prompt termination she puts to it

The mourning which our Lord declares blessed in this third Beatitude, is certainly not at all akin to the railing which has just been spoken of, any more than it is akin to the childish folly of the other method of avoiding the plain truth. It is not even, in any true sense, an unhappy state. When death visits our families, we do not mourn as those that are without hope or consolation ; our hearts may be full of thankfulness and holy joy, for those whom we have lost may have died the death of the just, they may have been delivered from great sufferings and anxieties, they may have had many opportunities of grace, and they may have been favoured by God with singular consolations and powerful helps, which have made their last days blessed to themselves and to all around them, and full of the promise of still greater joys hereafter. And yet we mourn in a Christian manner, and the departure of our friends affects our whole life, our thoughts and words and actions, it withdraws us from the world, and from even innocent enjoyments, from the society of our friends, for some time also from secular occupations, our houses are darkened, our food and raiment, our whole demeanour and conduct are coloured by mourning. It is a time for prayer, penance, almsdeeds, mortification, silence, abstinence ; delicacies, enjoyments, recreations, all that partakes of the show and glitter and dissipation of life, those that are truly mourners have no heart for. They have just been touched by the truths of the unseen world, the

in every individual instance, no human being ever comes into the world but another being is literally stretched on the rack for hours or days, not unfrequently issuing in death. . . . Everything, in short, which the worst men commit against life or property is perpetrated on a larger scale by natural agents. Nature has Noyades more fatal than those of Carrier ; her explosions of fire-damp are as destructive as human artillery ; her plague and cholera far surpass the poison cups of the Borgias' (*Essay on Nature*, pp. 28—30).

shortness and emptiness of life, the great account to be given to the Judge of all, the issues on which eternity depends, and these truths do not make them sad or depressed, but they make them serious, thoughtful, awake to the claims of God, the importance of time, the priceless value of grace, the nothingness of the world, and so unable to turn at once again to the dream in which all these things are forgotten. The life of a mourner has not more self-denial about it than the life of a man who is the slave of worldly business, who has to rise early and take his rest late and spend his whole day in the dry details of commerce, or law, or in passing as the physician from the bed of one sufferer of pain or disease to that of another. The mourner is engrossed with the truth, the others may ply their trade and spend their hours in toil merely for the sake of gains which they will never enjoy. The mourner, as our Lord promises, has his consolation, the toilers of the world may toil to no purpose either here or hereafter. ·

The motives on which the Christian virtue and practice of mourning are founded, are on every side of us, and when the mind is once turned in prayer to their consideration, they are enough to engross its whole attention. They are differently summed up by different writers. At the head of all must stand God, the Creator and Lord of all, Who has made man for Himself, and placed him in the world that all around him may help him to the attainment of this end, and Whose merciful designs are so constantly defeated and His honour trampled under foot. In this sense all sin, whether past or present, whether grievous or venial, whether known or unknown, whether of ourselves or of other persons, is a subject of mourning, such mourning and grief as that which overwhelmed our Blessed Lord's Soul in the Garden of Gethsemani. The higher we are raised in our conception and intelligence of the honour due to God, of His ineffable holiness, goodness, and loveliness, so much the deeper must be the grief with which the slightest offence against Him must pierce our souls, so much the more imperative shall we feel the duty of mourning over it.

Again, the more we dwell upon and learn to understand the marvellous love of God which is shown in the dispensation of the Incarnation, in our Lord's Person and character, in His love and sufferings for us, in the provision which He has made for us in the Church, her sacraments and priesthood and doctrine, the more we come to know about His tenderness for each single soul and the manner in which He watches over it as that for which He has given the whole of His life-blood, and would, if necessary, give it again—so much the more must the manner in which His love has been rejected, the outrages to which He has been exposed from His enemies, the coldness and ingratitude which His own friends have shown Him, the unfaithfulness of many of His ministers, the utter disregard with which His precepts and examples have been treated by the great majority of those for whom He has done so much, furnish us with fresh reasons for continual mourning.

The two considerations of what our Lord has done and suffered, and how His love has been corresponded to, are in themselves closely connected, and yet they may well be separated as matters of Christian mourning. It has pleased God that very full narratives should remain to us, from the hands of the Apostles and Evangelists, concerning every detail of His Sacred Passion, and the Church has, if we may say so, caught the thought of her Divine Spouse in making the contemplation and remembrance of that Passion her constant occupation, the subject of her liturgical worship and of most of the numberless devotions which she adopts for the use of her children. The Passion is the one great theme of her services, its memorials are stamped on every portion of the public life and of the private existence of all Christians. From the very beginning she has honoured the traces and the scenes of that wonderful sacrifice which was consummated on Calvary, and the whole tone of her existence has been attuned thereto. It is not wonderful therefore that we should have to place the Passion of our Lord by itself as one of the great sources of the continual mourning of her children, as a history that has left its mark on all that comes after it, the memory of which ought never to be laid aside; so that it has been said by some of the saints that we have not as yet begun the spiritual life until we have ever present to us the sufferings of our Lord on the Cross. There are instances in ordinary life of persons who have experienced some great blow, some sudden and shocking bereavement of which it is said that they never forget it. They return to their duties and occupations, they mix with their friends and resume their outward life as before, but those who know them see that they are changed, that there is a sorrow in their heart which is never spoken of, yet which is never lulled to sleep. And it is not too much to suppose that the Passion of our Lord can never be forgotten, that Christians never can and never ought to live as if for them it was over, a thing to be put aside, instead of an ever-living memory, silently present, affecting every part of life and every moment of time.

Another ground of mourning is found in considerations concerning the blessedness and glory to which men might have been raised hereafter, and the marvellous benefits to society and to the souls of men one by one which are, as it were, folded up in the gift of the Incarnation and of our Lord's example, and in the Church which He has left behind Him to bring these blessings home to men, who have nevertheless either rejected them entirely or used them very partially. There is continually going on all around us, there has been continually going on from the beginning, a waste of grace, a cheating of God of His honour and of man of his happiness, over which souls that can understand the beauty of God's work and the glory which it might produce may well weep tears of blood day and night. Meanwhile, there are generations perishing for want of the light and grace which God intends for them, because there are no apostles to carry the Gospel to them. There are large portions of the world which have once been the inheritance of the Church and which have been wrested from her, so that the frontiers of her empire have receded instead of advancing, tracts of country which once were studded with flourishing churches, where martyrs have bled and holy doctors have taught, have long been handed over to the desolation which marks the dominion of the false prophet, while in others the fatal principles of Protestantism have borne their natural fruit in the extinction of belief and the corruption of morals. Nations which were meant to be brought into the fold have perished before the face of Christian invaders and conquerors, whose manner of dealing with them has been such as to link the name of Christ with the utmost tyranny, licence, and avarice. Thus, outside themselves and their own lives, and in that large range of subjects to which the interests of God and the Church and religion belong, the Christian mourners have so much to occupy themselves upon that it seems as if their grief could never be assuaged.

But, even in the natural order, in consequence of the fall of our first parents, the world in which our lot is cast is in truth 'the valley of tears' of which the Psalmist speaks. And we find that our Blessed Lord, in the course of those actions of His which He has chosen to be recorded for our benefit in the Gospels, did not think it beneath Him to let His own mourning for natural evils be known to us for our example. He wept in agony in the Garden of Gethsemani, over the dishonour done to God by the sins for which He was to atone, over the misery and mischief to man which they involved, the loss of grace and Heaven and of the vision of God hereafter, as also over the particulars of His own Passion and the cold and poor return which He was to meet with, in His own Person and in His Church, for all that He has done and provided for those whom He loved so much. But He could mourn and did mourn also for the temporal evils and miseries with which human life is beset. He wept over the grave of Lazarus as well as over the spiritual ruin of Judas, and over the future destruction of Jerusalem, which was to be the chastisement inflicted on the apostate nation for His own murder. Compassion is a kind of mourning, and our Lord's whole life was a life of active compassion. He could not bear not to relieve the desolate widow whose only son was being carried out to burial, and He pitied the multitudes who flocked out into the wilderness to hear His teaching, and provided for their temporal wants by the miraculous multiplication of the loaves and fishes, knowing that they had come from far and would faint by the way if they were not supplied with food for the body as well as for the soul. In these actions of our Lord we have, as it were, His authority for mourning and compassion over the various kinds of temporal calamities to which our condition is subject—the great scourges of God, such as war, famine, pestilence, the desolation of provinces, the destruction of cities, and the like; and again, bereavement, family afflictions, sickness, death. There is scarcely any motive for mourning which did not affect the tender Heart of our Lord, and even when He could not mourn, as, for instance, for sins of His own, we have the examples of those most dear and near to Him, like the blessed Magdalene and the Prince of the Apostles, and St. Paul. And in the last-named Apostle we have an instance of another motive of mourning which is found in the saints of God, the groaning and longing desire after their heavenly country and the consummation of their blessedness in the presence and home of their Father.

CHAPTER XV.

The Consolation of the Mourners.

St. Matt. v. 5 ; *Vita Vitæ Nostræ*, § 31.

It cannot be said that any one of these and the other minor motives for mourning which are assigned by Christian writers, is imaginary and chimerical. On the contrary, no serious consideration of the condition of human life can lead to any other conclusion as to the facts than that which is the ground of Christian mourning, although, if such consideration be made without the light of faith and by men who reject even natural religion, it may certainly lead to a line of conduct very different indeed from that which is declared by our Lord to be blessed. The miseries and uncertainties of life, the fleeting and unstable character of prosperity, the unsatisfying nature of the lower pleasures, or even of the intellectual and philosophical pursuits which are among the noblest occupations of the mind, are things which are universally felt and complained of even by those who will not use the Christian remedy for the evils which they deplore. The two other remedies, so to call them, of which mention has been made above, are obviously unreasonable and unworthy of the higher parts of man's nature. It is not reasonable for a creature to set himself up to find fault with and rail against the arrangements of his Creator, nor again, is it reasonable to endeavour to escape the elementary conditions of existence by forgetting them or rather shutting our eyes against them. It would revolt a man of sense and courage to be told that he must hide his diseases and dangers from himself, and that that was the only remedy which his physician could recommend to him. Our Lord is the true Physician of all the evils of human life, of those that are incidental to its natural condition as well as of those which are generated by its moral shortcomings. He does not bid us fly from their contemplation or consideration. He bids us look them in the face, meet them in the light of faith, shape our conduct with regard to them as reason and truth require, and then He promises us, not that they shall be taken away, but that they shall be made the sources of consolation and joy. And surely in nothing can He show better His royal power and the transforming influence of His grace, than in taking up the very evils which in themselves tend directly to unhappiness and sorrow, and turning them into the sources of joy. Thus He said to His Apostles when He was preparing them for the great blow of His own separation from them by His Passion, 'You shall lament and weep, but the world shall rejoice, and you shall be made sorrowful, but your sorrow shall be turned into joy.'[1] This is the great triumph of His power, that He

---

[1] St. John xvi. 20.

does not take away sorrow or hide it from our eyes, but He sanctifies it and blesses it, and so turns it into joy. Some of the Christian commentators on the Beatitude before us have asked why our Lord does not tell us in what the consolation is to consist, what shall be the special reward of those who mourn. And the answer seems to be that their mourning itself shall be blessed, and that, on whatever subject it may be grounded, that same subject-matter itself shall be made the matter of consolation.

There is thus to be a general and a particular blessing on the virtue of mourning. It may be called a virtue, because it is not a transient grief or a mere affection of the feelings, shown or not shown outwardly, of which our Lord speaks, but a solid habit of grief, contrition, compunction, desire, and the like, which has its constant issue in acts and in a tone of thought and line of conduct which change the whole life. 'The sorrow that is according to God,' St. Paul says, 'worketh penance, steadfast unto salvation, but the sorrow of the world worketh death.' And he goes on to congratulate the Corinthians on the fruits of their mourning in one particular case, when they had been sharply reproved by him. 'For this self-same thing, that you were made sorrowful according to God, how great carefulness it worketh in you, yea defence, yea indignation, yea desire, yea revenge !"[2] His language proves sufficiently that it was not a mere feeling, but a practical and active sorrow, that he was glad to have caused in the converts, who were so especially beloved by him. And the mourning, which is declared by our Lord to be blessed, must at least lead to and involve the acts of a life of penance, even though it may in strict language be distinguished from them. For holy writers tell us that

[2] 2 Cor. vii. 10, 11.

heartfelt and sincere mourning has a power of its own in bringing down a blessing from God, Who loves His children so much that He cannot, as it were, resist their tears. Thus mourning is a satisfaction for sin, and the pardon which it wins from God is accompanied by a calm deep sense of forgiveness which sets the soul at peace, and this peace is in itself the most perfect comfort. Christian mourning for sin, whether our own or that of others, is an act of love, and so every true mourner may take to himself the words of our Lord about the blessed Magdalene, that many sins were forgiven her, because she had loved much; and the forgiveness which is here spoken of is that complete and full forgiveness which remains to be won even after the guilt of sin has been cancelled, the remission which does away with the whole of the pain due by way of satisfaction, whether here or hereafter.

Again, Christian mourning is inseparable from the spirit of prayer, and prayer is the consolation of the human soul in any trial or trouble whatsoever. Prayer, again, accompanied by mourning, is irresistible with God, Who often does not grant what is only asked in a manner which seems to cost us nothing and does not prove that we are in earnest, but when He sees us afflict ourselves and put ourselves to pain in our petitions, He no longer refuses what is asked. Indeed, mourning is in itself a most powerful prayer, like the tears of the widowed mother of Naim, who, as it seems, did not even think of asking for her son's restoration, or again, the ears of St. Mary Magdalene, who in like manner asked for nothing. Again, the habit and nature of mourning is a sure safeguard against sin. It at once separates us from the world, not only in body, but in spirit, because it shuts out the greater number of worldly occupations, it fills our mind with serious and heavenly thoughts, even when we go about our daily duties, which cannot be laid aside, it raises us above temporal things, the emptiness and misery of which are a part of the truth which the mourner has always before him. And in this way mourning of every other kind, the mourning of contrition, or compassion, or for the evils of their life, or for the dishonour of God, the persecutions of the Church, or the waste of grace, leads men naturally to an intense desire for the rest and peace of Heaven, which is in itself a great consolation, as well as a protection against the allurements of false joys, pleasures that cannot satisfy, the occupations and interests of the world which lead to nothing.

These are considerations which show us that the state of mourners, with all that it implies in the Christian system of life, the faith on which it is built up, the hope which supports it, the charity which it exercises, is in itself a state full of consolation and the tenderest happiness, a state which might be much coveted and embraced for its own sake, for the sake of the truth which it embodies, and the joy to which it leads, even by those who have no occasion for special mourning over sins and calamities of their own. It is the rational and practical answer which faith gives to the history and condition of humanity, as poverty of spirit is the practical answer of faith to the question silently put to us by the good things of the world, and meekness the same answer to the question as to the rights of man to honour, independence, and the gratification of self-love. It may also be considered that it is at this point in the chain of the Beatitudes that our Lord touches, as far as He touches at all, the other great concupiscence which works so much havoc among the souls and lives of men and in society at large, the concupiscence which feeds itself upon sensual pleasures of every kind. Our Lord, indeed hardly stoops to mention this concupiscence so directly as the others, because by those who are even beginners in His school it must have been already conquered. Still, the state of the mourners is utterly inconsistent with and contrary to any indulgence of the more animal parts of our nature. It not only supposes a condition of heart and a manner of life in which even lawful enjoyments are laid aside in the presence of the great solemn truths of existence, but far more, it raises the soul, as has been said, to higher thoughts and to desires of consolation which are as pure and spiritual as those which the lower passions yearn after are shameful and carnal.

There is also a more special fulfilment of the promise of consolation to the mourners, in that for each kind of sorrow there is its special comfort in the good Providence of God. For the sorrowing of contrition, inasmuch as it is founded on the love of God, brings with it its own reward and comfort in the vision and possession of Him, which is the fruit of such love, and although the time has not yet come for the fulness of vision and possession, still there is even here and now a degree of union with God which is the beginning and foretaste in the Holy Ghost of that consummate happiness. And the tears of compunction will always win the grace of forgiveness and peace. The mourning over the Passion of our Lord, the sufferings of the Church and her children, the waste of grace, the loss of souls, and the like, has the comfort that those who so mourn are allowed to see and taste, as it were, the fruit of the Cross and the power of the prayer which is joined to self-affliction for the honour of God and the good of the souls of men. Such mourners are taught by the light which their prayer and compassion bring to them, how all things work together for good, and how the adorable will of God is accomplished in everything. Those who mourn as exiles from their heavenly home and on account of the miseries of this valley of tears, will have the consolation that their hearts and thoughts are occupied with Heaven and spiritual things, and their mourning is made by the Holy Spirit Who guides them the ground of a great gift of enlightenment, which lets them discern the value of time and grace, the beautiful wisdom by which all the conditions of human existence are framed for the acquirement of merit, which is to last for ever in its fruit of glory, the blessing of being allowed to work works of justice and mercy, and of zeal for souls and for God's glory. So that we find some of the saints who have been, as it were, burnt up by the desire to be freed from their exile, still ready to forego the certain possession of their bliss of God, if it were more useful for His glory and for men that they should remain a while longer on earth in order to labour more. Such traits are recorded of St. Paul, and again, of St. Martin and St. Ignatius, and they show how perfectly our Lord fulfils His promise, in that even this longing and yearning desire for Heaven and the ineffable happiness there, can be, as it were, at once satisfied and unsatisfied— unsatisfied as to the direct possession of its object, satisfied by the consolation which floods the soul which is devoted to the advancement of God's glory, in suffering any delay, running any risks, and undertaking any labours which are imposed upon it by His will and the interests of His service.

CHAPTER XVI.

The Beatitude of Hunger and Thirst after Justice.

St. Matt. v. 6 ; Vita Vitæ Nostræ, § 31.

IT is not difficult to see how the Beatitudes lead us on by a regular and beautiful advance, the virtues which are mentioned as the earlier links of the chain introducing those which follow. This connection between these principles of our Lord's legislation has been a favourite subject of contemplation to many devout writers, who have loved to seek out reasons why poverty of spirit and detachment from this world's goods prepare the soul for the practice of meekness, and how meekness, in its turn, fits the heart for mourning, with its appropriate reward of sweet and deep consolation. It is not necessary here to go further into this matter, and it is enough to refer to what has already been said as to the great elementary truths on which are founded the Beatitudes which have been hitherto considered. Our Lord hides nothing from us. Rather, He sets before our eyes without any flattery exactly what we are and what we are entitled to, and the conditions of the world in which we live and the existence which we now lead. And He bids us see how blessed a thing it is to recognize these truths, and to arrange our thoughts and conceptions and conduct according to the light which streams from them. And now that He has put us face to face with the many solemn truths on which the

motives of Christian mourning are founded, He does
not leave us there, as if our lives were to be spent in
a plaintive though blessed grief, in a passive state of
sorrow and longing and lamentation. He has His
blessing for action as well as for suffering. Rather it is
more true to say that it is the characteristic of Christian
mourning to rouse us to Christian activity, just as much
as it is the characteristic of poverty of spirit to engender
meekness, and of meekness to open the springs of
mourning.

If we examine the considerations which have been
assigned as the grounds of mourning, we shall find that
they are all, when looked at in the light of faith, motives
and spurs for Christian activity. For it is by this that
the honour of God is restored, the Passion of Jesus
Christ repaired and its merits applied in the way of
fruitfulness, it is by this that our past sins are redeemed
and the empire of evil under which the world groans
assailed and overthrown. It is by virtue and justice,
in the largest sense of the words, that the precious
legacies which our Lord has left behind Him are rightly
used and His Kingdom advanced, the shortness of time
turned to good account, the calamities and sufferings to
which flesh is heir made the occasion of God's glory
and man's spiritual profit. It is by these that the weariness of exile is relieved, and the joys of Heaven for which
we are yearning increased in intensity and brought within
our grasp. Mourning and the practice of justice are
as nearly akin as poverty and meekness. The mourner
rises from his prayer with his heart on fire with sorrow,
which can best be relieved by the exertion and devotion
which spring from a great desire. The mourners of the
world are sometimes made to forget their sorrow by
being engrossed in political strife, or scientific investigation, or some other intellectual and mental labours

which leave no room for the indulgence of excessive grief; and others are tempted to dull the remembrance of what they have lost in a whirl of pleasure. The Christian mourner, however, has already had his mind and heart purged from foolish conceptions and inordinate desires as to earthly goods, while at the same time his perceptions of the value of spiritual treasures have been made vivid and keen, and his appetite for all that concerns the glory of God has been sharpened. The glory of God is then set before him as the end to be reached through the practice of justice, and thus it is that he learns that eager desire which our Lord speaks of under the name of hunger and thirst.

And it is to be noted, that in other pursuits it is the gaining of the end and not the straining after it which is blessed, not the hunger and thirst, but the satisfaction of the appetite. But in spiritual matters the blessing lies where our Lord's words place it. For our Lord considers the heart, and blesses the wish and desire even if they go no further, and are prevented by external hindrances from issuing in action. And again, if they were not blessed in themselves, they would still be blessed in that they cannot, by the mercy of God, be bootless and fail of success. In other matters it is possible to yearn with all the energy of which nature is capable, to labour and toil night and day, and, after all, to miss the object of all this desire and exertion. Human objects of ambition and desire can only be won, perhaps, by a few out of many that seek them, as St. Paul remarks when speaking of the pains which the athletes of the Greek games took in order to secure the prize, and it does not depend upon any exertions, however great, to obtain what is sought. But in the Kingdom of Heaven there is no such thing as labour in vain, nor again, anything that corresponds to the emptiness and

worthlessness of the prizes of earthly toil and ambition
when they have been won, their utter incapacity to
satisfy, and the disappointment which follows as the true
issue of all those labours. For spiritual goods are more
desired the more they are enjoyed, the soul can never be
cloyed with their possession, their sweetness and richness
are infinite, they enlighten the eyes and expand and
spiritualize and inflame the heart, so that those who gain
them are raised by them to a higher intelligence and a
more entrancing and penetrating desire, always seeing
more to love and learning to love more. For 'he that
eateth them shall yet be hungry, and he that drinketh
them shall yet thirst.' This hunger and this thirst are
in themselves satiety, and yet to be satisfied in their
cravings is to hunger and thirst still more.

If we now turn to the consideration of the special
object of the hunger and thirst of which our Lord
speaks, we find ourselves in the presence of an immense
range of virtuous actions, reaching over our whole life,
interior and exterior, and regarding all our relations and
duties, whether to God, our neighbours, or ourselves.
The word justice is used in a two-fold sense in the New
Testament, as representing either the particular virtue
which consists in giving to every one his due, as it is
classed with temperance, prudence and fortitude, or
again, as representing the whole range of virtues, inasmuch as all may be said to fall into the category of
justice. It would seem that our Lord uses the word
here in the latter sense, and we may combine the two as
far as they need combining by following some of the
holy writers who consider all virtues under this aspect.
Thus St. Bernardine tells us that the eager justice which
is here commended by our Lord renders three things to
God, three things to ourselves, and three things to our
neighbour. To God, honour as our Creator, love as our

Redeemer, fear and reverence as our Judge. To ourselves, purity of heart, custody of our tongue, discipline of our body. To our neighbour, obedience if he is our superior, concord if he is our equal, and beneficence if he is our inferior.

The honour which we are to give to God as our Creator consists in a due knowledge of Him, which is to lead to three practices, adoration or subjection to Him and humiliation before Him in all things, interior and exterior; prayer, by which we betake ourselves to Him in order to obtain His mercy; and veneration, by which we honour Him and all that is His with pure and fitting homage both of soul and body. Our Redeemer must be duly loved also in three ways, with sweetness, with prudence, and with fortitude, preferring Him and His service to all the delights of earth, giving up our own sense and opinion for Him, and letting no will or wish of our own interfere with our service of Him. Our Judge is to be feared in three ways, likewise, by keeping His remembrance always before us, on account of His infallible discernment, on account of His inflexible justice, and on account of His irresistible power from which there can be no escape.

The same holy writer goes on in like manner to the other heads of justice. To ourselves, as he says, we are to be eager to render the three things already mentioned, purity of heart, custody of the tongue, discipline of the body. The heart must be cleansed from three things, according to that saying of the Psalmist: 'Who can understand sins? From my secret ones cleanse me, O Lord, and from those of others spare Thy servant.'[1] He says that the sins which cannot be understood may be considered as chiefly those of omission, and the faults of slothfulness or vanity, which may infect

[1] Psalm xviii. 13.

works which seem to be in substance good.   There may be want of due diligence, or there may be a want of perfect and simple intention.   Our hidden sins are those which we have forgotten, or which have escaped our notice when they were committed.   The faults of others are those which are committed by us either by the suggestion of the devil or out of human respect; or again, they may be considered as the faults of omission or commission which we have occasioned in others by bad example, or neglect of warning, or in any other way.   Purity from all these, then, is the cleansing which is due to ourselves as regards our heart.   The custody of the tongue of which he goes on to speak is also three-fold, and he founds his explanation, as in the former case, on a verse in the Psalms: 'I said, I will take heed to my ways, that I sin not with my tongue.   I have set a guard to my mouth, when the sinner stood against me.'[2]   In these words, as he remarks, there is in truth a three-fold custody spoken of, of life, of tongue, and of patience.   That is, a man's thoughts, affections, words, and actions are all to be guarded, the intentions and aims and desires of the heart as well as the actions, for out of the abundance of the heart the mouth speaketh, and unless our thoughts and affections and actions are right, we shall offend with our tongue.   The whole must be kept in order, and any disorder which is permitted will manifest itself in word.   This is the guard of life.   But, he adds, there is another special custody, after all, to be set upon the tongue, because a man cannot restrain it from evil by himself, without the assistance of God, and thus it is said in another Psalm, which is repeated by the priest while he incenses the altar at Mass, 'Set a watch, O Lord, before my mouth, and a door around my lips, incline not my heart to evil words.'[3]

[2] Psalm xxxviii. 2.   [3] Psalm cxl. 3, 4.

The guard over the lips is reason illuminated by faith, because the tongue is the instrument of reason. The door around the lips, he quaintly says, is the guard that can be opened or shut, because there is a time for speech and a time for silence; and this 'door' in the Latin version is called *ostium circumstantiæ*,[4] and so the circumstances must be considered, who it is that speaks, and wherefore, and what, and to whom, and when, and how much. And the difficulty as to all these things is very great, so that the Son of Sirach exclaims, 'Who will set a guard against my mouth and a sure seal upon my lips, that I fall not by them, and that my tongue destroy me not!'[5] This, then, is the special custody of the tongue which is needed. And then in the third place, the Psalmist repeats, that he has set a guard to his mouth when the sinner stood against him, because the prosperity of the sinner, or his insolence, or the many provocations which he gives, the manner in which he challenges our indignation or anger, or attacks the truth or the Church which we are bound to defend, or detracts from the character of his neighbour, or uses words disrespectful to God or against good manners, and the like, make up a series of occasions on which a servant of God, who does not very patiently guard himself, may slip, so as to lose his peace or speak inadvertently and unprofitably. This is the custody of patience.

And, lastly, we owe to ourselves the discipline of our bodies. For, in the first place, there is a perpetual antagonism between the spirit and the flesh, as St. Paul tells us, and the works of the flesh, which he enumerates in the Epistle to the Galatians,[6] must be mortified by those who would obtain the Kingdom of God. And this discipline, in the second place, must go beyond the

---

[4] So also the Septuagint, θύραν περιοχῆς.

[5] Ecclus. xxii. 33.   [6] Galat. v. 17.

mere restraining of the flesh from open and grievous sins, such as those which are spoken of by St. Paul in the passage referred to, because the weakness of the flesh not only weighs down the whole man to evil, but shackles the readiness of the spirit unto good, and it must be braced up and strengthened by holy severity and the denial of all delicacy and softness, in order to make the body at least no longer an impediment to the service of God. And then beyond this there is a still stricter discipline, which amounts to positive mortification, in order that the lower part of our nature may be made subject and become a fit instrument, which may even help the soul in its spiritual enterprises and in the undertaking of great labours and dangers for the cause of God; for, as the Saint whom we are following says, as the potter cannot make beautiful vessels of earth unless it be first very well beaten and prepared, so also God will not make our bodies vessels of glory unless they be first diligently disciplined and reduced to subjection.

The virtues towards our neighbour which justice obliges us to, according to St. Bernardine, are also three. We must render obedience to our superiors, peace and concord to our equals, and beneficence to those beneath us. For love lifts us up, it makes us cling to those around us, and makes us also incline to pour down benefits on any who are below us in any way. As to obedience, he tells us that this it is which turns the practice of ordinary virtue into something more excellent and heavenly; for obedience is better than victims. He quotes St. Augustine, who says, in reference to the precept imposed on Adam in Paradise, that God could not more perfectly have shown how great a good lies in obedience than by forbidding a thing which was not in itself bad, because in that case it was obedience alone that could win the crown, and disobedience alone that incurred the penalty. As to the blessing of concord and harmony, he dwells at length on the beautiful description, given in the Acts, of the first disciples, who had 'one heart and one soul,' such charity being the special commandment of our Lord, and the badge by which He desired that His disciples should be distinguished. He says that in Heaven God dwells in His saints by the glory of charity; and on earth He dwells in those who are as one 'by the grace of charity.' For St. Paul tells us that we are to bear one another's burthens, 'and so fulfil the law of Christ,'[7] the law, that is, of charity, which is mentioned by St. John. And so it is in Heaven, as he explains in illustrating the words of Job, 'He maketh peace in His high places,'[8] that is, He has arranged and bound together His higher creatures, the hierarchies of the blessed spirits and the celestial bodies, by a bond of concord at once most enduring and most tranquil. For there is no conflict among them, no mutual opposition to separate them or corrupt them, that so we might be taught spiritually that he that abideth not in this life in the concord of charity shall not hereafter ascend to the concord of the citizens of Heaven. And, lastly, the justice of which we speak makes us practise all beneficence to those below us, as is imaged in the physical world, in which the higher creatures rain down a blessed influence upon those which are lower, or again, in the little world of man, in which the heart supplies life and motion to all the limbs. And this true paternal charity on the part of superiors to those below them, loves all most sincerely in God, gains to God all whom it can gain, makes no account of temporal interests for the sake of the brethren, is becoming and exemplary

[7] Galat. vi. 2.   [8] Job xxv. 2.

in its conversation, humble in condescension, gentle to foes, kind to friends, and always discreet, sociable to all, solicitous for all, and bearing the burthens of all, even the least; and, what is better and greater than what has already been said, it never fails or grows weary, but perseveres faithfully to the end in its practice of beneficence.

This, then, is one way in which we may form to ourselves some general notion of the justice after which our Lord bids us hunger and thirst. There are other ways by which the same general view may be gained, especially that which has been followed by many who love to cling to the footsteps of our Lord as they remain to us in the Gospel history, who have made a catalogue of the virtues which He practised for our example, and especially in those states and duties which are the same as their own. It is enough here to indicate these general methods. It must next be remembered that as to all these virtues thus set before us as making up the picture of perfect justice, there must be different degrees and even kinds of hunger and thirst, according to the state of the soul in which the blessed desire has to be enkindled.

There is, in the first place, the state of the soul which feels itself at a distance from God and under the ban of His justice, as the poor Prodigal, whom our Lord has painted in the parable, felt himself an exile from and an offender against his father. Our Lord says there came a great famine in that land, and that the Prodigal began to be hungry, longing for the food even of the hired servants in his father's house. Thus, when God touches the heart in order to arouse patience, when the light of faith, which has long been dimmed, streams in in all its power, and the remorse of conscience which has been lulled to sleep wakes up to agitate and terrify the unhappy soul, there comes also by His mercy, like a ray of light from Heaven, the longing for peace and reconciliation which already contains the germ of hope and returning charity. There is a journey before such a soul; the land of misery must be left, the ties of sin must be broken off, the desert must be crossed, there is humiliation, confession, penance to be undergone; but all these things seem as nothing, because of the hunger and thirst with which the soul is consumed, and which can have no satisfaction until peace has been won. In this way, even of those who are afar off, the words are true, 'Blessed are they who hunger and thirst after justice, for they shall have their fill.' The father of the Prodigal, who sees him afar off, and runs to meet him, and falls on his neck and kisses him, and restores him at once to his former state as his son, is but a faint image of the ineffable tenderness of God towards sinners, and of the richness of the mercy with which He welcomes them.

But again, when the Prodigal has been welcomed home with so much tenderness by his father, and clothed and adorned anew with the robes of grace and restored to his former place as a beloved child, there arises in his soul another great thirst which it was not to our Lord's purpose to describe in the Parable of the Prodigal, but which He has hinted at elsewhere, as when He says that the Kingdom of Heaven is like a treasure hid in a field or a pearl of great price, for which a man who desires them sells all that he has. This hunger and thirst we may well imagine in the case of the Prodigal himself after he had been restored, as if henceforth he desired to spend himself entirely in the service of his father, and as if nothing was too great or too hard for him to undertake or to bear for his sake. This is the thirst after ever greater perfection, the restless and yet calm desire to be more and more cleansed from sin, more and more full of good works, more and more devoted to the service of God, more and more united to Him in all the degrees of union that are open to men upon earth. St. Paul describes himself as forgetting the things that are behind, and stretching forth himself to those that are before,[9] and it implies the not being content with any kind of service to God, but only with the best possible, an unwillingness to rest in a lower vocation when a higher vocation is open, to go so far and no further in works of mercy, zeal, mortification, charity, and the like, the seeking, as the Apostle says elsewhere, to know and to fulfil the good, the acceptable, and the perfect will of God—not to know it only, or to desire it only, but to desire it and long for it with a yearning which will never rest until it is satisfied. And of this desire, again, it is true that it is blessed, because it shall have its fill.

And even when this hunger and thirst may have been in some measure satisfied, and the soul is in the state of which St. Paul spoke when he said that he knew nothing against himself, or again, that he had fought a good fight, and finished his course, and kept the faith,[10] there will still remain in such servants of God two great sources of hunger and thirst which have yet to be satisfied. The first of these two is the desire to see the justice of which we have been speaking spread and increase and flourish in the world at large and in the souls of the faithful. This desire yearns for the conversion of all sinners, the reclaiming of all heretics, the destruction of all schisms, the peaceful advance of Christian principles in society until the kingdoms of the world become the kingdoms of the Lord and of His Christ, the triumph of the Church over all her enemies,

[9] Philipp. iii. 13.   [10] 2 Timothy iv. 7.

and her splendid adornment with the choicest gifts of ·
grace and the glory of the sanctity of her children. This,
in brief, is one great desire which burns in the hearts
of those who are already, more or less, perfect; it is
an echo of those words of our Lord Himself, 'I am
come to cast fire upon the earth, and what would I
but that it be kindled?'[11]   And the other great desire,
which can have no full satisfaction in this life, is that
which longs after the perfect robe and crown of justice
which is the lot of the saints in Heaven. For until
then they are not made perfect, or at least, however
high their faithfulness may have raised them, they have
not yet, except in special cases, the certainty of their
perseverance or of their crown, they do not possess the
vision of God to Whom all justice looks as to its end,
and Who is to be for ever the object of their love and
desire, which will then be no longer able to swerve or
faint or fail.

[11] St. Luke xii. 49.

NOTE III.

*Some arrangements of the Christian Virtues for the purpose
of meditation.*

As it is one of the objects aimed at in the present work
to assist meditation by furnishing the matter on which it
may be fed, without drawing out formally the 'points' into
which that matter is usually divided, or suggesting the
affections and resolutions which may be drawn from them,
it may be useful to add here one or two of the classifications
of the virtues at which a Christian may aim, as they are
given in the works of a great master of the spiritual life,
the celebrated Alvarez de Paz. This holy writer gives two
different lists, so to speak, in different parts of his great
work. In the second volume, where the subject of the
virtues naturally comes in, he adopts the ordinary arrangement as it is found in St. Thomas and others, taking the
three theological and the four moral virtues as the heads
under which all others are grouped. In the case of each
virtue he explains what it is, then what are the incitements
to move us to seek it, thirdly, what are its actions, and
lastly, how it is to be asked for. 'The definition of the
virtue will be useful that men may know it, the motives
will help in meditation upon it, the actions in which it is
exercised will avail to its practice, and the manner of asking
will help in prayer for it.' He then warns his readers that
for certain reasons, which he assigns, he does not exactly
follow the usual theological arrangement as to the subor-
dinate virtues. It will be enough for us to set forth the
arrangement as he has given it.

First of all, of course, comes the virtue of Faith, which
has under it, as it were, four others to which it leads,
Meditation, Contemplation, Contempt of the world, and
Purity of heart. The next theological virtue is Hope, which
has for its subordinates Confidence and holy Fear. Then
comes Charity to God and to our neighbour, under which
he ranges Zeal, Joy (in God's presence with us and in
His infinite perfections), Peacefulness, Mercy, Beneficence.

The first moral virtue is Prudence, on which follow Discretion, Docility, Solicitude, and Circumspection. Then follows Justice, on which depend Religion, Penitence, Piety, Observance, Obedience, Gratitude, Truthfulness, Simplicity, Friendliness, Liberality. The third is Fortitude, which leads to Magnanimity, Security, Magnificence, Patience, Longanimity, Perseverance, and Constancy. Lastly, the number of the moral virtues is filled up by Temperance, under which are ranged Abstinence, Sobriety, Chastity, Virginity, Decency, Self-affliction, Meekness, Clemency, Humility, Poverty, Self-restraint as to curiosity, Taciturnity, and Modesty. This catalogue must suffice in this place, and the hints given above as to his method as to the motives and various actions in which the virtues may be exercised may suffice for such persons as are able to draw out points for themselves. Others must be referred to the work itself, or rather, it may be hoped that portions of this and other great ascetical works of the sixteenth and seventeenth centuries, which are either inaccessible from their rarity, or formidable on account of their great length, may be translated or abridged in the series of ascetical works which has been commenced under the same management as that to which the present volume belongs.[1]

In his third volume, in which he treats of Prayer, Alvarez de Paz gives another and a very beautiful classification of the virtues. He bids his reader divide them into five heads, that he may consider them in the Five principal Wounds of our Blessed Lord, and beg them of Him, by the love with which He endured those Wounds. The Five Wounds he arranges in an unusual way, one for our Lord's feet, one for His head, one for His Heart, and the two others for the right and left hand. Through the Wound of His feet we are to ask Humility, and as humility produces Obedience, Patience, and Silence, we are to ask those virtues also through that Wound. Through the Wound of His head we are to ask for Wisdom and the virtues which accompany it, namely, the Fear of God, Discretion, and Simplicity. Through the Wound of His Heart we are to pray for Charity and her adjuncts, Perseverance, Faith, and

---

[1] The passages referred to above are to be found in Alvarez de Paz, t. ii. *De Exterminatione Mali*, lib. ii. p. 2, c. 2—9.

Hope. Through the Wound of His right hand we are to ask for Justice, and Mercy, Truthfulness, and Gratitude as following therefrom. And through the Wound of His left hand we may beg for Fortitude, and three other virtues which are akin to that, Chastity, Sobriety, and Poverty. He explains that he has taken this arrangement from a Flemish author, Eschius, and he draws out briefly the manner in which the connection which he has assigned to the several virtues may be accounted for. The truly humble man thinks himself the least of all, and so he obeys readily ; he thinks himself worthy of punishment and infamy, and so he is very patient, and he thinks himself by no means wise, and so he easily holds his tongue. Thus obedience, patience, and silence spring from humility. The truly wise man, on the other hand, is very much afraid of the greatest of all follies, that is, the offence of God, he knows how to keep the mean and measure in all things, and he desires to avoid multiplicity of desires, and to cleave to the one true and highest good. Thus fear, discretion, and simplicity come from wisdom. In the same way the man who truly loves God desires never to be separated from Him, believes Him at once, knowing that He cannot deceive, and hopes in Him, knowing that He cannot forsake. And thus perseverance, faith, and hope come after charity. Again, the truly just man will never refuse to relieve misery, he will express things as they are, or as he believes them to be, and he will be careful to repay benefits, and thus mercy, truthfulness, and gratitude proceed from justice. Lastly, a man who has true fortitude will never let himself be cast down by impure pleasures, or overcome by too much indulgence in good, or trampled under foot by the possession of fleeting goods, and thus chastity, sobriety, and poverty come from fortitude. The very beautiful meditation which the author draws out upon the outlines which have here been sketched, is far too long to be even analyzed in these pages.[2]

---

[2] See Alvarez de Paz, t. iii. *De Inquisitione Pacis*, l. iv. p. 2, Ex. 5.

CHAPTER XVII.

The Hungry and Thirsty filled.

St. Matt. v. 6; *Vita Vitæ Nostræ*, § 31.

OUR LORD promises to those who hunger and thirst after justice that they shall have their fill, and we may be sure that the promise of Him Who is Truth itself cannot fail. But we have already seen that it is characteristic of these Beatitudes that the virtues which are commanded in them are in themselves blessings, and would deserve to be sought as such even if there were no further reward attached to them by God. Before, therefore, going on to consider the full satisfaction which our Lord promises, it may be well to pause a while on the thoughts which are suggested by the blessedness which the virtue here enjoined possesses in itself.

In the first place, it is a most blessed thing to have the hunger and thirst of the soul fixed upon justice. The condition of man in this life is one of craving and desire. The world is full of restless unremitting activity. If an ant-hill is disturbed, we see the hundreds of ants which belong to it running to and fro in what seems to us to be wild confusion, and as far as it appears they do nothing else but run about. Do not the blessed citizens of Heaven look down thus upon the world of men below them, and might they not wonder at what is the end and what the gain of all the actions which they behold? The external activity of mankind, whether it be in pursuit of wealth, honour, or in pursuit of pleasure—for the silly butterflies of the world are as busy in their way as the working bees—is yet nothing in comparison to the seething confusion within, the perpetual straining of desires, hopes, ambitions, the constant working of the passions of every kind towards their objects, indifferent or bad, shameful or gainful, so that it would seem that the mind and heart can never live without some food in the way of complacency or desire, aversion or displeasure. Our merciful Father, Who knows the restlessness of our nature, because it is always striving after its end under some form or other, true or false, fantastic or rational, has met our needs by giving us what to love and what to aim at, and so He has made it possible for our desires to work themselves in perpetual activity and at the same time ennoble themselves, elevate us, place us nearer and nearer to Him, and heap up for us infinite treasures and ineffable joys, which are indeed true treasures and true joys, in the life to come. Even in the natural order it is constantly seen how a noble ambition, or some sudden call of duty or patriotism which requires devotion and self-sacrifice, or even the having a new purpose given to a life by means of some deep personal attachment, makes men out of boys, and serious workers out of triflers and fops, and in this way developes and improves whatever is good and capable of being made better in the character of those who are thus possessed. And it is of the nature of such ambitions or desires as are thus generated to become engrossing and absorbing, and to extinguish, by excluding, all other concupiscences. What must it be, then, when this hunger and thirst after all the mighty and fertile range of virtues rise up in the soul? The lower passions are at once lulled to sleep, the appetites are tamed, reason regains her sway, the voice of conscience is louder and clearer, the mind becomes illuminated by faith, the will becomes robust and decided, the whole man becomes larger and stronger and nobler, his thoughts and principles and aims are insensibly changed till they become the thoughts and principles and aims of the children of God. This is a wonderful benefit, to be understood best by comparing the misery of a soul which is left to grovel in the filth of lower desires with the pure and lofty activity of the saints whose conversation is in Heaven.

In the same way, the pursuit of justice clears away the impostures of self-love and self-confidence, and puts the mind at once on the true foundation of humility. It learns its own strength, or rather its own weakness and nothingness, and its entire dependence upon God both to will and to do, to conceive, design, and execute anything in the spiritual order. Again, to hunger and thirst after justice is incompatible with the miserable state of tepidity, for to yearn after a thing and to be indifferent to it cannot be together. Those whose hearts are indeed on fire will not live on without any correspondence to grace or any attention to inspirations, they will not be tempted to make light of little matters, their use of the means of grace will be intelligent, eager, and profitable. They will not confess without amendment, or communicate without interior union with God, or hear His word without profit, nor will they find time to be keen-eyed to the faults of others, or to bemoan their state and vocation, as if their coldness could be charged to anything but themselves. In truth, the direct tendency on the soul of this hunger and thirst is to make it perfect and happy. It raises the mind to true wisdom, and enables it to interpret the world and its own condition and prospects and duties with the serene eye of a spiritual philosopher. Thus it secures peace at the same time that it inspires the noblest and most difficult undertakings, makes self-conquest easy, and by the generosity which it kindles, wins the most abundant streams of grace from the invincible generosity of God.

These are blessings which come to the soul along with the hunger and thirst after justice of which our Lord speaks. But, as is easily seen, they are blessings which are independent of the actual satisfaction of the longing which that hunger and thirst create. In this sense it would be well to crave for and seek for justice, even if it were not to be found; as it may have been a blessing to many a poor heathen to have wearied himself in desires after greater truth and light than were within his reach. But in the Kingdom of God there are no such unsatisfied desires. It is the will of God that they that seek should find, and therefore those who seek justice shall find justice. Its works are the works for which we are intended, and it is not likely that God would deny us them when we desire them. 'We are His workmanship,' St. Paul says, 'created in Jesus Christ in good works, which God hath prepared that we should walk in them.'[1] Man is made for justice, and justice is made for man. God has put us in the world and arranged the circumstances and conditions of our life, both as to what He Himself ordains, and what, according to the general laws of His government, He permits, with a distinct end in view, that of our practice of virtue and good works. The Beatitude before us thus fits on most naturally and most consolingly to that which precedes it. For in the Beatitude of the Mourners, the world and human life are presented to the mind in that aspect of sorrowfulness, misery, pain, exile, and affliction of every sort which belongs to them in consequence of the fallen state of man. But now we are to look on the same human life as beset indeed with causes for mourning,

[1] Ephes. ii. 10.

and yet at the same time most blessed in its multitudinous occasions of virtue and justice. Justice indeed is
the key of the riddle of life. At no hour and under no
circumstances are we not surrounded by opportunities of
virtue, nor is there anything which comes across our
path, good or bad, spiritual or material, which cannot be
as it were turned to gold for the enrichment of our souls
in the true treasures of Heaven. Man's life is short and
feeble, and he can do but little in any other way. The
loftiest intellectual flights are not in themselves very
much; the discoveries of science, the guesses of philosophy, the feats of statesmanship, the grand achievements of art, the material conquests of the physical
forces of nature which can be compassed for the service
of man, these are great indeed in their degree, but they
are but little, after all, above the common actions and
works of men. The loftiest mountains of the earth are
but the most insignificant elevations of its surface when
compared to its circumference; and in the same way
the noblest things which genius and industry have
brought about are altogether insignificant in relation to
the nature and end of man, except as far as they partake
of the character of moral or spiritual elevation. Man is
one of the weakest of God's creatures, except that he
can use grace and choose good and merit the eternity of
Heaven. And this he can do in every moment of his
life, this all men alike can do, young and old, rich and
poor, learned and ignorant, this is the one dignity of
humanity, a dignity more precious than diamond-mines
or streams flowing with gold, more fertile and fruitful
of blessings than the cornfields or the vineyards of the
whole earth.

It is not difficult to understand that the words of our
Blessed Lady, who sang *Esurientes implevit bonis*—'He
hath filled the hungry with good things'—have been

fulfilled in abundance in the Kingdom of which her Son is the Founder. In it, as history and the lives of the saints tell us, the sinner has indeed received pardon, and what is more, the assurance of his forgiveness, the just man has received continual increase in peace and virtue, the perfect have gained that union with God which is their great desire, and those who have burnt with zeal for God's glory have been enabled to see it advanced, even by their own exertion and instrumentality, to an extent which can be accounted for only on the supposition of the working of the power of God. The great gifts which are the common possession of the children of God in the Catholic Church have, moreover, a direct influence in the way of the satisfaction of desire. For the gift of faith is an imparting to the soul of a firm though not an adequate possession of the truth, the gift of hope is in the same way a direct satisfaction of the yearnings of what is called the irascible part of the soul, while the gift of charity, in proportion as it is cultivated and developed, satisfies the soul with a love which is something far above the selfishness of passion and the disturbed restlessness of ordinary concupiscence, a love which gives peace. The moral virtues which are imparted to the soul are also, in a direct manner, the satisfaction of the needs from which the hunger and thirst after justice spring, and the same may be said, in a still higher degree, of the gifts of the Holy Ghost. The true demonstration of the fulfilment of our Lord's words in His promise to the hungry and thirsty after justice, would lie in nothing less than an examination of the interior perfection and manifold beauty of the souls of the saints, and of the solid and fruitful virtues in which their perfection has been exercised. It would be necessary for this to be able to show how, not one or two in a generation, but many thousands and hundreds of thousands at any time in the Church, have been enabled by Divine grace to keep their hearts and minds pure, to rise altogether above the love of temporal things, to reduce the appetites of nature to peace and tranquillity, to keep their tongue from hasty, indeliberate, or unbecoming speech, to occupy their minds continually with holy and pious and lofty thoughts, to be on fire with desires for good and the glory of God, to practise the whole range of moral virtues for which their vocation gives them occasion, and to do all their works in the perfection of charity. We should have to trace out their practice of the passive as well as the active virtues, their heroic patience under adversity and disappointment, the wonderful intensity of their interior acts, the perfect union of their wills with that of God, that transformation, in fine, into God of which St. Paul speaks when he says, 'I live, but not I, it is Christ that liveth in me.'[2] These and other considerations of the same sort would show us how truly the hunger and thirst of the servants of God have been fulfilled even in this life.

Or again, it would be easy to take the characteristics of Christian society and the effect which our Lord's religion has produced upon the world as an exemplification of the fulfilment of this promise. This is too wide a subject, however, to be entered on here. It is not only that the grace of God has enabled those who hunger and thirst most eagerly after justice to attain to a level of virtue which was all but unknown before, save in the case of the most favoured and exceptional saints. It is not only that what may almost be called new virtues, virtues of which the heathen had no idea, and the Jews but an inadequate notion, such as humility, or again charity, have been introduced and brought within the reach of all. More than this, the standard of the whole range of moral and domestic duties has been raised, and these duties have been discharged by multitudes with a correspondence to that new standard which has not only affected and changed the whole face of society, but has elevated whole classes which before were either enslaved or despised, while, on the other hand, vices and abominations which, among the heathen at least, were not considered disgraceful, have either been extirpated altogether, or at least made the object of public execration and even legal penalties. The amount to which purity, piety, devotion, zeal for good works, and the advancement of the faith, have come to be surrounded by general respect and to rule the verdict of public opinion, is a sign how far these virtues have been carried by particular persons in large and influential numbers. No doubt, much has always remained undone, and the influence of the Christian virtues on domestic, social, and political life, might have been greater than it has been. Modern times, moreover, have been distinguished by a reaction of the pagan principles in many conspicuous instances, nor is the tendency of the immediate future likely to be less in favour of those principles than that of the immediate past. Still, on the whole, Christian society as such has borne a witness to the satisfaction of the hunger and thirst after justice, all the more wonderful because it is evident from recent experience, as well as from the study of pagan antiquity, that the standard which has been generally acknowledged is one against which the natural passions and the blind, because proud, intellect of man are necessarily in continual revolt.

It must, of course, be added that the full satisfaction of those who thus yearn after justice can only be attained in the Kingdom of Heaven which is to come. The abundant reward which may be gained even here in the way of the increase of justice by a life of faith and prayer, the daily conquest of ourselves and careful practice of virtue, aided by faithfulness to Divine grace and by the stores of spiritual power which are contained in the sacraments, is not all that is to be given to the hungry and thirsty by the bountiful mercy of God, carrying out His promise as expressed in this Beatitude. It may be said that even in Heaven there will be hunger and thirst, as even upon earth there is the fulness by which they are relieved. For thus is sometimes understood the saying of Holy Scripture: 'They that eat Me shall yet hunger, and they that drink Me shall yet thirst.'[3] But in Heaven the desire is not the craving for a thing which is absent, but the delighted enjoyment of a thing which is present. 'For,' says St. Bernardine, 'the desire of Divine glory in the blessed is not after a thing absent or at a distance, but rather after a thing which is intimately their own and which belongs to them with full power of enjoyment for the whole eternity which is to come. Nor does it come like earthly hunger and thirst, from any interior consumption or fire, but rather from a disposition of most excellent vigour which is always the same, and thus it hath in it nothing of pain, but always a most sweet and delightful satisfaction, which satisfaction never begets any cloying or lack of taste, and thus the desire of him that loves after this manner is always kindled to one uniform glow. And hence it may become clear to us, that the more glorious any one of the blessed is in his blessedness, the more he is satiated and as it were inebriated with delights, so much the more does he desire to be delighted in God and by God.'[4] And the same holy preacher goes on to explain how the intellect of man, which had been enlightened and in a manner satisfied here below by

---

[3] Ecclus. xxiv. 29.
[4] *Advent. de Christiana Vita,* Serm. viii. art. 3, § 1.

faith, is in Heaven satiated by the vision of God ; how the memory, which here had been fed and in a measure satisfied by hope, is there satiated by the certainty of a Divine security of the possession of God throughout all eternity ; and how the charity which in this life has been the satisfaction of the will, is there made perfect and consummated in itself, and also in its power of making man perfectly happy, because there the love of God will be brought to its perfection for ever.

CHAPTER XVIII.

The Beatitude of the Merciful.

St. Matt. v. 7 ; *Vita Vitæ Nostræ*, § 31.

WHEN we remember what has been said of the power which belongs to such words as those of our Lord when uttering the Beatitudes, it may seem as if the blessing which follows next on that of hunger and thirst after justice, must have given Him a special joy when the time came for Him to pronounce it. It has been said that the words of our Lord are in a certain true sense creative and prophetic, as well as the words of a Legislator and King. That is, they create what they pronounce to be blessed, and they are predictions of what was to be after our Lord's departure in His Church. The beautiful morality and philosophy of the Beatitudes, as they seem even to worldlings, would have been no more than the speculations of Plato or Aristotle in their practical effect on the world, if they had not been laws as well as maxims, uttered by one Whose words are always with power, Whose example was to teach men how to act up to His precepts, and Whose Life was to be a means of grace as well as a pattern. As to this point there was a difference between our Lord's legislation and all others that had preceded it even in the Kingdom of God itself; because the Old Law was not only severe and prohibitory, instead of gentle and full of promise, it was also inefficacious, because it did not convey to those to whom it was addressed any new power to keep its commandments. In this respect our Lord's words differ from those which were spoken by Moses. They are the words of God Himself, living, life-giving, full of grace.

Our Lord's own Mission on earth was essentially one of mercy. He will come again in judgment, but His Incarnation was the highest work of the mercy of God. He became Man out of pure mercy. He became Man in order that the Manhood which He took upon Himself might, at the cost of His life, be the instrument of God's special mercy in the redemption of the world. The great work which He accomplished, besides making atonement for all mankind, was the foundation of the Church, in order that it might remain on earth after Him, and be the organ and instrument and channel to the world of that great mercy to successive generations. The Church herself is a vast organization of mercy; and she has regenerated the older human society upon which she is engrafted by means of those principles of mercy and charity of which every one of her lineaments is the expression. These considerations show us how dear the practice of mercy must have been to the Sacred Heart of our Lord, which existed and exists for and through mercy. When, therefore, our Lord reached this point in the chain of the Beatitudes, He had come near to the accomplishment of His own dearest wishes. He came as the Creator of the new world and the new society, the characteristic badge of which was to be

Q 2

mercifulness. He was now to add to the unchangeable and fruitful laws which were the foundation of His Kingdom, poverty of spirit, meekness, mourning, hunger and thirst after justice, this new and crowning commandment in which the end and object of the whole dispensation was summed up. The glory of God, the happiness of man, the formation of a new generation of God's children, who were to share His own Sonship, and to have on their souls the impress of His own character—as dear as all these things were to Him, so dear must have been the moment when He came to promulgate the great principle of Christian mercifulness, and to sanction it by His promise which specially belongs to it, 'Blessed are the merciful, for they shall obtain mercy.' The former Beatitudes were to this as the sowing of the seed, and the natural processes by which it is prepared for fertility and generation: this is as the springing of 'the blade, and the ear, and the full corn in the ear.'

The place which the Beatitude of the merciful occupies in the series to which it belongs is to be explained in this way. Why is it, it might be asked, if mercy is thus the special characteristic and main end of the dispensation of the Incarnation, that mercifulness does not fill the first place among these new principles of the Kingdom of the Incarnation? Mercifulness appears at first sight one of the most natural and most easy of the beautiful chain of virtues which our Lord recommends both by precept and by example. It does not win the hearts of men less powerfully than meekness itself. It appeals to the natural sense of dependence and misery which belongs to our condition, which makes us, even if it be only out of a kind of selfishness, love and honour the merciful. It was the first thing in which the world around the early Church began to imitate her rules and copy her institutions. Even her enemies in all times, who

see superstition in her piety, idleness in her prayer and
contemplation, folly in her love of the Cross and renunciation of earthly delights, and a cruel destruction of the
rights of nature in her purity, have still a word of homage
and admiration for her developments of the principle of
mercifulness. The Filles de la Charité and the Sisters
of Mercy are in honour, even among men who think that
all priests must be torturers of consciences, and that
monks are worse than drones. The seed, too, of a kind
of mercy lies very deep in the soil of human nature, and
may often force its shoot to the surface when all hope of
fruitfulness or good has been abandoned. Thus sinners
are exhorted in Scripture to 'redeem their sins with alms,
and their iniquities with works of mercy to the poor,'[1]
and the same advice is constantly given to Christians
whose lives have been a disgrace to their profession, that
they may win for themselves mercy which may issue in a
true conversion, by means of the prayers of the poor
whom they may benefit, and the compassion with which
God has promised to regard those who are themselves
merciful. Nor is the privilege of mercifulness confined
to the instance of great sinners, who, as it seems, can be
brought to practise no other virtues. For in the New
Testament we find it said to Cornelius, the Gentile
centurion, that his prayers and alms had ascended as a
memorial before God,[2] and had won for him the wonderful grace of being the first of his nation solemnly admitted
into the Christian Church by the Prince of the Apostles.
We cannot doubt that he and others like him, who have
great graces conferred upon them by God in the way of
high vocations and the like, have had other virtues and
perfections besides that of mercifulness, and yet it seems
as if it were to this that is attributed the special power
which opens the gates of God's signal mercies. All these

[1] Daniel iv. 24.   [2] Acts x. 4.

are reasons for wondering at the position of mercifulness, which comes comparatively late in the chain of these Christian excellences, after poverty of spirit, after meekness, after mourning, after the hunger and the thirst after justice.

The answer to this question leads us to a fuller understanding of what that mercifulness is which our Lord here so highly commends. Just as meekness and other beautiful Christian virtues have their natural counterparts, which are fair in themselves and may even be made the foundation upon which the true supernatural virtue is built up by the grace of God, so there is a natural mercifulness and compassionateness which is a kind of instinct in persons of good and soft dispositions, which has a charm of its own to all the world, and which yet cannot bear the weight or strain of the works which are required of the true Christian virtue. It is not this natural virtue, nor is it a single act or a few acts of the Christian virtue of mercifulness which our Lord blesses in the Beatitudes, but something far higher, more solid, more enduring. The mercifulness of which He speaks could not come sooner, we may venture to say, in the chain of Beatitudes than He has placed it. It can only exist in those who are already detached from the love of earthly things, who are already masters of themselves by the possession of meekness, who habitually look on the world around them with that view of faith which makes them true mourners, and who are already inflamed with that hunger and thirst after justice which prompt them to make the most of the thousand occasions and means of which human life is made up, for practising the manifold virtues of which St. Paul says that God has prepared that we should walk in them. Those who have gone thus far are prepared for the further illumination, if we may so speak, which the Holy Ghost, the Perfecter of the elect of God, has in store for them, by means of which, having already learnt so much about God, and His ways, and themselves, and the world around them, they come to see all as it were under a new aspect, in which God is revealed to them as pre-eminently rejoicing in mercy, and in which they see a number of other truths, which may be drawn out presently, which are dependent and consequent upon this primary truth regarding Almighty God. And the same Holy Spirit, Who sheds this light upon those who have already so far followed His blessed guidance as to rise through the degrees of the Beatitudes which have already been spoken of, inflames their hearts also with a new desire which corresponds to the fuller perception of the truth which their minds have received.

And thus they become capable of this new virtue of mercifulness, which rejoices alike God, and Heaven, and earth. For it is a joy to God that His children imitate Him in that special perfection in which He so much delights, and are merciful, as our Lord says, because their Father Who is in Heaven is merciful. And the angels are specially rejoiced by the same virtue, because they are themselves pre-eminently the ministers of God in His works of mercy to the children of men. And earth also is rejoiced by mercifulness, because it is above all others the virtue to which God has, as it were, entrusted the execution of His own compassionate intentions towards the untold and innumerable maladies and miseries of the world. In His own providence, by the hands of the angels or in other ways, He takes care of His lower creatures, and clothes the lilies, and feeds the young ravens when they call upon Him. But human misery, poverty, indigence, ignorance, sickness, helplessness, weakness of every kind, these indeed He has cared for, and cares for with the tenderest love as the Father of all, but He has willed that their relief should be in a great measure and ordinarily entrusted to the ministrations of human mercifulness.

Mercifulness has thus a work of its own entrusted to it, as we may say, by God the Author of human society, and it is a work on which the comparative happiness of a very large number of the members of that society is made to depend. And as we rise into the higher sphere of the supernatural aids which God has provided for His children in the Church, we find the same rule prevailing. For men, not angels, are the ministers of the sacraments and the other ordinary means of grace which are the inheritance of Christians, and these blessings are to be brought home to them and made easy of access to them by charity working through mercy. It may, then, be well said that earth and Heaven are alike interested in this beautiful virtue, that the welfare of thousands of souls, both of those who are to receive mercy and those who by administering it are to win it for themselves, is involved in the enactment of this great law of our Lord's Kingdom, by which Christians are bidden to go even beyond the thirst for justice and the care of their own souls, and pour out the treasures of mercy with a free hand upon all that are around them.

The virtue of mercy lies in compassion for the ills of others, of whatever kind those ills may be, and in giving them relief to the utmost of our power. It thus lies in a certain degree in the sensitive faculty and affections, by which the afflictions of others are felt by us as tenderly as if they afflicted ourselves, while it dwells in a far higher degree in the will, which is roused and guided by the reason to consider in charity the evils of others as our own, grieving for them, and desiring with an efficacious desire to relieve them and substitute the contrary goods in their place, and to proceed, as has been said, to the utmost of its power actually to do this. This account enables us to take in the immense range and extent of the acts of this virtue, which, as has been said by some of the saints, makes men like to God. For His mercifulness is the great truth of faith on which this Beatitude is founded, just as poverty of spirit, meekness, mourning, and hunger and thirst after justice are founded upon the recognition of His supreme dominion as Creator and Preserver and End of all, of His dignity, of the abuse made of His gifts, and of His ineffable holiness. It may be well, therefore, to draw out the truths concerning God which must be grasped by a special gift of faith in order that the virtue of mercifulness may be placed upon its true basis.

There are three principles concerning God which are stated in various places of Holy Scripture, and which may be considered as having especial reference to the subject now before us. The first is contained in the words of the Psalmist: 'His tender mercies are over all His works.'[3] These words do not imply that God is more merciful than He is holy or just or true—for all the perfections of God are infinite—but that all His works are the occasion to God of a special exercise of His mercy, and are in a particular manner the sphere in which that loving attribute manifests itself. The original act of creation, whereby all things were called out of nothingness and endowed by a free gift of God with being, existence, life, and all its properties, in accordance with the capacities of the various natures in which they were created, was an act of pure mercy and, so to speak, compassion, on the part of their Maker. Their continual preservation by God, and His co-operation with them, which enables them to exist and

<hr>

[3] Psalm clxiv. 9.

live and act, may also be included under His works of mercy. Much more is His mercy shown in the elevation of the whole creation to a supernatural state, which is an act distinct from creation and preservation, however immediately it may have been connected with the others in decree and in execution. For neither angels nor men were left by their Creator in their native beauty and excellence, but were raised by Him to a state of grace which was to issue in that intimate possession of God throughout all eternity which is the blessedness of Heaven. And, as the whole visible creation is made for man, that also is destined to a higher state, and is now waiting and 'travailing,' according to the forcible imagery of St. Paul, for its own deliverance from corruption through the adoption of the sons of God. Mercifulness, again, is the rule and law of God's providence in His government and management and designs over all His creatures, and finally, the act of redemption, by which all things are raised and restored, and the consequences of the Fall obliterated, through our Lord's Incarnation and Passion, by greater glories than might otherwise have been their portion, is the crowning and most excellent of God's works of mercy, unfolding itself in an infinite variety of gifts the tale of which can never be told, and the fruits of which will fill Heaven with fragrance and beauty throughout all eternity, which will thus be what it is on account of God's mercifulness. The order of the world, then, the whole creation in which we live, the acts of God in which it depends, and the laws by which it is governed are all in an especial manner the outpourings of His mercifulness.

If the mercy of God thus clothes, like the mantle of Heaven, the whole of His works, it must necessarily follow that, as far as the administration of the universe is committed by Him to the creatures which He has made, the law of mercy must guide and rule their actions also. We see this in the first instance in the care which the holy angels have it in charge to take of men and the material universe, and we may consider also that the unmercifulness and love of destruction which mark all the actions of the evil spirits, in relation to other creatures of God, and notably to man, is a characteristic in those fallen angels which is particularly hateful to God and contrary to His intention in making them, though He may use them as the instruments of His anger and justice. This law of mercifulness is mentioned in Scripture in the great passage in which the Wise Man may be said to have laid the foundations of Christian theology as to the state in which man was first created, at the close of which he says that God 'gave to every one of them commandment concerning his neighbour.'[4] When Cain, in his miserable self-defence, uttered the words, 'Am I my brother's keeper?'[5] he said what implied a neglect of the law of mercy, as well as of the natural law written in every man's heart, which forbids the crime of murder.

This leads us to the second great Scriptural doctrine on this subject. The law of mercy is more than once quoted by our Lord as it is expressed by the Jewish Prophet, 'I will have mercy and not sacrifice;' and He speaks of it in each case as a truth which was not understood by the Jews, who were led into a line of conduct displeasing to God in consequence of their want of light concerning it. He implicitly rebuked the Pharisees who found fault with Him for eating and drinking with publicans and sinners, by bidding them go and learn what that saying about mercy and sacrifice meant, and a little later in the history He said still more strongly, that if they had known what that saying meant

<hr>

4 Ecclus. xvii. 12.   5 Genesis iv. 9.

they would not have condemned the innocent, in the case of the disciples who rubbed the ears of corn in their hands on the Sabbath-day.[6] In each case, as it appears, the persons whom our Lord reproved were sticklers for the letter of the Law and the strictness of observance, whereas God, in the words of the Prophet, had declared His preference for mercy over sacrifice. Yet sacrifice was the highest form of the worship of God positively instituted by God Himself. It was an act of religion, the virtue of which ranks highest in the scale of virtues, because it has immediate reference to God. In the first case, the Jews thought that a teacher who professed to come from Him ought to avoid the contamination of contact with sinners, who were commonly held as such; and in the second case they thought it right in themselves to censure and remonstrate against laxity as to the law of the Sabbath-day. Our Lord told them implicity that God was more honoured by His own condescension in making Himself, out of mercy and compassion, the companion of sinners in order to win them, than He would have been by His abstention from their society, and also that if they had understood God's love for mercifulness they would have considered it more pleasing to Him to form a compassionate judgment of the disciples than to be scandalized at a material breach of a positive law. We thus get an idea of the paramount authority in the Kingdom of God of the law of mercifulness in action and in thought, an idea which, if it be well meditated and developed, will lead to a far higher conception of the duty than is usually entertained. Self-love is ever narrowing the minds and hearts of men, making them forget God's rights and their own position in His world, persuading them that, while their property in a legal sense is their own, in a moral and

<hr>

[6] St. Matt. ix. 13; xii. 7; Osee vi. 6.

religious sense they have no strict obligations as to their poorer neighbours, but only those of charity, which it is well to observe but not sinful to leave aside, and that the works of mercy are beautiful and holy, but not enjoined by a positive law of God. Nothing can scatter this delusion better than the light of truth which our Lord sheds upon the subject of mercy when He puts it, on the authority of God Himself, even above His own worship.

There is yet another revelation concerning God in Holy Scripture with reference to the subject of mercy which it requires a large gift of faith to take in in its full practical importance. This is the revelation of God's method of dealing with us which is summed up in that petition of our Lord's Prayer, which alone is in a manner conditional, when He bids us pray that our trespasses may be forgiven as we forgive them that trespass against us. The law thus taken for granted by our Lord in His prayer, and so forcibly insisted upon by Him in other places, and especially in the Parable of the Unmerciful Servant,[7] is not absolutely new, for we find it in the Old Testament in the same 'Sapiential' book to which reference has already been made on the subject of the law of mercy. 'Forgive thy neighbour if he hath hurt thee, and then shall thy sins be forgiven to thee when thou prayest. Man to man reserveth anger, and doth he seek remedy of God? He hath no mercy on a man like himself, and doth he entreat for his own sins?'[8] Indeed, the truth here declared might have been drawn by meditation out of the consideration of the rights of God, the needs of our own souls, and the power of prayer, much as our Lord represents the worldly and iniquitous steward, in another parable, having the prudence to make himself friends by propitiating the debtors of his

<hr>

[7] St. Matt. xviii. 21, seq.   [8] Ecclus. xxviii. 2—4.

lord. But much more than this is implied by the insertion of this condition by our Lord in the prayer which He has made for the children of God in the Church. That insertion implies that it is the normal and legitimate claim which is to be pleaded before God, that we have shown mercy in our turn. And in this respect the Lord's Prayer throws light upon the description of the Day of Judgment which our Lord gives at the end of His public teaching, in which the works of mercy alone are mentioned as having been the passports to the Kingdom of Heaven in the case of the blessed.

These considerations may serve to show how much the doctrine of mercifulness is founded on the character of God as revealed to us in His government of the world and in the Incarnation, and how much that doctrine requires a firm grasp of faith upon the truths here mentioned. Without such faith, mercy becomes an instinct of humanity, of no more authority than any other natural sentiment. It follows from this, as will be seen more clearly hereafter, how much every attack upon faith diminishes the power of mercy in the world. We may now go on to consider, in the second place, how powerful the grace must be that is to enable men of passions like ourselves to exercise the virtue of mercy in all its fulness. The mercifulness which our Lord speaks of is a virtue which requires at every turn the conquest of ourselves. Self-love is its destruction. We may follow once more the loving guidance of St. Bernardine, who draws out what he calls the twelve fruits or perfections of mercy in one of his sermons. He divides them into three sets, each of which includes four acts. The first 'quaternion' of mercies he calls compassion, condonation or forgiveness, deploration, or the weeping over the ills of others as our own, and exoptation, or the heartfelt desire of good for others. Of compassion, he says that a man who is truly merciful feels all the miseries of others, and carries them in his heart, as if they were his own. He quotes the words of Job— 'I wept for him that was afflicted, and my soul had compassion on the poor,'[9] in which the two acts of compassion are included—the 'weeping with them that weep,'[10] and the interior sympathy of the heart. Compassion is even more than simply to give relief, because compassion gives something of ourselves, instead of what belongs to us, and a person who gives without compassion, in a certain manner refuses what he gives, while a compassionate man, if he does not actually give, at least does so in his heart. As to condonation or forgiveness, he says that the truly merciful man most easily forgives all injuries, past or present, and hardly feels them, or takes account of them, and he quotes the passage of Ecclesiasticus which has lately been mentioned as to the forgiveness of our own sins on condition of our forgiveness of others. Both these acts of the virtue certainly require the mortification of passion and self-love as well as great faith, for there is no true tenderness of heart except where such mortification exists, and the conquest over the feelings of resentment and of the desire of revenge is most difficult. The other two acts which St. Bernardine classes under this head, by which the vices and ills of others are wept for as our own, and by which we desire from our heart all kinds of good to our neighbour, are not more easy. For the first requires a very keen sense of the injury inflicted by sin upon God and upon man, or, in the case of others' evils, a tender sympathetic love for those who suffer them, while the second cannot be without the absolute extinction of all envy, all reluctance to see others on an equality with ourselves, such as was shown by Moses

<hr>

[9] Job xxx. 25.   [10] Romans xii. 15.

when he refused to forbid Eldad and Medad to prophesy in the camp, saying to Josue, 'Why hast thou emulation for me? Oh, that all the people might prophesy, and that the Lord would give them His spirit!'[11] It certainly seems strange that it is almost less easy to wish all kinds of goods to those who are like ourselves than to wish them deliverance from evils, and yet there is scarcely any of the manifestations of the spirit of mercifulness which seems to require greater mortification of self-love than this.

The second 'quaternion' into which St. Bernardine divides the fruits of mercy contains those acts of the virtue which require more large and practical action than those which have been already enumerated. These fruits he calls 'supportation,' or bearing with one another; 'coadjuvation,' or active assistance; 'communication,' which means the imparting to others of everything that we possess or that they have need of; and 'congratulation,' the rejoicing in all the good of others as if it were our own, whether spiritual or temporal. This last fruit may be dismissed at once before the other three, as it obviously belongs to the same ungrudging temper of charity which wishes all good to others, and grieves for all their ills. St. Bernardine refers to the joy of Achior and Nabath, the kinsmen of Tobias, who 'came to him rejoicing, and congratulating with him for all the good things that God had done for him.'[12] He also quotes the traditional saying of St. Francis, that a man who rejoiced in the goods of another as if they were his own, enjoyed them without sin or labour, and with great merit. And here we find the virtue of mercy opening the door, as it were, to those beautiful affections of prayer which consist in rejoicing in the goods which God and His saints and our own brethren possess,

<hr>

[11] Numbers xi. 29.   [12] Tobias xi. 20.

affections the practice of which are found to bring much light and peace to the soul. Returning to the three first members of the 'quaternion,' we find them such as to require in the soul which can practise them fully, a large amount of perfect virtue and disinterestedness. We are to bear with one another in charity,[13] as St. Paul bids us, or as he says in another place, 'to bear one another's burthens, and so fulfil the law of Christ,'[14] which is the commandment of charity. For it may be understood in the last passage as well as the first that we are all burthensome one to another, and that in this life we must all draw upon the charity and compassion of our brethren, and in return, to bear what we have to bear from them with equal charity. And if this field of mercy is so large, much larger still is that which is opened by the other fruit of 'assistance and communication,' the precept of which rests on the doctrine of the same Apostle, that we are all members one of another and of the body and head, Who is Christ. The manner in which he has drawn out the mutual duties of the members of the body of Christ is enough to show us how large are the demands which this duty makes upon us, and how contrary to our self-love.[15] And as to the fruit of 'communication,' St. Bernardine remarks, that our Lord's command is 'to give to every one that asketh,'[16] and He does not say what, in order that the generality of the aid which is enjoined may be understood. Give him, he says, your heart by love, compassion, and congratulation; give him your tongue by instruction, consolation, and prayer; give him your hand by bountiful aid, service, and defence. Give to every one that asketh, what he asks, if you have it, if not, at least compassion and consolation.

[13] Ephes. iv. 2.

[14] Galat. vi. 2.   [15] 1 Cor. xii.   [16] St. Luke vi. 30.

There are, according to St. Bernardine, four other points or acts of the perfect virtue of mercifulness, which it will be enough simply to mention. Mercy gives no offence to any one, as the Apostle says,[17] much more does it refrain from taking an undue advantage of or overreaching any one, as St. Paul says, 'that no man overreach or circumvent his brother in business,' a rule which carries the law of mercifulness into departments of life from which it is generally excluded. The demeanour and carriage of the perfectly merciful man is therefore free from all roughness and overbearingness, so that no man's feelings can be hurt by what he says or does, while in the worldly business upon which it may be his duty or calling to be employed, he is to deal not only with chivalrous honesty, but with all regard for the interests of those across whom he comes as if they were his own. Lastly, St. Bernardine places two states of the heart which imply the perfect absence of all self-love. The first is that absence of all affection for temporal things which belongs to those pilgrims to the heavenly country who 'have not here a lasting city,[18] but seek one which is to come,' that perfect detachment which is theirs who 'having food and wherewith to be covered, are therewith content.'[19] And the other is what he calls a kind of fatherly and motherly love which looks on all around with a tender compassionate pity and affection, and which is an image of the love of the Father of all, of which our Lord speaks when He says that 'He maketh the sun to rise upon the good and bad, and raineth upon the just and the unjust.'[20] For the man in whom perfect blessedness dwells must practise this mercy towards every rational creature, in order that the mercifulness of God may be copied and

<hr>

[17] 2 Cor. vi.

[18] Hebrews xiii. 14.   [19] 1 Timothy vi. 8.   [20] St. Matt. v. 45.

reflected in man. True mercy does not consider the deserts of him who is miserable, but his wants, it acts according to its own laws and instincts, not seeking for merit but for misery in its objects, nor looking to what it may receive, but to what it may give. The rays of the sun do not consider whether the bodies which they illuminate are clean and good, but shine on them indifferently, as far as they are capable of receiving light: and such is the mercy, as St. Chrysostom says, which is the guardian of salvation, the adornment of faith, the propitiation for sin, which proves justice and strengthens sanctity, and shows the true worshipper of God.

To have gone through, however slightly, the qualities which are required in those who are to receive the blessing of the merciful, is enough to make it clear how high a standard of interior perfection and self-control is required in such souls. The same conclusion would follow from any other examination of the same subject-matter, as for instance, from a consideration of the qualifications required, not for the practice of a single act or of repeated acts of the corporal or spiritual works of mercy, but for a life spent in them.

In truth, mercy is a virtue which has its own severe pains and crosses, and which involves immense and long-continued exertions. The more we understand the world to be full of miseries, the more and the heavier are the pangs which those miseries inflict on the heart of the merciful. Sympathy and compassion are in themselves swords which pierce more deeply, in proportion as the soul is more tender and quick to feel the woes of others. A great part of mercy lies in compassion, which is a great gift of God, and which we find in its perfection in the saints, as in St. Paul. It is a great help to promptness and energy in the works of mercy, it enables men to gain great spiritual riches from the miseries of others, and to earn from God much consolation and strength. Thus our Lord Himself chose to have experience of so large a range of human sufferings, though it was His right to be free from them, and He chose for His Blessed Mother the special cross of compassion. To this it must be added that the promptitude, the good-will, the pure intentions, the prudence, the perseverance, the indifference to human respect, and the many kinds of self-sacrifice, that are required for the due performance of the works of mercy, especially such spiritual works as instructing the ignorant, counselling the doubtful, administering fraternal correction, and the like, are all circumstances which point to the same conclusion, that mercy is a difficult virtue, and that it requires all the force of the charity which our Lord has left behind Him to enable men to practise it continually and in perfection. Much more does it require a high super· natural grace diffused largely through society to bring about anything like such a common and systematic practice of this heavenly virtue as may really give a character to a people or to an age.

Mercy, as a practical element in society, hardly existed before the foundation of the Christian Church, unless we except its partial development among the Jews, many parts of whose laws were intended to turn their hearts in the direction of mercy. The needs of the world, the calls which human misery make upon human compassion, were even greater in heathen than in Christian times. Yet whole classes of the community were oppressed, trampled down, ill-treated, while there was but scanty hope for the weak and the unfortunate. As it was Christianity which first turned the streams of mercy upon the arid wastes of society, so it has always been the noblest and highest and most unworldly of the Christian vocations to which some greater and more durable works of mercy have been specially entrusted. In Christian countries mercy has penetrated all classes, raised the condition of the most abandoned, made its way as a ray of light into the dungeon or the madhouse, and softened, if it could not altogether put an end to, the furies of war. But the Church, which learns from her Lord to lay the law of mercy upon all her children, has yet seen the wisdom of organizing special religious institutions for the more heroic works of mercy, and in such matters heroism is to be measured not so much by the danger or the magnitude of the enterprise, as by the detachment from worldly ties and secular cares which is required in those who devote themselves to it. The whole atmosphere which she created was one of mercy, and there was no part of life, no sphere of society to which it did not penetrate. No Christian, young or old, great or little, in the rudest community and lowest rank, but was in his degree far more merciful than he would have been, if he had been born and brought up a heathen of the most cultivated and enlightened stamp. Mercy was taught to children as a duty like the duty of prayer, it was practised by monarchs in their palaces, and by soldiers on the field of battle. And yet it was felt that the higher ranges of the virtue of mercifulness might be beyond the strength of many, that it was a virtue which required the solid foundation of the habits which our Lord has placed before it in the order of the Beatitudes, and was most likely to be secured by the consecration of a religious life. We thus find many of the greater works of mercy, such as the redemption of captives, or the care of persons sick of dangerous diseases, made the special objects of religious orders, while the more ordinary works of mercy were constantly committed to the care of religious confraternities organized for the purpose.

This is not the place to dwell upon the contrast between the modern spirit of philanthropy and the Catholic virtue of mercy. But it may be certainly concluded that this mercifulness which, in our Lord's design, was to play so great a part in the relief of the temporal and spiritual miseries of life, which made so deep an impression upon His Heart, has two great and principal enemies—a false creed and a vicious life. The decay of the spirit of mercy in Europe was contemporaneous with the breach of Catholic unity at the so-called Reformation, and the destruction of the religious institutions in this country was followed by the immense increase of unrelieved pauperism, which has never yet been fairly met and grappled with. There are now current among the educated classes, perhaps not among them alone, theories about the origin of the world and of the human race, which are contradictory to the doctrine of Creation, the Fatherhood of God, and the brotherhood of men, while the philosophers of the time have long ago satisfied themselves that the Incarnation is a dream. The inevitable result of these tenets has been seen in the advocacy of suicide as a laudable act, under certain conditions, and the argument for the violent removal of useless members of society, the aged, the poor, the helpless, all who can be looked on as a burthen to the community, is already contained in the approval of suicide. The doctrines about population, poverty, and other kindred subjects, which are not uncommon, have a distinct tendency to countervail the claims of mercy. At the same time, the rejection of revelation is to a great number of men only the first and logical step to the rejection of the moral law, and thus they are led at once to the indulgence of passion, and the hardness of heart, already engendered by opinions as to man and his position here which leave him without a God, is fostered and made more stony and cruel by a thousand vices. The sentiment of Christianity will, no doubt, long survive in the minds of the masses the loss of the true Christian doctrine, for it is difficult for the perverse and frivolous world to get rid in a few generations of the blessed influences which our Lord has shed over society. But the tendency of unbelief is certainly the same as the tendency of self-indulgence, and the manifold fruits of the virtue of mercifulness will disappear from the world which is a stranger to those truths of faith on which alone that virtue can be securely based.

CHAPTER XIX.

The Merciful obtaining Mercy.

St. Mark v. 7 ; *Vita Vitæ Nostræ,* § 31.

WE may follow the same holy writer who has taught us the fruits of the virtue of mercy, in drawing out the reward which is promised to that virtue by our Lord. The merciful are blessed, 'because they shall obtain mercy.' Their state in itself is full of blessing, and they shall moreover have the special reward which corresponds to their virtue. God will show mercy to them as they have been full of mercy to others.

St. Bernardine tells us, in the first place, that the merciful are promised three rewards in return for their virtue : the reward of glory, the reward of the forgiveness of their sins, and the reward of special grace in this life.

We may pass over the first mentioned for the present,
as it comes more naturally after the other two. The
holy preacher takes the Psalm which has already been
referred to as furnishing the text on which he comments,
in order to draw out the doctrine he is insisting upon—
'Blessed the man who understandeth concerning the
needy and the poor.'[1] In the word Blessed, he sees
the promise of future beatitude; and he notes that the
reward is promised to the affection of the mind and
heart, even before the work of mercy is done, for compassion and mercy begin in the heart; and he compares
the beautiful words of Isaias—'When thou shalt pour
out thy soul to the hungry, and shall satisfy the afflicted
soul, then shall thy light rise up in darkness, and thy
darkness shall be as the noonday.'[2] The next words
of the Psalm, he says, refer to the remission of sin—
'In the evil day the Lord will deliver him.' The evil
day is the day of death, and in that day God will deliver
the merciful man, giving him time and heavenly light
to lead him to true contrition. For, as the Proverbs
say, 'By mercy and truth iniquity is redeemed.'[3] And
St. Jerome writes to Nepotianus, that he never remembers
to have read of a man dying badly, who had cheerfully
practised works of mercy. Such a one has many to pray
for him, and it is impossible that the prayers of many
should not be heard. And, on the other hand, St. James
says, 'There shall be judgment without mercy for him
who hath not done mercy.' And then the Psalm goes
on—'The Lord preserve him and give him life, and
make him blessed upon the earth, and deliver him not
up to the will of his enemies.' Here are four kinds or
acts of grace, St. Bernardine says, for God will first preserve him as he is, then He will give him this life, as piety,
according to the Apostle, 'hath the promise of the life

[1] Psalm xl. 2.　　[2] Isaias lviii. 10.　　[3] Prov. xvi. 6.

that now is, and of that also which is to come.'[4] Thirdly, He will make him blessed and happy in hope, on the earth, and again, He will not deliver him up unto the will of his enemy, the devil, freeing him from sin and its punishment. Such a man is sometimes handed over to his enemies for trial, as was the case with Job, but he is not given up to their will, just as the same holy Patriarch was preserved by the express order of God, Who forbade Satan to touch his life. For the natural power of the evil spirits is in many things restrained by God, and it depends on Him in each case to decide how far He will allow them to do all or less than they can to our detriment. And in the case of the merciful man, we have the promise, that God will not permit him to be tempted and assailed to the full desire and power of his enemies. He will watch over him with a special Providence, as being one who has done his part in carrying out the providence of God's mercy towards others.

The Psalm continues, 'The Lord help him on his bed of sorrow, Thou hast turned all his couch in his sickness.' This whole passage, as explained by St. Bernardine, gives us an idea of the special consolation and protection by which mercifulness is rewarded. It will be comforted, for there is a holy joy and a delight not to be described in labouring to relieve the sufferings of others, of whatever kind they may be, which is in itself a great reward and a sort of promise of the mercy of God to those who thus practise mercy. It need not be denied that God will often in His providence allow merciful men to be afflicted, but it is only that He may make them more conspicuous examples of His own mercy. If He allows them to suffer, it is because suffering is for them a higher good than immunity, and

<hr>

4 1 Timothy iv. 8.

a good which He takes care to crown both by interior
consolations, abundant graces, and by rewards hereafter.
In many cases in the histories of the saints we find a
single act of mercy or compassion, such as those of
St. Peter Damian and St. John Gualbert, rewarded by
a very high vocation and a large treasure of grace.   In
other cases it is an almsdeed or a kind word in defence
of some one in trouble, or an act of clemency, which
wins for the sinner the grace of penitence and contrition,
either at the time or afterwards.   Some of the dealings
of God in this respect are manifest to us, as in the case
of the conversions or vocations just now mentioned,
or even in the external peace and prosperity which seems
to haunt merciful persons or their descendants.   In the
greater number of cases it must certainly be that the
workings of God are hidden from us, but the language of Holy Scripture warrants us in concluding
that a thousand dangers are averted from the merciful
because of their mercifulness, that it wins them sorrow
for their sins and grace to avoid more, that it cancels
the debt of punishment that they owe to the justice of
God, that it wins for them a happy death and a speedy
entrance into the true life.   Mercifulness in judgment
is, in the Sermon on the Mount itself, promised the
reward of immunity from judgment—'Judge not and
you shall not be judged.'   Mercifulness in speech is
promised a special reward in the Psalm quoted in a
former chapter, 'He that would love life and see good
days, let him keep his tongue from evil and his lips that
they speak no guile.'   And mercifulness in action has
the promise contained in the description given by our
Lord of the Judgment to which reference has already
been made.

The promise of future glory, which St. Bernardine puts
by the side of those other two mercies, that of forgiveness

of sins and that of protection and grace in this life, is said by the Saint to be apportioned according to the degree of mercy which has been shown by the merciful. There is, he says, a great mercy, and a greater mercy, and a greatest mercy. The great mercy is to give to others of our goods, and this shall be greatly rewarded, according to the words of Isaias, ' Deal thy bread to the hungry, and bring the needy and the harbourless into thy house ; when thou shalt see one naked, cover him, and despise not thine own flesh ; then shall thy light break forth as the morning, and thy health shall speedily arise, and thy justice shall go before thy face, and the glory of the Lord shall gather thee up.'[5] The greater mercy is to give all our goods to the poor, as our Lord said to the rich young man, ' If thou wilt be perfect, go sell all that thou hast, and give to the poor, and thou shalt have treasure in Heaven.'[6] And the greatest mercy of all is when one gives himself, either for perfection, as in the religious state, or for the sake of charity, as St. Paul was ready to die for the sake of the Jews. To each of these mercies the Saint tells us there is a corresponding reward in the next world. The great mercy shall be rewarded by a very great indulgence and compassion as to all that requires mercy at the hands of the Judge. And those who practise the greater mercy shall not only find mercy in the day when they are judged, but, as our Lord says, they shall find that they have laid up a very great treasure in Heaven, which they shall enjoy in glory. And for the greatest mercy of all there is the reward which is like that of martyrdom, that it cancels all the debts which may be owing to God's justice, and that the soul which thus enters the next life in perfect charity shall at once and without any delay enjoy the vision of God.

[5] Isaias lviii. 7, 8.　　　[6] St. Matt. xix. 21.

St. Bernardine concludes his commentary upon this Beatitude by expounding our Lord's strong words in St. Luke, 'Give and it shall be given unto you; good measure, and pressed down, and shaken together, and running over, shall they give into your bosom.'[7] All this he finds fulfilled in various ways in the reward which is given hereafter to the merciful. All that they have earned by their mercy is paid them, he says, faithfully, equitably, largely, and superabundantly: faithfully, because God fulfils His pledge to give them His great glory; equitably, because the reward is allotted according to the merit; largely, because there shall be nothing, no thought or word or action, that shall not be rewarded; and superabundantly, because the reward shall far exceed the desert in every way. In these four qualities of the eternal reward of the merciful we are to see the good measure, pressed down, shaken together, and running over, of which our Lord speaks. And the bosom, St. Bernardine adds, into which this reward is to be poured, is the mind which is filled with the highest truth, the affections which are fed upon the chief good, the memory which is filled with God's own magnificence. All these things the merciful shall possess in entire security, and this is signified in our Lord's words, because what a man holds in his bosom, of that he is secure. Or again, the words are taken to signify the wonderful rewards which St. Paul describes as what the eye hath not seen, nor the ear heard, nor hath it entered into the heart to imagine them, and God Himself is in them all. Or again, the measure is good, because it is more than the merit, and pressed down, because it is more than was hoped, and shaken together, because it is more than was desired, and running over, because it is more than was conceived. Or again, the reward is

7 St. Luke vi. 38.

divided according to the degrees of mercy spoken of above. He who gives of his goods to the poor, shall have good measure; he that giveth all his goods, shall have measure pressed down; he that giveth himself in religion, shall have measure shaken together; he that gives himself in perfect charity, shall have measure running over.

It has been noticed above that our Lord has not said, in assigning the rewards of the several Beatitudes, that He will give the Kingdom of Heaven, or the possession of the land, or consolation, and the like, and that the reason which has been given for this is, that it was His intention to show, among other things, that the rewards of the virtues which are here commanded grow naturally, as it were, and of right, out of the virtues themselves. This is undoubtedly true, and yet this remark may be here supplemented by another, which is suggested by our Lord's language in the passage of St. Luke on which we have just been commenting. This other remark is, that it is our Lord's way to speak but little of His own part in the blessings and mercies which He confers, as if even in this He would set us the example of perpetual reticence and modesty as to anything in which we are the agents. How little, for instance, He says when He confers His greatest gifts, such as the Blessed Sacrament, or the power of the Keys, or the promise of His perpetual Presence with the Church! And so in speaking of His own joy over the recovery of sinners, He says, ' There shall be joy in Heaven before the angels of God over one sinner doing penance,' and the rest, when in truth it is His own joy of which He speaks, the joy which the angels shall witness and be invited to share. And so here, when He says that all this wonderful measure of mercy shall be given in return for the mercy which men have shown to others, He is speaking of Himself, of the blessings which in this four-fold manner of multiplied and excessive magnificence He and His Father and the Holy Ghost will confer upon the merciful. God will do it Himself, or rather He Himself is the abundant and overabundant reward which He will give to those who have understood the love with which He regards mercy, and have done their best to make that love the law of their own actions in relation to their neighbour. It is seldom that our Lord uses so many words to characterize the same thing as in the passage which St. Luke has recorded as to the reward of mercy; and if He allowed His own Sacred Heart to pour Itself out, as it were, in heaping one image upon another to express His own beneficence, it must be certain that no human words can possibly be adequate to describe the blessedness of those on whom He sheds His loving bounties in full measure, shaken together, pressed down, and running over.

CHAPTER XX.

The Beatitude of the Clean of Heart.

St. Matt. v. 8 ; *Vita Vitæ Nostræ*, § 31.

IT is unnecessary to repeat what has more than once
been said as to the manner in which the Beatitudes
gradually rise higher and higher, the preceding steps
leading naturally on to those which follow. The point
which we have now reached has, however, been noted
by some writers as that at which the eye of the soul
is turned more directly upon God. The three first
Beatitudes may be considered as in some sense disci-
plining the soul as regards itself, and the two which have
followed as perfecting our action towards our neighbour. Poverty of spirit, meekness, and mourning are
virtues which indeed bring us across our neighbour in
many ways, but they are not so directly occupied with
him as justice and mercy. The interior man is first
brought to perfection, and then we are taught how to
exercise ourselves in virtuous actions, and especially in
mercy. And, when this has been done, the soul, as
has been said, is turned away from earthly things, and
is taught, as far as possible, to purge itself from all
dross and stain, that it may see God in the sixth
Beatitude, and after that, go on still further to work
His own peculiar work of peace, and to suffer for it,
in the seventh and the eighth. We have seen that
the thought of God, the active exercise of faith in a

number of truths concerning Him, must be the foundation of the earliest Beatitudes as well as of the latest, and the mind must be turned to Him and grasp what He has revealed concerning Himself and make Him the object of its every aim and endeavour, in order even to enter on the path along which the Beatitudes lead. But it is also true that the Beatitude at which we have now arrived is the point at which the union between God and the soul is more directly and continually sought, because such union is a higher grade of perfection even than justice and mercifulness, and the Vision of God is a nobler reward, so far as it can be distinguished from them, even than to be filled with justice, and to experience His ineffable mercy. 'Blessed are the clean of heart, for they shall see God !'

It may be noticed that this great Beatitude comes after those two others which, as has been said, regulate the actions of the perfect Christian with regard to his neighbour—justice and mercifulness. It follows, then, that in the intention of our Lord, the Lawgiver of the Beatitudes, the active exertions of justice and the devotion of self in every kind of the works of mercy, do not indispose the soul from union with God, nor overlay it, as it were, with the dust that accumulates, in the case of the imperfect, from those exercises of virtue which carry those who practise them into frequent communication with men and the world around them. No doubt there is danger in all such works, that those who are given up to them may, if they neglect prayer and the exercises of the interior life, become merely external workers, and lose their recollection and their peace. But this is not the effect of works of justice and mercy where they are done, however multifariously and continuously, with a pure intention and such other circumstances of perfection as to method and manner which our Lord requires. Rather, such activity and such energy, even when they fill a large space in a life and occupy the greater part of its time, help the soul to rise into regions higher than their own works, for if they are done for God and in God they are perpetual strainings towards Him and so preparations for His sight. Works of mercy in particular are, as we have seen, a sort of special commission from Him, and a carrying out in the sphere of human action of the law which He has chosen to reign over all His own dealings with His creatures. In the next place we must be prepared to find in this, as in the other Beatitudes, a two-fold blessing as well as various degrees of the virtue and of its reward. Cleanness or purity of heart, that is, is in itself blessed, and it is blessed also in its reward, which is the discernment of God. And there are various grades in which this blessed virtue may be practised or possessed. A certain degree of cleanness of heart is of course necessary for the state of grace itself, and so for salvation. There are other higher and still higher degrees, rising one over the other until the soul is endowed with the purity of the angels. And in like manner, the discernment or vision of God is of various kinds and degrees, and will be made perfect at last in Heaven, where, as St. John says, 'we shall be like Him,' in His ineffable purity, 'because we shall see Him as He is.'

The heart, which is to be cleansed or kept pure by him who would gain this Beatitude, stands in our Lord's words for the whole interior man, the soul with all the faculties of intelligence and volition. It includes, therefore, the memory, which retains the knowledge concerning the past, present, or future, which has been communicated to the mind, the reason or intellect, which considers, reflects, compares, and concludes, and the will, which chooses and decides and resolves. It embraces the affections, the feelings, the emotions, the imagination, the whole varied working of the intelligence and the will. This is the true man, and the life of this is his true life; and it is capable of the utmost foulness and corruption, as well as of the most sublime purity and activity. Out of the heart are the issues of life. Our Lord on one occasion broke out, if we may use such words of Him, into a sort of enumeration of the evils and miseries which have their birth in the heart. The Pharisees had found fault with the disciples for eating with unwashed hands, and our Lord called the multitude to Him and declared that what came out of the mouth was that which truly defiled a man, 'For from the heart come forth evil thoughts, adulteries, fornications, murders, thefts, covetousness, wickedness, deceit, lasciviousness, an evil eye, blasphemy, pride, foolishness.'[1] He ranged from great to small in the list of sins, and found them all rising up out of the heart. Thus St. Ignatius, in one of his meditations on sin, bids us consider ourselves like some foul wound or running sore, out of which so many sins and impurities, and so much of the foulest venom have welled out on all around. This is the dark side of the picture—dark indeed when we consider that the heart is never at rest, that it needs no company or presence of occasions or temptations and provocations to sin, but can create them for itself at will, that it must always be feeding upon thoughts and imaginations of some kind or other, which must take their character from the passions which are predominant at the time, or the habit of the soul as to the regulation of its own interior life, while, on the other hand, it is utterly unchecked by any created power but itself, its movements and complacencies and desires are known

[1] St. Mark vii. 21, 22.

to no one but itself, and may be black as night and foul as Hell itself, in the holiest places, at the most sacred moments, and while the exterior man is at work upon the best and noblest occupations. Even in sleep, the mind is in a sort of way at work, though its working is mechanical, and the will has no control over it. And there are very large portions of the waking life of all men which are little better than dreams, as to any attempt of the will deliberately to regulate or restrain the ceaseless action of the mind, which writes, as it were, its own character of childishness, frivolity, worldliness, pride, anger, envy, sensuality, the darkest or the most shameful of vices, upon the moments which stream by it, to meet it again once more when it has to be judged by its Creator.

If the thought of this continual action and working of the heart is so humbling and so alarming when we come to consider what a tale it is continually telling of us before God, Who has chosen to reserve to Himself the prerogative of reading its every motion, or even when we reflect how we should be inclined to shun the face of any friend like ourselves who had received the power of knowing it, it may be remembered, on the other hand, that there is nothing in the whole creation of God that is capable of a more perfect beauty, a more heavenly and sublime fertility of good and noble fruits. If we set aside the intellect and will of the angelic host, nowhere has God made for Himself a garden of delight in which to rejoice equal to the mind of man. Its power of ranging at will from Heaven to earth, over the past, present, and future, its gifts of imagination and affections, its desires and aspirations which count before God for deeds, without being limited by the halting capacities of human action which lag so far behind its passionate wishes and intentions, give to it a breadth and might and compass for what is holy and noble, which seem ever to transcend its miserable fertility in evil and corruption. When the memory is indeed purged from foolish and wicked thoughts, and peopled with images of all that is beautiful and holy; when the intellect is ransomed from the blindness which has fallen upon it, like a cloud, in consequence of the Fall, a cloud deepened and made heavier by personal transgressions; when it is delivered from ignorance and error, and flooded with the light of faith, the knowledge of God, and the intelligence of His ways, and when the will, freed from all perversity and inclination to lower goods, is fixed upon God alone, then indeed the heart of man can be fruitful of thoughts, imaginations, conceptions, contemplations, desires, and affections, which may present to God a fairer and a better world for Him to bless and rejoice in than the material universe, which, at the beginning, He created and declared to be good. The spiritual beauties and glories of which every single human soul is capable, under the influence of the supernatural grace which is its inheritance through our Lord, are known to God alone. But we are able to see that as all kinds of wickedness, as our Lord has said, can proceed out of the heart, so also there is nothing lovely or magnificent in the spiritual order of which the heart cannot be made the continual and inexhaustible source. There are some among the saints of God, like the blessed St. Aloysius, of whom it has become known that a great part of their merit consisted in the intensity and beauty of their interior acts. And from the nature of the case it follows that what is known to be true of a few is probably the truth with regard to thousands upon thousands whom the world has never heard of, while of those with whose great deeds and heroic sufferings the Church upon earth has rung, there will

be few indeed whose interior affections have not been
more precious in the eyes of their Lord than their
outward works.

The heart, then, is the centre of the whole life and
action of man ; it is open to God alone, Who delights,
as it seems, in Sacred Scripture in the Name of Him
'Who knoweth the heart.'[2] He alone sees it, and He
can see in it, such is His providence, and such the power
of His grace, things that are more pleasing in His sight
than anything which the lower order of creation can
produce. It is but fitting, as it may be said, that the
hearts which make this blessed return to their Creator
should, on their part, be rewarded with the crown
promised in this Beatitude, that they in recompense
should see Him. We have now to go on to the stages
of the purgation, or of the cleanness, of the heart, of
which our Lord speaks. It is natural to begin with
sins, which stain the heart in which they are conceived,
and which leave behind them, when they have gone
forth and become consummated in action, a wound and
weakness which form a miserable legacy, infecting the
character, making it prone to similar excesses in future,
as well as a debt due to God's justice, which is distinct
from the guilt and the stain. All this is to be purged
away if the heart is to be cleansed. The guilt of sin
is done away when the precious Blood of the Immaculate
Lamb of God is poured upon it in the Sacrament of
Penance, or is applied to it by the grace of contrition,
which avails even when this sacrament cannot be applied.
But in the greater number of cases the sinner may be
justified, and the guilt wiped away, without that perfect
cleansing from tendencies and inclinations and dispositions and affections and habits which belong to the
state in which he has placed himself, and he has

<hr>

[2] καρδιογνωστῆς θέος.

need, not only of the Sacrament of Penance, which is
transient, but of the virtue also of penance, which
abides and gradually produces the effect of more perfect
purification upon the soul. Penance must be aided by
prayer, by the constant use of the means of grace, by
the careful flight of danger, by the diligent practice of
virtue. These will purify the soul from its weaknesses
and habits of sin, by perfecting and strengthening the
contrary habit of virtue, while the debt which is due
to the justice of God, without the cancelling of which
neither forgiveness nor purification can be quite complete, is gradually done away with by the same means,
but especially by the works of penance, almsdeeds, and
mercy of every kind.

It must be remembered also that the sins from which
the soul has to be cleansed are not only those grievous
offences or bad habits which entirely destroy the life of
grace. For the soul is to be made a beautiful garden, in
which the Eternal King is to take His pleasure and set
up His abode, and nothing less than this is included in
the promise of our Lord : 'If any one love Me, he will
keep My word, and My Father will love him, and We
will come to him, and make Our abode with him.'[3] But
a soul that is thus to be made fit for the sojourn of
the adorable Trinity, must not only be free from the
poisonous weeds and deadly growths which represent
mortal sin. There must be nothing in it which can
offend the eye; nothing out of order; nothing, at all
events, wild, or hideous, or deformed, or stunted, or
half-withered. It must be free also, therefore, from the
sins which are called venial, because of their lightness
in comparison with mortal sins, but which are still greatly
displeasing to God, and altogether unfit for the soul in
which He is to delight. There are various kinds and

[3] St. John xiv. 23.

degrees of these lesser sins, so called ; for some are only not mortal, because there has been want of full advertence or deliberation, but for which want they would constitute grievous offences ; others, again, are in their nature lighter, being on a subject-matter which is not important enough in itself to bring down the greatest anger of God ; while a third class are the effects of inattention, or surprise, or even of the weakness of nature, and so are neither deliberate, like the second class, nor grievous in their character, like the first. All these kinds of lesser sins are more or less purged away by the faithful use of the sacraments. The former class must, moreover, be dealt with severely, as mortal sins are dealt with, and their occasions must be avoided, and penance must be done for them. The second class of sins, such as those of vanity or inaccuracy in speech, and the like, must be removed, among other things, by such meditation and consideration as may open the eyes of the soul to the extreme indecency and deformity which really belongs to them ; for it is often want of light and reflection that makes persons who are in the main bent on serving God fall into such faults. The third class of distractions, negligences, surprises, and weaknesses, will also be gradually conquered, in proportion as the soul becomes more and more enlightened in prayer, more advanced in the practice of virtue and in union with God, Whose service and presence require the most perfect and accurate homage from them who are to be the favourites of His Heavenly Court.

We are thus led to the truth which is expressed in the saying of the Old Testament, part of which has already been quoted, 'With all watchfulness keep thy heart, for life issues out of it.'[4] The continual vigilance which is implied in the Christian practice of self-examination,

---

[4] Prov. iv. 23.

which has been made the matter of so much special legislation by the teachers of spirituality, can never be carried too far, so long as it does not touch upon scrupulosity, by those who wish to make their hearts pure in the sense of this Beatitude.   There is much to be found in the writers to whom reference has been made on the subject, of what are called technically the various 'temperaments.' The whole of this doctrine seems to rest on the truth that men are differently constituted as to character and disposition, and that the varieties can be more or less reduced to classes, the peculiarities of which can be noted, and their appropriate remedies assigned. Certain it is that what are called 'faults of character' are often the faults to which persons who have long given themselves to the service of God and the cultivation of their own souls remain the longest blind.   The acts of such faults of disposition are so congenial and natural to the soul that it takes no account of them, except when its attention is arrested by their effect on others. Men are quick and sensitive, slothful or irritable, impatient or indolent, impetuous or cold, self-asserting or shy, and these various characters issue in a number of daily actions, or perhaps in an habitual manner of performing daily actions, which other people see not to be according to the standard of perfection, and, indeed, far below it, while there is no change or progress in respect of them in the souls which they infect, because they are not recognized as faults.   These faults are often the causes of serious evils, or at least they hinder great good in the souls in question, or even in the Church, as, for instance, when a superior is indolent, or a confessor impatient, or when narrow-mindedness hinders great enterprises for the glory of God, or when the natural feelings of jealousy are not altogether subdued among persons whose work lies in the same part of the vineyard of our Lord.   Eli,

Saul, Caiphas, Pilate, are instances in the sacred history of persons of high position who in very various degrees indeed have either done or not hindered great evils, on account of faults of character uncorrected, and perhaps unrecognized. And it seems even to be sometimes the will of God that when these faults are recognized by those who have them, and when they are striven against they should not at once be removed, but allowed to remain, like St. Paul's thorn in the flesh, in order that humility may be strengthened, or again, as has been seen in some servants of God, in order that the loving patience of others may be exercised upon them. But perfect purity of heart implies the removal—at least, the earnest desire for the removal—of all these defects, as far as it may be the will of God, for they are in themselves enemies of the peace of the soul, and flaws which mar its perfect beauty in the sight of God. Everything that is in any way disorderly in thought or in affection must be set right before perfect purity can be attained. Thus we are told by St. John that our Blessed Lord had a special love for St. Martha, as well as for St. Mary Magdalene and Lazarus; and yet in the scene in which the two sisters are put before us, the one as careful about the serving, the other as sitting at the feet of our Lord, the over-anxiety of St. Martha is reproved by Him, as having led her into the fault of censuring her sister. This is an instance in which a defect of character led even a Saint dear to God into an unwise speech and judgment just as truly as, we may suppose, the characteristic and untamed ambition of Caiphas led him to jealousy, and from jealousy to the enormous crime of compassing the death of our Lord.

Perhaps the easiest way to gain some idea of the faults and defects which do not always amount to sins, from which the heart must be purified before it can be fit for the vision of God, of which our Lord here speaks, may be to turn to His own Sacred Heart, which has in these later ages of the Church been so providentially set before Christians as the special subject of their study. The Devotion to the Sacred Heart of our Lord has, indeed, a character of its own, that of sympathy, condolence, and reparation for the coldness and neglect with which He is treated by the world at large, by many Christians, and even by souls who are in a special manner consecrated to Him. But this does not shut us out from the study of the Sacred Heart under other lights also, and we shall find much to help us in our present inquiry into the consideration of what holy writers have left behind them concerning the perfect purity of that Sacred Heart. We find the following arrangement of a number of the disorders from which our Lord's Heart was so pre-eminently free, and the freedom from which is a matter of imitation for us, who must aim at immunity from all sorts of disorder, whether of mind and thought, or of heart and affection.

The Heart of our Lord, then, in the first place, was free from all love of temporal things. There was nothing in the whole world, however innocent in itself, and good in its own kind, but of a merely temporal character, to which His Heart had any attachment at all. Thus He used what temporal things were necessary for the sustenance of His Sacred Humanity with the utmost simplicity and sparingness, utterly rejecting all superfluities, and taking what He did take in measure barely sufficient. Here we have His example for freedom from care for all visible things, all superfluities and curiosities and delicacies and ornaments, which, trifles and knicknacks though they be, are often enough to entrap a part of our affection, and are at all events incongruous in those who wish to imitate His perfect detachment and poverty, as far as is agreeable to the conditions of the state of life in which they are placed.

Another and a kindred kind of the perfect purity of the Sacred Heart was Its entire detachment from all worldly delights. For we may be without superfluities and vanities in our own possession, and yet we may delight with a refined sensuality in what we have, and may share the world's enjoyments as far as they are open to us. Food and sleep and dress, human friendship and conversation, the pleasure of beautiful sights and sounds, the news of the day, the latest of the novelties of amusement and curiosity—these are all matters which form the subject of sensible delight. And our Lord, Whose Heart was always conversing with heavenly things, and occupied with them alone, could not but turn away from all these lower and false attractions with the sort of distaste which a philosopher might feel if invited to join a party of educated persons in playing with dolls or blowing bubbles. And all these are things which may entangle the thoughts and even the affections of persons whose hearts, if purified from sensible pleasures, might have a clear perception and a close familiarity with God of which they are now deprived.

Another kind of freedom which our Lord's Heart enjoyed in perfection was the freedom from the desire of pleasing men. Human respect, in its more gross forms, is often the cause of many sins both of omission and commission, and in a less degree it may act as a shackle and restraint on the perfect liberty of the soul in the service, and so in the contemplation of God. For human friendships and regards, the fear of displeasing or the hope of gratifying, may often make it difficult to do just what the heart knows to be the most right, the most pleasing thing to God. Human considerations must have their due weight, because God has placed us in society, and has willed that the claims of kindred or of friendship should be observed. But all these affections and relationships are to be kept under and dominated by the pure love of God, the overpowering passion of the soul. Natural love is to be turned into supernatural love, equal charity is to be dealt to friends and foes, to those who are dear to us, and to those who have thwarted us or who are disagreeable to us, the vices and follies and bad qualities of some are not to revolt us any more than the contrary qualities in others are to make us partial, and in all we are to preserve our perfect independence and liberty, wishing and praying good for all, and helping all as far as our power extends, not according to the inclinations of flesh and blood, but according to the universal law of charity which is based upon the love of God.

Again, the Heart of our Lord was absolutely free from another source of distraction and imperfection, which lies in the want of a perfectly direct intention. He had but one single and most pure aim, the glory of the Father, and in pursuing this He was never turned one hair's breadth to the right hand or to the left by any desire of His own glory or good. Thus His intention was not only pure and right in its aim, but entirely simple also, and most perfect too, in that it was the same to Him whether to aim at the glory of His Father was to Himself a matter of consolation or desolation, of pain or of joy. These then are the qualities which we ought to seek to gain in our own intention after the pattern of our Lord : rectitude, to seek His honour and glory purely in all, as a child the honour and glory of the Father ; simplicity, that everything may be referred to this one single intention, the mind and heart and whole man occupied with God, and then that perfection which consists in indifference to our own consolation or desolation in what we do for the glory of God.

Again, our Lord's Heart may be considered in Its perfect purity from all useless thoughts. All our Lord's thoughts were regulated and deliberately chosen. No thought entered His Heart which was not holy, pure, beautiful in itself, and admitted, as it were, into that sacred abode for the glory of His Father and for the benefit of our souls. Here we find an immense field for self-humiliation and prayer. We are very tepid and very careless, and hence our minds are like the streets or market-places into which all sorts of creatures pass unhindered, thoughts of positive evil, or empty and superfluous thoughts, of which we should be nearly as much ashamed as of the others if they could write themselves on our foreheads for our friends to read, or thoughts of over-anxiety, or of too many matters to be attended to calmly and seriously at once. Even the thoughts which are necessary to us, such as those about our duties, are to be moderated in their intensity, as children whom their parents are bound to feed are yet to be restrained in their greediness for food. Such thoughts are to be so dealt with that God may be the end in view, and so they may not separate us from Him. All the peace of the soul in prayer depends upon self-discipline in these matters, and hence the value of the virtues of the love of silence and solitude, as far as they are compatible with the duties of our calling, and when we go among men and open our minds to the many thoughts which must invade them in consequence, it must be for charity to them or to ourselves, not for simple and sensible consolation. On the other hand, we must keep our minds, as far as may be, for the holy and pure and sublime thoughts which will not be wanting to those who love our Lord, for the simple thought of Him is full of treasures of contemplation enough to feed the minds of all the inhabitants of Heaven.

After freedom from useless thoughts it is natural to place freedom from superfluous cares. Our Lord's Heart was always perfectly tranquil, and thus His liberty of spirit was marvellous. Nothing disturbed Him, or moved the simplicity and quiet of His Heart. We are told that He sometimes chose to be troubled, but then He deliberately took up the grief or sorrow or displeasure, and allowed it to work upon His Heart just as much as was best and as He chose. We, on the other hand, as long as our passions are not perfectly mortified, as long as we have not perfectly gained the blessed practice of the presence of God, are the servants and not the masters of our cares, and they tend in consequence rather to separate us from Him and disturb our peace than to unite us more closely to Him. Some holy writers speak of the 'mordacity' of cares, and the word expresses the idea of an influence which we ought never to allow them to gain. Nothing is great or difficult with God, and all ought to be regarded in Him. We are to do our part, and take the advice of prudent persons, and then leave the event to God. The actions which are duties to us we are to perform without strain or over-solicitude, and as far as their nature allows, keep our minds and hearts fixed on God as we do them. Thus our minds will not be over-clouded, as is sometimes the case when men take up too great a number of occupations, an evil which has for its result the growth of tepidity. Temporal things become interesting, and spiritual things distasteful, unless this liberty of the soul is reserved, which in its turn helps to the perfection of all the actions which are required by the cares which lawfully fall to us, and makes them all the means of our advancement and spiritual strength instead of weakness and distraction.

Again, we are told to consider that our Lord's Sacred Heart was always full of sweetness and kindliness, and altogether free from bitterness of every kind. St. Matthew draws attention to this characteristic of our Lord when he relates how He retired from before His enemies in order not to obtrude upon them what might provoke them to sin, and he sees in this a fulfilment of one of the prophetic notes concerning the Messias, 'He shall not contend or cry out, neither shall any man hear His voice in the streets; the bruised reed He shall not break, and smoking flax He shall not extinguish.'[5] He had more to provoke Him in this way of ingratitude, of malignant hostility, of disingenuous and captious criticism, of envy under the cloak of zeal for God's honour, of baseness and brutality on the part of enemies, and of faithlessness and cowardice on the part of friends, than any one else had to suffer since the world was. It seemed as if His ineffable holiness, by the splendour of its light, revealed an amount of blackness and deformity in the human hearts which were ranged against Him which had before been unsuspected. But there was never the slightest bitterness in the Heart of our Lord. It is for the imperfect servants of God, who have pride and presumption on their own merits still uneradicated, to become indignant and pass severe judgments, judgments without compassion, on the enemies of the truth. Bitterness comes from want of mortification, from self-love, which fosters rancour and hatred against opponents, or from envy, or from tepidity. And all these are so many impurities which must be removed from the heart that is to see the King in His beauty.

[5] Isaias xlii. 2, 3 ; St. Matt. xii. 19, 20.

It is not much, in the next place, to say that our Lord's Heart was free from all vainglory; but by this is meant that He thought very little of His own works, exquisitely perfect as they were, that He had no complacency in His own words or deeds as being perfectly virtuous, but did them all in the utmost humility, submitting them all to His Father, and taking no credit for them. This return upon themselves, whereby they take up what they have done for the service of God and their neighbour, is a great danger to spiritual men, and is directly contrary to our Lord's precept as well as to His example. For He bids us not let our left hand know what our right hand doeth, lest by contemplation of it and self-satisfaction regarding it, we should have our reward here and not hereafter. Rather, we are to think ourselves the lowest of all, unprofitable servants even when we have done all that is commanded us, and much more unworthy of notice on account of the sins which we have committed, or those which, if left to ourselves, we should have committed; or again, of the many gifts of God which we have left unemployed, the many opportunities of grace and holy inspirations which we have neglected.

There are yet other kinds of purity in the Sacred Heart on which devout writers have loved to linger. Something has been said already as to our Lord's indifference to consolation or desolation as a part of the perfect purity of His intention. It may be added, that as to any created consolation or comfort, He was ever free from any delight therein. He delighted even in sorrow and affliction. His Soul from the first moment of its existence possessed the Beatific Vision, and was plunged in infinite joy. But the lower part of His Soul was no stranger to anguish and affliction. On the contrary, it endured them to such an extremity on the

Cross, that He could use the words of the Psalmist, and call on His Father to say why He had forsaken Him. No anguish can surpass what our Lord then endured. He might have chosen to undergo external poverty and all the other circumstances of bodily suffering which belonged to our condition, or to the execution of the work of redemption for which He came, and yet all the while have retained joy and delight in His Heart, and made It the home of unmixed exultation and gladness. But for the love of us, and to become our example, He chose to add to bodily torments the sorrows and sufferings of the soul. And in this He has set us an example of this purity of heart, that we may not cling to consolation when we have it, but only use it and value it as a means which enables us to serve Him more easily because more gladly ; and when we have it not, that we may persevere in all fervour and never betake ourselves to seeking comfort in creatures. For true holiness does not consist in the subtle investigation of the secrets of Heaven nor in any sensible devotion, but in charity and humility, and the perfect observance of the law of God.

It is further remarked that our Blessed Lord did all that He did for the service of His Father with a wonderful confidence and absence of all anxiety, knowing with absolute clearness that such was the will of His Father, and performing it fearlessly, joyously, exultingly, as a Son and not as a servant. The quality opposite to this freedom would be a timid scrupulous anxiety, as if God were a hard taskmaster, and might make us responsible for the failure of our efforts, as if the success depended upon us and not on Him, and it might also be a subtle self-love, which is afraid to venture lest it should fail and so win discredit to itself instead of glory to God. This would produce that pusillanimity which is sometimes the hindrance to many great attempts for the honour of our

Lord, such as St. Francis de Sales exclaimed against when there was a question of stopping a conference between some Catholic and Protestant doctors, for fear that the latter might perhaps seem to have the best of the argument.

Another head of the purity of our Lord's Heart is His absolute freedom from impatience. This is a different quality from that liberty from all bitterness which has been noticed already, because impatience has reference to the things which are suffered, and bitterness has reference to the person through whom the suffering comes. But our Lord with the most perfect meekness welcomed all the contumely and mocking and derision to which He was exposed, all the spitting, and scourging, the insults and torments of His Passion and Crucifixion, and was so far from having any vindictive feelings against His persecutors as to pray for them as He hung in His agony. God visits those who serve Him with many things which are far less hard to suffer, but which yet require much patience. Some things come from men, as insults, injuries, and neglect, others are inflicted in the course of His own providence, such as sickness, bodily pains, bereavements, desolation of spirit, and the like, and in all these things the heart that is not perfectly pure may be moved to impatience and murmuring, or again, to some desire of revenge upon the persons who may be the instruments of God in thus chastising us or putting us to the proof.

Lastly, our Lord's Heart was absolutely free from all self-will, not, of course, only those manifestations of self-will which amount to disobedience, but even from the slightest movement of discord or deviation from the will of His Father. He came into the world, as St. Paul tells us, to do the will of His Father, and indeed He Himself declared the same more than once. The will of the Father was the one purpose for which He lived. And He showed this perfect conformity most conspicuously in His Prayer in the Garden, when His human will had conceived the desire that the chalice of the Passion might pass from Him, and when He had expressed this desire in earnest prayer, while yet the prayer was made with the condition, expressed with equal earnestness, that not His will might be done, but that of His Father. And here is a kind of purity which is not easy of attainment, even by those who are heartily bent upon serving God. They wish to have their own way in some respects, as Moses, or as Samuel in his grief for Saul, and so far they are liable to disturbance, or disappointment, or chagrin, when the will of God turns out to be not exactly what they have wished it to be, inverting, as St. Ignatius says, the order of Divine Providence.[6]   .

It must be obvious that the many subtle manifestations and struggles of self-love which must be put down and kept under if the heart is to be fashioned after our Lord's pattern in all these measures of interior purity, require nothing short of the most continual vigilance in the practice of self-examination, the most constant attention to the presence of God and to His glory, as the one aim of life and of every action in it, as well as very powerful assistance indeed in the way of enlightenment of the mind and conscience, and fortifying of the will, by theological virtues and the various means of grace. And yet it may safely be said that the faithful use of the Sacraments of Penance and of Holy Communion, added to diligence and prayer, to recollection and self-restraint of body and mind, can hardly fail to produce in the soul some such results as those which have here been

---

[6] The substance of the foregoing paragraphs will be found in an Exercise by Alv. de Paz, t. iii. *De Inquisitione Pacis*, l. iv. p. 2, ex. 4, *Quomodo ad Christi similtudinem cordis affectus compones.*

sketched. That is, this high perfection of purity of heart is within the reach of those who make the most of the ordinary means of grace, and it does not require the more special favours which are reserved for the chosen saints of God. Thus an astonishing purity of heart is sometimes found in the simplest and humblest Christians, whose lives, to the outward eye, present no appearance of a strain after extraordinary modes of serving God, no astonishing practices of penance, no eremitical seclusion from the paths of common life. Thus, again, we find that high as we may rise in the scale of the Beatitudes, we do not leave behind us of necessity any class of men as such or any lawful vocation, and that the heart of any Christian may be made pure, after the pattern of that of our Lord, though its purity must fall so short of His in its intensity. Nor is any one shut out from what seems to be the choicest of all the rewards which are here allotted—the blessed vision of God, which is the crown of the clean of heart.

CHAPTER XXI.

Purity and the Vision of God.

St. Matt. v. 8 ; *Vita Vitæ Nostræ,* § 31.

IT is obvious to any one who considers the degrees of
cleanness and purgation of the heart which have been
already spoken of in reference to the sixth Beatitude,
that each of them implies the removal of some cause of
disquiet, of blindness to the mind, and of hardness to
the heart. All sin has the effect of impairing the keenness
for their lawful purposes of the faculties which it abuses,
while it also fosters pride and self-love, which have a
direct tendency to darken and sour and stunt the souL
We have but to recall to mind the various phases of sin
or imperfection which have been counted up in the
preceding chapter, to see that to be free from them
must be a blessing in itself. It cannot be but that to
get rid of them must bring to the soul liberty and calm,
security and peace. It must set it free to occupy itself
upon the highest and noblest subjects with which it has
the capacity to deal ; it must make it quiet in itself,
mistress of its own emotions and thoughts and imaginations, able to aim at lofty ends and conceive great plans,
to understand noble speculations and sublime arguments. So that if a philosopher had at his command
the power of grace, if he could at will enforce upon his
various faculties the law of peace which comes from
purity, he would certainly endeavour to cleanse his heart

in the manner which has been traced out, if it were only for the tranquillity which he would thus gain and the ten-fold strength which would ensue to all his intellectual faculties.

It would follow from this that cleanness of heart is happiness in itself, even if it were to lead to nothing beyond itself, and that the labour and exertion which are required to gain it would not be wasted, if they resulted in nothing else than in securing it. But, on the other hand, it is certain that even in this life, and much more in the next, the extrinsic rewards which are gained by purity are of that transcendent beauty and value which our Lord has summed up in the words which express the formal cause of the blessing of Heaven itself, when He says that the clean of heart shall see God. There are various degrees of this vision of God, as there are various degrees of purity of heart, and we must now endeavour to set these shortly before ourselves. The change from blindness to sight is the greatest boon that can be given to any one who has been deprived by nature of any of the common gifts of sense, for the world of sight is the most beautiful and varied of all the spheres on which the senses can be occupied, and the gift of sight enables us to compensate in some measure, at least, for defects as to the other senses. We may naturally feel pity at the sight of a blind man, knowing how much he loses of the glorious works of God and man around him, how little he can know of the world in which he moves, the persons with whom he converses, the pleasures and delights of other men, of how many external helps or incentives to intellectual cultivation or development he is deprived. And when we hear such a one told, as in the case of the man born blind, to go wash in the Pool of Siloe, as the single condition on which he is to receive the boon of which we know how precious it is, we are ready to rejoice for him that at so little cost he is to gain so great a blessing.

But there is no blindness to the external things of the world that can be compared in its misery to the blindness as to God, there is no loss to the mind which is consequent upon such external blindness which is like the loss which the soul suffers from ignorance of God. There is no condition so hard and painful that it would not be wisdom to submit to if it were to lead to the taking away of blindness as to God. And, on the other hand, just as a slight wound in so delicate a member as the eye is enough to destroy its power of sight, or as a mere mote may make it useless, as the smallest atom which comes between it and the object to which it is directed is enough to veil it, so what seems a comparatively slight flaw or stain upon the soul may prevent it frcm recognizing and contemplating God. God is in His own universe as if He deserved that title above all others which St. Paul, in his walk through Athens, found inscribed over an altar—the Unknown God. And yet, as the Apostle told the Athenians, He is not far from any of them, for in him all men live and move and are. As the eye is made for light, so the soul is made for the knowledge of God, and as, when the impediments are removed and the diseases healed, the eye comes at once into the use of its natural power of seeing all things in the light which is all around, so when the purification of the soul is effected, there is no longer any impediment between it and its God, and it becomes at once, by His mercy, capable of using its natural powers concerning Him and of receiving also the immense supernatural illumination which comes to us through our Lord.

When, therefore, our Lord promises to the clean of heart that they shall see God, His words do not imply, in every sense in which they may be understood, that

He was about to give them a new faculty, or raise them to a new state of existence, as if a stone were suddenly to be endowed with sight or enabled to think. There is, indeed, a vision of God which is to be the lot of the pure in heart which is a supernatural gift, and for which the soul has no capacity of itself. But God is all around us in many ways, and He can be seen and known in many ways which do not transcend the powers with which man is here and now endowed, assisted by the ordinary aids which are denied to no man. For, as has often been said, it is the very accusation which the same Apostle who spoke in the Areopagus about this unknown God brought against the heathen world generally in his Epistle to the Romans, that they had not known God in the revelation concerning Himself which He had written in the physical universe. Here, then, is a vision or discernment of God which is open to all men, and which those who had long lost the light of primitive tradition, and been aliens from the covenant of God, were still blameworthy because they had not recognized. In another place we find the same St. Paul, speaking to another assembly of heathen, far less cultivated than those who came to hear him at Athens, reminding them how God the Creator of all things had not left Himself without witness to His creatures who had forgotten Him, 'doing good from Heaven, giving rains and fruitful seasons, filling our hearts with food and gladness.'[1] The Apostle here implies that the ordinary providence of God, which is full of beneficent mercy, is a testimony concerning Himself that all mankind can and ought to recognize. Thus we have a second way in which God can be seen by men, in His providence, besides the revelation of Himself which is contained in the works which He has made.

[1] Acts xiv. 16.

In his Epistle to the Romans, also, St. Paul speaks of the voice of conscience as having been recognized by many heathen as speaking with the authority of God and with a sentence which is a sort of anticipation of the future Judgment which He is to hold.[2] God therefore may be recognized in conscience as well as in the creation and in the order of the world, and we are thus led up to the doctrine that His dealings with us in His particular providence, as also His government of the world in the great drama of human history, are full of signs and marks by which we may recognize Him and learn more concerning Him.

We find all these heads of knowledge concerning God continually dwelt upon in the Psalms, which were the familiar prayers and praises of the people of God, and which have passed naturally into the use of the Church from our Lord and the Apostles, the vision of God which they revealed being the common heritage of His children in all ages and under all dispensations. The Psalms are full of the works of God in the material universe, of His dealings with His people in history, and of His counsels as revealed in prophecy, as well as of the purity and perfection of the moral law which He has given, and of His manifold and intimate dealings with the soul in its various conditions of sin, penitence, hope, fear, gladness, sorrow, and consolation. They also open to us another source from which we are meant to draw a large and most wonderful stream of knowledge concerning Him, for they speak of His wonderful doings in His saints, and so point to us the revelation concerning Himself which is contained in the creation of grace. But here we at once are struck with the great expansion, so to speak, which the knowledge and recognition of God which are to be gained from the study of the

2 Romans ii. 15, 16.

Kingdom of grace, has received in consequence of the Incarnation, our Lord's Life and Passion, and the establishment of the Church. Our Lord's own Person and actions form a mighty and inexhaustible store of teaching concerning God, His wisdom, His power, His mercy, His justice, His ineffable love for His creatures, which it is necessary to pass over here in the briefest words, because if we once began to enter on the details of all this magnificence, we should never end. Our Blessed Lady, the angels, the saints, the Catholic Church, her wonderful array of weapons for the spiritual warfare, her provisions for the needs of her children, her unfailing springs of grace in the sacraments, the great notes by which her Divine mission is attested in the world, the providential arrangement of her history, her triumphant issue from every possible form of trial and affliction, her power of healing all the ills of society, and of reclaiming to her own allegiance and care all the stray elements of good which were floating like the scattered relics of a wreck upon the stormy waters of the heathen world; or again, the beauty and Divine innocence, the sublime, intellectual achievements, or the heroic acts of virtue which mark her genuine children as the princes of the Heavenly Kingdom—all these and many more such features in the Catholic Church are full of teaching about God, Whose darling creation she is.

And again, another page which is open to us, full of the most precious revelations of God, in which His ways and works and character and attributes are to be read in letters of light, is to be found in the Sacred Scriptures, which embrace the whole history of His dealings with our race from the beginning to the end of time. Here too is a wealth and abundance of truth concerning Him which can only be mentioned, and which it must be left to meditation and reflection to draw out.

There are several ways in which God may be dis-
cerned, learned about, studied, and known by men,
even in the Church upon earth.   They are all reflections
of the light, rather than the light itself, except when
the direct light of the Godhead falls upon us from the
face of our Lord Himself, the Eternal Son, but even
the Sacred Humanity of our Lord is given to us as
a way to lead us up to the knowledge of the Godhead.
'For now we see through a glass in a dark manner,
but then it shall be face to face.'[3]   This is the one
intrinsic and essential difference between the beatific
vision of God which is promised hereafter to the clean
of heart, and any kind of vision which can be ordinarily
gained here below.   There are more special kinds of
the knowledge and vision of God which are vouchsafed
from time to time, and sometimes in a very large measure
and in a very high grade indeed, to God's favoured
servants on earth, accounts of which are given us by
mystical writers in the state of prayer.   These methods
of communication of Himself on the part of God are
as true and as much matter of fact as any outward
events or actions that meet the senses, and those to
whom they are familiar live in a world which may
almost be called their own, as much as the world in
which politicians, or artists, or men of science live.
The phenomena, the incidents, the effects, the results
of these methods of seeing God are as true and actual
as those of any other range of life which is open to
mankind.   But the narratives which treat of them are
technical in their terms, and seem to the mass, even
of ordinary Christians, like a story read to them in an
unknown tongue, and we may for the present content
ourselves with the other ordinary methods by which the
knowledge of God is obtained in the Church.

[3] I Cor. xiii. 12.

A very little consideration is needed to show us how purity of heart, in the sense in which it has been explained above, is what we may call the natural condition on which alone we can avail ourselves of all the great mass of the cognizance of God which is included under the various heads enumerated above. For in all these things God is revealing Himself indeed, but revealing Himself as the truth concerning Him is revealed by our Lord in His wonderful system of parabolic teaching. That is, there is an outside which must be penetrated, a veil which must be lifted, a secret teaching which must be brought to the surface. And this precious teaching is addressed to men, who live in the midst of a world of sense, with the clouds which are raised by passions all around them, with the falsehoods of the world painted, as it were, on every wall, with its lying maxims and principles ringing in their ears, and repeated and enforced by the example of all among whom they move, and echoed by all that is grovelling and rebellious in their own hearts. It is cleanness of heart alone that can silence the din and disperse the cloud. Even before God and the truths which concern Him are made the direct object of formal prayer and contemplation, there must be purity of heart and the humility which is its inseparable companion, or rather a part of it, before we can recognize the teaching of nature or of Providence concerning God, or listen to His reproofs or inspirations in the secret sanctuary of our own conscience. For those whose hearts are not clean, the glories of our Lord's Sacred Humanity, the perfection of the saints, and the rich beauties of the Catholic Church, are all without attraction. Nay, to such men they are too often the objects of a mad hostility which seems almost to reveal that they are under the mastery of a foe of our Lord who is more than human. The hatred with which the creation of grace inspires the slaves either of sensual passion or of intellectual pride, is such as fully to justify our Lord's warning words about casting pearls before swine. 'They trample them under their feet, and turning upon you, tear you.'[4]

When we go on to consider that it is prayer, in its largest sense, which is the means by which we take to ourselves the rich fruits of truth which are collected for us in the various stores of knowledge concerning God which have been spoken of above, it becomes still more intelligible that the condition of their enjoyment should be purity of heart, and that purity of heart should be crowned by that enjoyment as a matter of right. Prayer is the exercise of the spiritual faculties of the reason and the affections on the highest objects, indeed, which those faculties can grasp, but still the objects which, in the intention of God when He created us and when He elevated us, are their proper and destined occupations. As we have seen that man is made for justice and justice for man, so also is it true that prayer is made for man and man for prayer. But when we begin to inquire what are the conditions of the soul which are favourable or requisite for the exercise of prayer, and especially for what is more particularly known as contemplation, in which the mind and heart are fed upon God and His works, we are at once met by an answer which describes the purity of heart on which we have been engaged. Contemplation requires a quiet, calm, serious state of the soul; it is the exercise of men who carefully avoid the least deliberate fault, and have carried on the war against sin in themselves so far as to have destroyed, as far as may be, its roots and its results. These are the men who guard and mortify their senses most completely, who free them-

<hr>

4 St. Matt. vii. 6.

selves as far as possible from temporal cares and possessions, who carefully regulate their occupations, so that there may be no excessive strain or anxiety or multiplicity of affairs to distract them, while they are equally diligent in their practice of the virtues, in the constant exercise of humility, and of purity of life. These are the men who by constant practice and prayer, and often by the special grace of God assisting them, have secured the blessed gift of the continual presence of God and an almost unbroken remembrance of Him, the gift which may be said to be the practical 'sight' of God, and of which some holy writers have spoken as if it were the beginning and the middle and the end of perfection. For it is the weapon by which we are easily enabled to avoid sin, to resist temptation, to conquer bad habits, to restrain and subdue our affections and appetites, and by which we can turn even adversities and afflictions into good. It helps us to keep the fear of God in our soul, which will lead us on to true wisdom, to direct all our intentions to Him, and thus fill our hearts with all the virtues. It regulates even our exterior actions, and, much more, is a continual spur and incitement to activity and fertility in good works. Again, it prepares the soul for that peace on which contemplation is founded, chases away inordinate and unnecessary thoughts, keeps down the sensitive appetites, subdues curiosity, raises the affections to holy objects, and is, in fine, the most certain instrument for gaining all perfections. Thus its office very mainly consists in helping that purgation and cleansing of the heart of which we have been speaking, and in return, as it were, it is helped on by that very same purity. For the practice of God's presence, which seems in theory so easy, is in itself difficult, on account of the many impediments which beset us from the world, the things of sense, and most of all, from ourselves, and thus anything that sets us free from the thraldom and persecution of these impediments has a direct influence in enabling us to live in the presence of God.

In order to complete the subject of the reward of the clean of heart, it is necessary at least to allude to the various kinds of the 'sight' of God, as it may be called, which are sometimes vouchsafed to contemplative souls in the higher states of prayer, and also to refer to that blessed and Beatific Vision of Him which is the ineffable and eternal reward of the saints in Heaven. As to the first, it is very difficult to say a little without running the risk of omitting something that is important, and the language of holy writers on such subjects is hardly to be understood save by those who have some experience of these marvellous visitations of God. It must suffice here to point out that although it is true that the marvellous effects which are produced in the soul, and in some of the stages of prayer on the body also, may sometimes be the results of illusion, or again, may belong to the class of graces which are called *gratis datæ*, and so are not infallible proofs of the presence of sanctifying grace in the soul, nor evidence that they themselves proceed from God or a good spirit, still, what is enough to say for our purpose here, they ordinarily seem rightfully to belong to the high state of contemplation to which those who are pure of heart are carried when it pleases God that it shall be so. To speak of visions only, holy writers are agreed that the lowest kind, such as what are called corporeal visions, in which the senses perceive visions of our Lord or of His angels and saints, are the most liable to delusion ; whilst the highest kind, which is that of intellectual visions, cannot be produced by the evil spirit, but by God alone. These favours are bestowed by Him in that free and royal way which belongs to Him, no one has a right to expect them, it is better even not to wish for them or ask for them. But still purity of heart, in the sense in which it has been explained, is the general condition of the soul upon which these favours are bestowed by Him when He bestows them at all.

And as to that clear and intuitive vision of God which is to be the possession of the saints hereafter, which now makes the souls of the blessed in Heaven happy, and which is, indeed, the essence of their blessedness, it cannot be doubted that that also is the future reward of the clean of heart. It is indeed necessary that those who are to see Him shall be made pure. And if their purification has not been effected in this life, as to the remains of sin, the dross upon the soul, the debt due to His justice, and the like, it must be fulfilled in the flames of Purgatory, which have a necessary work to perform in fitting the souls which are committed to them for the presence and sight of God. The whole Christian doctrine concerning that blessed and merciful provision of God for enabling so many to enjoy Him for ever that would otherwise have to be banished from His presence, is a long commentary on this Beatitude. 'Blessed are the clean of heart, for they shall see God.' They shall see Him and none else shall see Him. And if there be souls which have the dignity of sanctifying grace, and the Divine adoption, and the indwelling of the Holy Ghost, and the inheritance of Heaven secured to them as a right, and which still have any stain upon them, so that they are not absolutely clean, this best and eternal good of the Beatific Vision must be denied them for a time, until they have been made perfect in their purification and so able to see God for ever.

CHAPTER XXII.

The Beatitude of the Peacemakers.

St. Matt. v. 9 ; *Vita Vitæ Nostræ*, § 31.

It might seem as if, after the Beatitude of the clean of heart, the reward of which is nothing less than the Vision of God, our Lord could go no further in His legislation and in His promises. The three first Beatitudes may be said to have regulated, according to His perfect law, the interior feelings and mental attitude of men as to their own position in relation to God, the world around them, and the conditions of life. After these three our Lord gave two more, which encouraged and commanded an immense activity in the practice of virtue of every kind, and especially in the practice of that blessed virtue of mercy which is the mainspring of the government of the world. And then He turns once more to the interior man, the affections and thoughts of his heart and mind, which are able to grasp worlds larger and nobler than that in which we are placed, and possess the power of an activity and life and energy which far surpass in range, in multiplicity, in intensity, and in continuity, the external and visible operations which lie within his reach. Over all these interior acts our Lord lays the law of perfect purity ; a law which not only forbids all obliquity of intention and perversity of action, but stimulates the energies and quickens the activity of the soul by removing the clouds and veils which float between it and the true objects of its contemplations and desires. Purity, as has been seen, gives peace, security, and liberty; it sets the faculties free from chains, so that they can leap forward to the life for which they were intended, and it opens to them new and immense fields of action, on which they would energize unceasingly, even if they had not the spurs which are supplied by the hunger and thirst after justice to urge them on, or a world full of objects of misery of every sort calling upon them for the practice of mercifulness.

It might seem, however, that now at last our Lord might pause. For after every kind of activity has been penetrated and vivified by the rays of perfect purity, it might seem as if all that man can do here below had been enjoined and regulated. And after the chain of wonderful rewards had been riveted, as it were, by the fastening of the last link, of the Vision of God Himself, it might seem as if all the crowns which can be assigned to obedience and holiness had been counted over. The sight and discernment of God have no doubt many degrees, rising from the knowledge of Him which is gained from the physical universe to that higher and intuitive contemplation of Him which is the lot of those who dwell in His home for ever. The regions which lie between these two kinds of vision, especially the regions of prayer, are wide and fertile indeed. But after all, what higher beatitude, what more intense sweetness or more lofty glory can be the lot of a creature, than that sight of God as He is, which is included in the promise to the clean of heart! And yet, as we know, our Lord has not exhausted His Beatitudes, or the rewards which He promises to the virtues of which they are the principles. God Himself is for ever essentially blessed in the contemplation of Himself, and yet God is, as our Lord says, always working, and the Incarnate Son, Who is in the bosom of the Father,

He is working always also, on a special work which is peculiarly the work of God in the present order of His providence. The blessed angels and saints who see His face, and are for ever blessed in consequence, they too are always occupied in this Divine work, in which they have their share committed to them, partly of active operation, partly of intercession and prayer. And the men who are most closely united to God in this life, those who most nearly resemble the angels and the saints in the continual occupation of their minds and hearts upon Him, men whose hearts are pure, and who so have the privilege of seeing Him in the highest manners and degrees which are within the reach of those who are still upon earth, these men are invited by this seventh Beatitude to occupy themselves also in that work of God on which the hearts of all Heaven are bent, that is, the work of peace in its highest sense. And as a reward for this work, our Lord has a crown to hold out which is in some respects nobler even than that which is promised in the last Beatitude, for it promises them a special share in that seemingly in-communicable privilege of His own, His Divine Sonship. All Christians, indeed, have power and authority given to them by Him to become the sons of God by adoption, and this sonship, therefore, must be claimed for all who have been born again in the waters of Baptism. But the sonship which is gained by that blessed sacrament may fall to the lot of many who have never had a share on earth in that work of which we speak, which is the special work of the Son, because there are millions of souls in Heaven who have died after Baptism and before attaining either the age of reason or the time when they could take their part in that work. But there are others who shall be, and shall be called the sons of God. They shall not only have the quality of brethren of Jesus

Christ inherent in their spiritual nature, recognized by the eyes of Heaven, and terrible on that account to the enemies of God and His creatures, but they shall exercise and prove their brotherhood by bearing a part in the eyes of the world in the work which is here called the work of making peace. The pure in heart may see God, and their secret may remain their own. The peacemakers labour in a business which lays them open to the eyes of angels and men, and proclaims to all who see them that they are the brethren of Jesus Christ because they carry on in a special manner the work which He came to do. So thus then, 'Blessed are the peacemakers, for they shall be called the sons of God.'

These last remarks lead us by anticipation to the very highest sense in which our Lord's words in this Beatitude can be understood, and we must therefore, before continuing the train of thought which they suggest, turn back to the more ordinary exercises of the virtue of the peacemakers. And we are struck at once with the truth that, as to the virtue which is commanded in this seventh Beatitude, the remark already made more than once as to others in the series must be repeated. There is a natural love of peace in the heart of man, and there are some persons who seem to possess in an eminent degree the natural virtue which corresponds to that love, and to desire peace, and so seek to discharge, after a fashion, the blessed office of the peacemakers. Again, like mercy, this devotion to peace is a virtue very attractive in the eyes of the world, and there can hardly be said to be any degree of civilization and culture among people where peace is not considered an object of desire, and where the peacemakers are not held in a kind of honour. We see the same in households, in families, and among nations. No one professes to make war except for the purpose of securing peace; no one ever professes to love contention for its own sake, or to be unwilling to make peace when just claims have been satisfied. Or, if this cannot be said of some wars of modern times, in which aggression and conquest have been almost openly the motives which have set in conflict hundreds of thousands of men on both sides belonging to nations which still call themselves Christian, the conduct of the ambitious men who thus wantonly cause so much bloodshed and such widespread misery is abhorred in secret by the public conscience, and where it is not abhorred, the fact is a sign of that advance of barbarism which has many other evidences to witness to it.

And yet, notwithstanding the apparent easiness and natural attractiveness of this virtue, our Lord places the peacemakers, as He has placed the merciful, late in the order of those who practise the virtues which He declares to be so highly blessed. For the true peacemaker, like the truly merciful man, must have gone through a long process of interior training, and must have practised many virtues which involve serious effort and resolute self-discipline, as well as a frequent use of the sacraments and close union with God in prayer. There must first be won the peace of his own heart and soul, and we have but to recall what has been said in the Beatitude which immediately precedes this in order to see how naturally, in the order of spiritual perfection, peacemaking follows upon purity of heart. For purity in heart and peace of heart are the same things under different aspects. Those who have got rid of sin and its remains, and of imperfect habits, and faults of character, and, as far as may be, even of the weaknesses of human nature as far as they are manifested in what infects or disturbs the soul, are enabled by the grace of God to see Him in the various manners and degrees which have been enumerated, and the sight of God, in whatever degree it is obtained, is the direct cause and security of peace. This peace as yet has only been considered as reigning in the hearts and souls of those who thus, after many internal struggles and by means of much prayer and toil, have been enabled to win the priceless grace of interior purity. But such persons do not win peace for themselves only. The knowledge of God and the joy which it generates cannot but produce in them the instinctive and almost unconscious tendency to spread around them their own light and joy, and thus to become centres from which peace may radiate on all around them. Still nothing short of purity can make a human soul a true cause of peace, because all passion and self-interest and prejudice and narrowness, all hardness and stiffness of character, indeed, all imperfections, are in a certain sense and to a certain degree the causes of positive dissension or of the absence of that active and energetic charity in which true peace consists. For the calm of death, when quiet reigns because there are no forces left to live or move or energize, when there is silence because there are no voices to break it, is not true peace. The peace of which God is the author is the peace which keeps in tranquil order and perfect harmony elements which, if left to themselves, might jar upon one another, forces, the conflict of which would issue in mighty shocks and terrible collisions, and which are yet made to work together in that smoothness and perfect balance which characterizes the operations of nature, and by their mutual concord to gain an efficiency and to produce a whole marvellous alike for its symmetry and for its might. We may thus easily understand how the men who are to earn the blessing of the peacemakers must begin by ruling themselves in absolute peace, and how the simple

tranquillity of their own hearts makes them also, first
of all, to be so entirely masters of themselves as to keep
perfect peace with their neighbours, and then to go on
to what is properly the office of those whom our Lord
here speaks of, the office of reconciling those who are
at discord among themselves, and spreading peace over
the world, not, as the Romans of old,[1] by the power
of their arms and the strong justice of their laws, but
by curing the diseases of the soul and removing the very
roots from which discord springs.

Another resemblance between the Beatitude of the
peacemakers and that of the merciful is to be found in
the immense multiplicity and variety of the works which
engage the exertions of both. A very large portion
indeed of the miseries of the world have their source
in discord, and thus an equally large portion of the
efforts made by merciful men to relieve those miseries
would fall under the head of peacemaking. Anything
that is strained and exaggerated in the relations of life
generates discord. If parents exceed their rights and
are cruel to their children; if the husband is a tyrant
over his wife, or the master over his servant, if, in a
political community, a certain class possessed of power
uses it harshly and selfishly to grind down the rest, the
fires of discord are lighted, and it is only a question
of time when they will burst out. Thus anything that
softens manners and introduces more just and equitable
relations either between class and class, or between the
members of smaller societies, such as the family, is a
work of peace, though not so directly as the interference
between enemies in order to bring about reconciliation
between them. Viewed in this light the action of the
Church on society has ever been the fulfilment of the

---

[1] Hæ tibi erunt artes, pacisque imponere morem,
Parcere subjectis, et debellare superbos.

command implied in this Beatitude. She it is who gradually put an end to the barbarities which prevailed even among the most civilized nations in the world, to whom it was the will of God that she should first address herself. It took her many years, even after the Empire had become Christian, to abolish the gladiatorial shows. It took her still longer to raise the condition of the slave, until slavery was practically abolished. It was before her influence that the horrible practices of abortion or of the exposure of infants, and of human sacrifices, died away. She regenerated the family, elevated woman, destroyed polygamy, established a holy Christian equality between husband and wife. Her influence has always been directed to the softening of the horrors of war, if she could not abolish altogether that great scourge of mankind which God keeps in His own hands to chastise public sins. The mediæval institution of the Truce of God is an illustration of this. It would be absurd to deny that the most Christian ages of Europe were miserably disfigured by wars, and that the wars which are related in the page of history give by no means an adequate representation of the violence and quarrelsomeness of times when the barons made war upon one another on their own account, and neighbouring cities were continually endeavouring to settle their differences or jealousies by private war rather than by arbitration or justice. But the work of the Church must be estimated by what she could effect, not by what was beyond her power. The Popes were the general pacificators, and the wars which they hindered might have been far more sanguinary than those which they could not prevent. Again, exertions were made by the Church to ransom captives, to soften criminal legislation, to put an end to duelling, and to produce other mitigations of the fruits of the want of peace in the world. It may be

said that in no department of her great work in the
world has the Church more clearly shown her Divine
spirit and her tender care for human happiness ; while
in no other has she had more difficulties to contend with
and been more resolutely opposed by human passions,
which in many cases had become almost canonized
in the minds of peoples and nations into objects of
worship to which it was wrong to deny homage and
obedience. The national spirit, everywhere, in its merely
human aspect, and apart from the true light which faith
sheds upon the origin of society and the brotherhood
of all mankind, has gathered under its flag a whole band
of enmities and malices, the traditions of hatred and the
creeds of revenge. The same spirit has even broken
large masses of Christian populations off from the unity
of the Church, and in our own days has been the power
invoked to bring about her slavery to the State in many
countries and her spoliation in others. The maintenance
of universal peace among a confraternity of Christian
nations has been the dream of many a saint as well as
of many a statesman, and it cannot be denied that the
principle of peace and of peacemaking which our Lord
has enshrined in His Beatitude contains within itself
no less splendid a result. But the fulfilment of such
aspirations can only be in a perfect state of the whole
Christian society, and human passions have as yet been
far too powerful to permit of such a consummation. In
such a state of the world the work of the peacemaker
would cease, because peace would reign universally.

It follows that the world, as it is always full of objects
on which the merciful may spend their labours and
energies, so it will always be full of work for the children
and messengers of peace. Every preacher or minister
of the religion of our Lord is in the highest sense a
peacemaker, because it is his office to reconcile man

to God and to his own conscience, and to enable him to maintain peace in his own soul and with all around him, by the knowledge of the truth and the use of the means of grace. In another sense also he is a peacemaker, because he teaches the truths which give repose and satisfaction to the restless mind of man, which is always striving to solve the riddle of his existence and of the condition of the world around him, and peer into the darkness which hides the mysteries of the past and of the future. And by imparting true light as to these necessary problems, the religion of our Lord also puts men at peace with their lot; it explains to them what seems hard and unjust, it softens the blows of adversity, it makes them accept pain, misery, bereavement, affliction of every kind, in a spirit of penitence and resignation, and, instead of the gloomy or rebellious anticipations as to the future which have borne such miserable fruit in the minds of unbelievers and sceptics, it reconciles them to the ordinances of God by the light with which Christianity opens to the mind the view of an endless eternity of happiness. Faith reconciles man to the government of the world, however hard it may press upon him here and now. Hope puts an end to his quarrel with the uncertainties of the future, while charity reveals to him a new law promulgated by a God Who hung for him upon a Cross, whereby his peace with all around him is enjoined by the precept of the forgiveness of injuries and of the love of enemies.

The mention of these two great acts of Christian virtue leads us to the work of the peacemaker as it affects the relations of men one to another, and especially of those who have either inflicted or received injuries. These are the two heroic acts of Christian peacefulness, and the multiplied instances in which they have been put into execution by the saints and by others whom·

their example and exhortations have led to this virtue are enough to make us understand that our Lord has here commanded nothing that, difficult as it may be, is beyond the power of man assisted by His grace. They show also that our Lord's words have been taken in their fullest and plainest meaning by His saints, who have not failed when themselves greatly calumniated, as St. Francis of Sales, or when it was in accordance with the laws of honour of the time to avenge a brother, as St. John Gualbert, or when they have been exposed to personal violence and their lives attempted, like St. Andrew of Avellino and St. Charles Borromeo, to carry out the commandment of the love of enemies to the letter, by showering the most prodigal kindnesses upon those who have inflicted the injuries, or upon their representatives. And the work of bringing about reconciliations, whether between man and man, or between families and communities, has filled a large space in the lives of many of the saints, such as St. Bernardine of Siena, St. James of the March, St. John of St. Facundus, and others, who have lived in times and countries in which traditional feuds were almost a part of every man's patrimony, and the duty of revenge considered as incumbent upon Christians. It has required all the authority of the saintly character, all the force and energy of the words which came from the mouths of men held in such high veneration, all the weight of the example and precept of our Lord, and sometimes even displays of miraculous power, to enforce the words of the pleader for peace, to enable even men who have the faith, and profess to live up to the Christian law, to conquer themselves so far as to submit to this law of forgiveness and of the love of enemies. On the other hand, such submission has been constantly rewarded by very great ·favours and graces, not the least of which is the confidence which the victory over self and human respect engenders in the heart. For all can understand the truth of what has been said by one of the servants of God, that if He were to reveal to us all the secrets of His most holy Heart, if He were to raise us day after day to the vision of the angelic choirs, if He were to give us the power of recalling the dead to life, all such favours would not make us so infallibly certain of His love as we should be if we could feel that with all our hearts we do good to those who have done us evil, and speak well of those who speak evil of us, and condemn us unjustly. For in the latter case the reward of the Beatitude would be ours, and we should feel that we were in truth the children of the Most High.[2] And if the blessing which results from obedience to the precept of forgiveness and the love of enemies is so great, even greater in proportion must be the blessing of those who not only obey this commandment, but bring others under its gentle yoke, for our Lord says, a little further on in this Sermon on the Mount, that 'he that shall do and teach shall be called great in the Kingdom of Heaven.'[3]

It must not, of course, be supposed that the Beatitude on which we are now engaged differs from the others in being reserved for any particular class of Christians, as, for instance, for those who are called to the duties of the ministry. On the contrary, all Christians have the duty and the blessing to be the messengers and propagators of peace, both by their example and by their influence. This may easily be seen when we consider what are the provisions by means of which God has ordained that peace should be maintained in the societies which He has established. One great provision to which

---

[2] B. Bapt. Verana, *Cronic. Sti. Francisci*, p. 4, t. ii. l. vii. c. 26.
[3] St. Matt. v. 19.

all are bound in the natural society as well as in the supernatural Body of the Church is to be found in the law against detraction. Detraction, as all know, differs from calumny in that the latter consists in a false charge against our neighbour's character, while detraction is the circulation of the truth concerning him to his detriment, without some fitting motive which overrides in his particular case the duty of silence. Thus the fault of detraction rests partly on the unlawful assumption on our part of the right to judge and condemn, which belongs to God alone, but it is also founded upon the duty which is incumbent upon us of guarding the reputation of our neighbour in the interests of peace. Detraction is thus a distinct violation of the law of peace, and that it should be classed among sins is a proof of the importance which God attaches to the maintenance of peace. The unkind thought, the uncharitable judgment, the evil wish, the malicious desire, do not go beyond the heart which conceives them, and although they stain it with sin, they do not directly violate the public peace. But when they come to be expressed in words, and are sent forth, never to be recalled, to work upon the minds and hearts and conduct of others, they thus acquire a grievous character in addition to their own intrinsic malice, because they affect peace. So it is in the natural human society, of which God is the author and the protector ; and other instances might be adduced of sins which are what they are, because they have the same character of assailants of the common good-will and good opinion of men towards and of one another. There are several virtues, on the other hand, such as truthfulness, faithfulness, the keeping of secrets, hospitality, and the like, the obligations of which rest in great measure on the duty, not only of preserving, but of fostering and increasing peace. And, again, the strong language of Holy Scripture about sins of the tongue, of which there are many kinds besides detraction, can best be explained by considering the tongue as the instrument which God expects us to use for the propagation of peace and charity. In the light of these thoughts we have a large range of actions opened to us as enjoined by this Beatitude. We are not only not to be contentious, arrogant, false, boastful, and the like, but we are to make the guarding and the advancement of peace, in the ordinary sense, a distinct and deliberate study, a work to be as much insisted on and cultivated as mercifulness itself, a work for the sake of which sacrifices are to be made, and many things foregone which it might be otherwise well to do, a work of prayer, and thought, and suffering, as well as of action.

In the supernatural society we gather in the same way the value which God attaches to all that serves to maintain peace and union from the penalties which are attached to those who in any way attack them. It has pleased God that the Church should be so far the city of perfect peace, even upon earth, that unity of faith and discipline shall be matters of distinct precept and peremptory obligation. Unity of faith is violated by heresy, while schism is the sin which lies in division of the one visible Body in which the Holy Ghost dwells. The schismatic may profess to believe all Catholic doctrines—except, of course, the doctrine of the obligation of unity—and yet he cannot be saved, because schism of itself, the mere act of division, as such, is a deadly sin. The precept of unity, for sake of argument, may be compared to the commandment of God given to our first parents, which forbade on the ground of simple obedience, something which in itself was not forbidden. As God by that precept showed, as has already been said, how much importance He attached to the virtue of obedience as such, whatever might be the subject-matter of the command, so it may be said that if schism had not, as it has, a number of fruits and consequences which give it a character of deadliness, the fact that it has been, as it were, made a special sin which Christians are bound to avoid under pain of forfeiting their chances of salvation itself, shows how intensely dear to God is unity of every kind among His children. In this view, we gain an idea of the enormity of the crime of those unhappy men who are the authors of schisms in the Christian body, just as by considering the penalties of the sin of detraction, and of other sins of the tongue, which do not seem grievous sins except when they are looked upon in the light of the charity which God has made the law of society, we come to understand how much His anger is provoked by those who infringe that law in any way. And the misery of those who are the authors of dis-union, whether in the natural society or in the Church, helps us to conceive the extreme blessedness of those who, on the other hand, by example and influence, are labourers in the cause of peace. By the blessing of the peacemakers, our Lord seems to give us to understand that He commissions us all to be guardians of peace in all the spheres in which we move, and that its preservation is to be as dear to us even as our own union with God, as important as the practice of virtue and of mercy. And as has been already said, we are to be not only guardians, but makers of peace, restoring it where it has been lost, and increasing it where it already exists only in an imperfect degree. We are to help men to keep or regain the peace of their own consciences, and that empire over their passions, which is the peace of the heart. We are to serve the cause of peace by our own use of the tongue, to make peace between neighbours or members of families who are at variance, and in general to labour to all that conduces to the peace of the State in which we live and the several classes of which it is made up, and of the whole world and all the States which compose it. Very dear indeed to our heart must be social peace, but still dearer the peace of the Church, and the peace of all men with God. Thus everything that advances the knowledge of God, every-thing that serves to destroy error and prejudice, to put an end to the rebellion of schism and the self-will of heresy, whether they have been inherited or deliberately chosen, all the work of enlightening ignorance and spreading truth of any kind, the work of true civilization as well as of Evangelical preaching, the work of putting an end to scientific pride and childish scepticism by helping men to reason logically and modestly in matters which concern revelation, as well as the work of reform-ing manners and checking un-Christian license and luxury—all these are the work of the peacemaker, which earn for him, as we shall see, the high reward of being called, with a higher right even than ordinary Christians, the son of God and the brother of Jesus Christ.

CHAPTER XXIII.

The Sons of God.

St. Matt. v. 9 ; *Vita Vitæ Nostræ*, § 31.

IT is not difficult to see that the work of the peacemaker, such as it has been sketched in the last chapter, must be a work full of happiness and blessing and consolation to those who are engaged upon it. In those who are peacemakers of the kind of which our Lord speaks, the passions have been conquered and the mind and heart filled with the noblest spiritual thoughts and desires. They are anchored upon the vision of God, and the work which they do is done with the purest intention for His glory, and, at the same time, in perfect resignation to His will, without which no success can be gained, and against which there can be no failure. The blessedness of the work of peace may be described in the words which form part of our Lord's instructions to the Apostles and the seventy-two disciples : " Into whatsoever house ye enter, first say, Peace be to this house. And if the son of peace be there, your peace shall rest upon him, but if not, it shall return to you.'[1] There can be no question, therefore, of the perfect peace which the peacemakers win for themselves. Their work is a constant exercise of the highest virtues, for it requires, as has been seen, a great amount of self-conquest and self-denial, and it is exposed in the present state of the

[1] St. Luke x. 5, 6 ; St. Matt. x. 12, 13.

world to much opposition and many storms, so that
the passive virtues of patience, humility, meekness, and
the like are not less called into play than the active
virtues of charity and zeal. It is a work which is
removed as far as possible from the danger of all lower
temptations and ambitions, and, on that account also,
is highly blessed. No more need be said to point
out its intrinsic happiness, the reward which it contains
within itself.

The special boon, however, of this Beatitude is one
which requires a more detailed examination. The peacemakers are blessed, because they shall be called the
sons of God. In the language of Scripture and of our
Lord, to say that a person or persons shall be called
this or that is the same thing as to say that they shall
be so, unless indeed, as has been already said, the
expression means universally, what it certainly means
in some passages, that the name applied shall not only
belong to the person spoken of, but also that it shall
be known that he is what the name denotes. Thus it
is used by the Angel to our Blessed Lady at the Annun-
ciation, 'The Holy which shall be born of thee shall be
called the Son of God.'[2] The promise, then, of this
Beatitude is that the peacemakers shall be in a special
manner the sons of God. It has already been said that
the adoptive sonship of God is the privilege communicated to all Christians in their Baptism, while the fulness
of the Divine Sonship can belong to no one but the
only-begotten Son of God Himself. We must therefore
look for some special reason why the peacemakers may
claim the name as a title of their own and in a sense of
their own.

Three things, says St. Bernardine, make a man the
son of God. The first is formed faith.[3] Lively faith is

---

[2] St. Luke i. 35.   [3] *Fides Formata.*

like a life-giving ray which descends as a free gift into
the human intellect from the Source of Life. He applies
to this the famous words of the Psalm, 'The light of
Thy countenance, O Lord, is signed upon us: Thou
hast given gladness in my heart.'[4] The countenance of
God, he says, is reason, because it is by the countenance that one man is like another, and that he recognizes
another, and it is by reason that we are like to God and
know God. But the light of His countenance is faith
made formal by sanctifying grace. For as a coin is
without form, until the image of the King is stamped
upon it by the die, so is our reason unformed, until it
is enlightened from Heaven by the grace of formal faith.
He quotes the words of St. Paul to the Ephesians, 'In
whom also believing you were signed with the Holy
Spirit of promise, which is the pledge of our inheritance,'[5]
and says it is to such faith St. John's words apply, 'To
as many as received Him, to them He gave power
to be made the sons of God, to them that believe in
His name.'[6] The second thing which makes men sons
of God, St. Bernardine proceeds, is perfect charity, and
on this he quotes the words of our Lord further on in the
Sermon on the Mount, 'I say to you, love your enemies,
do good to them that hate you, and pray for them that
persecute and calumniate you, that you may be the
children of your Father Who is in Heaven, who maketh
the sun to rise upon the good and bad, and raineth upon
the just and the unjust.'[7] And he says, this sonship is
not natural, but consists in imitation and grace. You
are already children in hope, be so in deed, and your
rewards shall answer to your merits. There is a two-fold
sublimity, he says, in this love of enemies, a formal and
a final sublimity. The formal sublimity is the share

[4] Psalm iv. 7.

[5] Ephes. i. 13.   [6] St. John i. 12.   [7] St. Matt. v. 44, 45.

V 2

which those who practise this lofty virtue have in the
Divine resemblance, because they perfectly imitate the
nature of God, for God is charity. And thus they are
the sons of God. And again, God will honour and
elevate such persons as His children, and this is what
He calls the 'final' sublimity, they shall have the right
of sons in the inheritance of their Father. And thus
this reward is assigned in the seventh Beatitude, that of
the peacemakers, because for any one to love perfectly
his greatest enemies cannot be without some ineffable
outpouring and abundance of Divine peace. And the
third thing which makes men obtain the reward of being
the sons of God, says the Saint, is the concord of peace.
And he quotes the explanation of St. Chrysostom of this
Beatitude, which amounts to this, that peacemakers and
peaceable persons, who have no hatred, who do not
quarrel, but rather reconcile those who are at variance,
are rightly called the sons of God, because it is the
work of the only-begotten Son to gather together what
has been scattered abroad, and to bring to peace things
that were at war one with another. Such sonship to God
implies likeness to Him, for it is the peculiar privilege of
God to enjoy His own felicity and to be at rest and
peace in Himself.

This last thought of the resemblance of the peacemakers to God, and of the work of His only-begotten
Son in the world, is sufficient to open to us a very wide
field of contemplation as to this Beatitude. It must be
remembered that it is not merely peaceableness which
is here blessed, but the virtue which lies in positive and
active peacemaking. Now this may be said to be in a
special manner the chosen work of the children of God.
As has already been said, God Himself is always working,
and His work is always the work of peace. That this
should be so is, as will be seen presently, a result of

His own nature and character. And because this is His work, it is the work also of His Son, and of all that are to share in this special way the relationship of sonship to the Father. 'The Son,' our Lord said to the Jews, 'cannot do anything of Himself but what He seeth the Father doing. For what things soever He doth, these the Son also doth in like manner. For the Father loveth the Son, and showeth Him all things which He Himself doth.'[8] We shall presently see what is the work of peace on which the Father is always employed. But it must first be understood how this work flows from the Nature of God. God is the essential and primal Peacemaker, because God is Himself Eternal and Uncreated Peace. Peace is the harmony and tranquillity of order and of union, and God Himself is the Eternal Peace, as He is the Eternal Light and Love, because the ineffable union and oneness and harmony and order which bind together the Three Divine Persons in the Unity of the Godhead is itself the essential and archetypal peace, and the fountain and pattern of peace to all who are not God. The mutual knowledge and love and unity and relations of the Father, the Son, and the Holy Ghost, each though a distinct Person, possessing the fulness of the Divine Nature, each God and yet the three not three Gods but one God—these constitute the Uncreated Peace which has been from all eternity, and will be throughout all eternity, and which is the foundation and model of all peace which is not uncreated and eternal. And when it pleased God, according to our modes of conceiving and expressing Divine things, that there should be others besides Himself to whom He would impart some of His own gifts, and make them be and exist and live and know and choose and love, according to the manner and character of the being, life,

[8] St. John v. 19, 20.

energy, and capacity of intelligence and will and choice which He thought fit to impart to them in their several gradations of being, then it was a part of His Divine counsel that, outside Himself, in the universe which He made, and in the creatures with which He peopled it, in themselves, and towards one another, and towards Him, there should be peace and order and harmony which might reflect His own tranquillity and unity. For the whole universe was designed in many various ways to reflect His attributes, and, as His Beauty and Wisdom and Power are imaged in His creatures, so also did He will that they should represent His Peace.

This reign of peace, which is secured by the observance of law, keeps the whole physical universe together. It is made up of an almost infinite variety and multitude of parts, of natures of every grade and kind, of an immense number of forces which have only to be let loose from the constraint of law to rush into confusion, conflict, and destruction. The balance is kept by the law which God has impressed upon the whole and on every part of it, and which is punctually and exactly obeyed. It is this variety and diversity among the creatures which makes it possible for them to glorify their Creator, not only singly by reflecting what each can reflect of Him, but also as a whole, by the harmony and order which reign among them. The homage of the universe as such is founded upon its peace. 'Great peace is to them who love Thy law,' says the Psalmist, and his words are true of all God's creatures, inanimate as well as animate, material as well as spiritual, whether intelligent or free, or guided by instinct and the law of nature inherent in them. God has given them a law which shall not be broken, and in doing this He acted and acts as a giver and maker of peace. This is the first sense, then, in which this name of Author of Peace applies to God. And it is this glory which He gains from the observance of His law by the physical creation which is often the subject of praise and exaltation in the Psalms and Prophets. And certainly God deserves great glory in this way, which Christians may well study in these days, when He is, as it were, put aside out of His own creation, the forces and system of which have never, perhaps, been better understood than now, while He Who made and sustains all has never been more for-gotten. The whole universe is a great and harmonious concert of praise to Him, each nature and each creature fulfilling the law of its being, keeping in its appointed place, and supplying what it is intended to supply in the harmony of the whole. It is the moral and human world alone that has broken the concert, and by its own dissonance has marred the harmony of the rest. And this truth is often witnessed to by the soothing and tran-quillizing effect which, up to a certain point, the more lonely and more uninvaded aspects of nature produce on minds which are ill at ease with themselves, with the world around them, and with God. Whenever we can grasp at one sight a comparatively large aspect of the natural world, as when we gaze up at the starry sky, or look over a landscape of wide plains or lofty mountains, or escape from the turmoil of society and life to the tranquil sea, the disquiet and restlessness and pettiness of our own hearts seem to be rebuked, as if we were in the presence of something which reminds us that the mighty and eternal peacefulness of God Himself is reflected in His lower creatures, and that there ought to be in the hearts and souls of those who have a spiritual nature akin to His, which raises even the lowest being of all those who share it so infinitely higher than the whole physical universe, something analogous to the same ineffable calm. ·

If so much glory to God is derived from the dominion of peace in the physical universe, it is clear that the unresisted prevalence of the same law in the world of humanity must be fraught with a still higher measure of honour to the Creator of all. God intended that it should be so, and that while the peace of the whole universe gave praise to Him and secured life and happiness to the lower creatures, the observance of the same law by the higher creatures endowed with intelligence and freedom, should render to Him a far higher amount of glory and secure to them a far nobler happiness, because far more near in its resemblance to His own. Every intelligent soul is a world in itself, the elements of which are to glorify God by peace under law. Man is to be at peace with himself, with God above him, and with all around him. He has various faculties, but all are to work harmoniously together, in due subordination and obedience. This harmony and peace of the interior kingdom of man, was to be secured by his obedience to the law of God, as witnessed to by his conscience, and as expressed to him by any declaration or revelation that he might receive mediately or immediately, from God Himself. Thus man was to be at peace with his God, and a lasting and deep happiness was to be his portion in consequence of that peace. Again, as man was created in society, he was also to be at peace with his neighbour, and the joyful discharge of all mutual duties was to be the means by which the charities of life were to be multiplied and intensified. Glorious to God as is the harmony of all the forces and elements of the material universe under the rule of the law which He has imposed upon them, far more noble and far more glorious to Him was to be the harmony of the whole community of free and intelligent beings whom He had made after His own image and likeness. Their service to Him was to be that of children, not of slaves, and the virtues in which their obedience to Him and their harmony with one another were to consist were to be far more pleasing to Him than the inanimate homage of the universe, because they are the exercise of the faculties of a spiritual nature like His own. As God had provided in the faculties with which He had endowed man, and in His own continual assistance to him, for the easy observance of the law of peace in the management of man's own soul, so also in the same constitution of man had He provided for the world-wide peace which was to be so fair a thing in the sight of Heaven. And the law of peace in which He thus provided the material universe, the moral world of mankind, and each single soul of the human race, was to rise still higher in the order of creation, and embrace the multitudinous orders and ranks of the heavenly host, the highest of all God's creatures in the order of their nature. They too, as was most meet, were to be at peace with themselves, with their Creator, and with one another, and, with man and the material universe, were to make up the great concert, so to speak, of all the works of His hands, each order of which had its certain relations to the rest, and thus by the one subordination and mutual interdependence of the several natures and of all the members of each, the peace of the Godhead itself was so represented and reflected to the glory of Him Who had made the whole, in this respect, as a shadow of Himself.

This is the account which may be given of the first great peacemaking on the part of God. We know that this first design of His was, in our way of speaking, partially defeated, because He allowed it so to be for purposes of His own greater glory, and that discord and its follower, ruin, were introduced by the perverse will of creatures to whom He had given the privilege

of freedom of choice, first into Heaven—where the havoc,
as far as it extended, was irreparable at least to those
who chose war rather than peace; then into earth—where
full and overabundant reparation was at once provided
by the promise of the Incarnation; and, through the fall
of man, even into the inferior creation of which he is
the lord. We need not now dwell upon the subject
further than to consider how it gave occasion to God
once more to 'make peace' in a manner which called
for the most glorious exercise of His Wisdom, Power,
and Love, than He has ever displayed. This was the
great work of the Incarnation, in which God made peace
between Himself and man, in which the losses of Heaven
were repaired by the admission of men to its glories,
and in which the lower creation has its share, as has
already been seen from the words of St. Paul to the
Romans. This peace on earth was the song of the Angels
at the Nativity of our Lord, in Whom, as the Apostle
says, 'it hath well pleased the Father that all fulness
should dwell, and through Him to reconcile all things
unto Himself, making peace through the Blood of His
Cross, both as to the things that are on earth, and the
things that are in Heaven.'[9]

Thus for the second time did God become the author
of Peace in His own Kingdom. The execution of the
great council of peace was committed to the Eternal
Son in His Human Nature, Who thus becomes the
Prince of Peace, the Angel of the Great Counsel. Thus
peace is the characteristic of the Incarnation, in a higher
sense than it was the characteristic of the creation and
of the government of God in the world. In the New
Testament God seems to delight in the name of the God
of peace, which St. Paul continually gives Him, and the
peace of which He is the God is the Christian peace,

<hr>

[9] Coloss. i. 19, 20.

the peace that is through our Lord.[10] Peace is the substance of the Gospel, for God sent His word 'preaching peace through Jesus Christ,'[11] and so we find it continually used by the Apostles as their salutation at the beginning of their Epistles, and it seems evident that in them it is an echo of the greeting of our Lord after His Resurrection, when He first saluted them in that way, having before promised that He would leave them His peace.[12] The working out of this peace in the world is the office of the Holy Ghost, Who uses as His instrument the whole Body of the Church, with all her hierarchy, sacraments, members, and means of grace, as well as His own interior action, for He, being God, has immediate access to the hearts and souls of men. This, then, in brief, is the great work of the Incarnation of the Son of God. And, as has already been more than once pointed out, it is the will of God that men should co-operate largely in this work, or rather that the visible carrying on of the work should be entrusted to men.

Here, then, we have the full meaning of the crown which is promised to the peacemakers. They are the 'workers together with God' in the great undertaking of the restoration of peace which He has committed to His Son. The whole Church is a vast organization of peace, penetrating the whole of society, spreading itself over the whole world, making peace in souls, peace in families, peace in kingdoms, giving peace to the mind

[10] Romans xv. 33, xvi. 20; 2 Cor. xiii. 11 ; Philipp. iv. 9; 1 Thess. v. 23 ; Hebrews xiii. 20.

[11] Acts x. 36.

[12] See the beginnings of all the Epistles of St. Paul, except that to the Hebrews, which is rather a treatise than an Epistle. The same salutation is used by St. Peter at the beginning of his second Epistle, and at the end of his first ; and by St. John, in his second and third. It is clear that the peace here spoken of is the Gospel peace, the peace of the new Creation.

and heart, satisfying intellect and conscience, answering all questions, healing all sores, pardoning all sins, soothing all complaints, quelling all murmurs, and removing even the roots and sources of disquiet as to the past and the future. The world and man without God are like a troubled sea, the waves of which know no rest. Rest and peace are the gifts of God, the gifts which no one but God can give. This is the one work on which God and Jesus Christ are engaged, which occupies alike the angels and the saints, the Church in all her ministrations and sacraments, all her missioners, all her prelates, all her priests, the hermits and monks in their retirement, the active Orders in their works of spiritual mercy, every Christian, high and low, at the altar, in prayer, and in daily life and intercourse with men. There is no work but this which is worthy of the attention and industry of the children of God. Well, indeed, may it have the highest crown, and those who advance it be called His sons. By the Word of God all things were made, and the children of God are His instruments in the building up of that new and far fairer creation, spiritual, moral, and material, which is to succeed to this, when the time has come for Him to establish at last the Kingdom of eternal peace, when heaven and earth shall be made new.

CHAPTER XXIV.

The Beatitude of the Persecuted.

St. Matt. v. 10 ; *Vita Vitæ Nostræ,* § 31.

THE Beatitude of the Peacemakers seems in one sense naturally to end the chain of these wonderful principles of perfection which our Lord is enacting upon the Mount. It sets before us that most blessed work of peace, which is the chosen work of God and of His Incarnate Son, as committed also to men who are enabled by the perfection to which the former Beatitudes have brought them to become His instruments in the execution of His great and eternal counsels, and who receive from the Holy Spirit of Peace a special guidance and a special power and consolation in the discharge of their commission. After the vision of God comes the work of peace, and the work of peace is so noble and so dear to Him that it gives to those who undertake it and further it the power to become, in a still more special manner than before, the sharers in the Sonship of the Word made Flesh. They are in a particular, and we might almost say, an official manner, fellow-workers with our Lord in that special Mission for the sake of which He became Man, the end of which was that men might become the children of God. Here, then, we might again expect that the stream of blessings would stop, leaving us before the throne of the Father in Heaven, beholding Him face to face, and acknowledged by Him as His children through the Son of His love.

But the unexpectedness and apparent strangeness which characterize so many of the Beatitudes have yet to be seen in one more instance, and in this case too it will turn out that when we look closely at what strikes us at first sight with wonder, we shall find that faith and reason alike concur in showing us new and beautiful truths where we did not expect them. The great peace between Heaven and earth, God and man, man and himself, man and Providence, man and his neighbour, which was the work of the Incarnation, was not like the peace which succeeds some earthly war of exhaustion and ruin, a truce or armistice which leaves the enmity and alienation of hearts with which the strife began only enhanced and embittered, though it is necessary for a time that open war should cease. The peace of God, like all that comes from His hand, is deep and solid and substantial, the enmity is done away with altogether, justice and love and charity are set up in its place. God is our Father and we are His children, the brethren of Jesus Christ, and in Him brothers one to another. The peace which has been won is not external only, but internal, peace in the heart and mind, peace without flaw, penetrating the whole man and the whole world. It is not transient, either, or partial, but universal and eternal. But it has all these qualities because it has been purchased at a great price. Peace has been made through the Blood of the Cross. This is what it cost to redeem the world, and reconcile man to God. Thus, as has been said above, our Lord's first recorded utterance of His own special salutation of peace was after His Resurrection, when the price had been entirely paid, and the victory was His own by right. It is on the Passion that the peace which our Lord brought with Him from the grave was founded. He entered Jerusalem in triumph on Palm Sunday, because He was

then about to consummate the work of peacemaking.
He was nailed to the Cross on Good Friday, and then
and there it was that peace was won. He rose again
on Easter Day, and then His peace, which He came
to spread over the whole creation of God for ever and
ever, was with Him, to give to whom He chose.

It could not have been impossible for God to arrange
that the peace which had cost our Lord so dear should
make its way over the world, without any necessity for
the repetition in the persons of those to whom the
spreading of it was committed, of the conditions of
opposition and suffering which had been necessary in
Him Who was the author and purchaser of this peace. It
could not have been impossible, but still it was not so to
be. The hostility which greeted our Lord, the outburst
of wilful passion and hatred against God which brought
about our Lord's condemnation and crucifixion, were,
in a sense, the inevitable issue of the appearance of
ineffable holiness under a form of weakness, in a world
without faith, in which passion reigned and over which
the powers of evil had established so firm a dominion.
Not Judas, nor Caiphas, nor Herod alone were enemies
of our Lord: the whole corrupt world was His enemy,
and fell upon Him as a madman falls upon the physician
who would fain cure or alleviate his malady. The strife
between good and evil was not put an end to by the
Sacrifice on Calvary. The world woke up on the morning
of Easter Eve as it had waked up on the day before.
The free-will of man involves his power of choosing evil
rather and good, of stifling the voice of conscience,
of selling himself to his lusts, and so becoming the
sport and slave of the evil one. This was not altered, it
could not be altered, since man was not to be saved
against his will. The lower elements of fallen humanity
which had raged and stormed about the Incarnate Son

when He came to make peace, were therefore to rise up in fresh fury against those who were to carry His message and His blessing home to every soul. The world had concentrated its hatred against Jesus Christ into the space of a few hours; it was to spend the same malice upon the peacemakers who came after Him through a period of untold centuries, until the number of the elect was accomplished, and the day and hour came at last which the Father had kept in His own power. And therefore to the Beatitude of the Peacemakers was to succeed, by a kind of necessity, the Beatitude of the Persecuted, that the Cross and the victory of the Cross might not be wanting in the chain of the choicest spiritual blessings which God has to bestow, that the disciples might be as the Master, and that none of the footprints which He had left upon earth might be untrodden by those who were dearest to Him. The crown which our Lord had won for Himself was to be imparted to them. And as the Passion had been to Him the cause and means of His greatest triumph and greatest glory, so this Beatitude of resemblance to Him in His Passion is to crown and end the series, because by means of it those who share His sufferings become the partakers of His glory, and owe their greatest spiritual graces and their most intense joys hereafter to their participation of His Passion.

It was not and could not be by an accident, as men speak, that the Passion of our Lord became the healing of the world and the source to Him of glory and power so infinite. All was done, as the Apostle tells us, according to the determinate counsel and foreknowledge of God, Who chose His way for the exaltation of His Son in His Human Nature to that Kingdom which as God He already possessed. Meditation on the Passion reveals the transcendent wisdom and power and justice of God in that mystery, in which those attributes are displayed as in nothing else. The Passion is the greatest work of God. In like manner, the spiritual virtues which are stored up in the last Beatitude must be studied by meditation, and thus we shall come to see that it is not, as it were, an addition to or an excresence upon the perfect system of principles of spiritual power which is contained in the other seven, but that it crowns and completes them, and in a certain sense rises above and passes beyond them, while, like the rest, such is the marvellous mercifulness of the Legislator of the Gospel, it is within the reach of all Christians of whatever grade or vocation. All may have their share in the riches of the Cross, as all may have shared in poverty of spirit, in mercifulness, in purity of heart, or in the work of the peacemakers. The special crown of this Beatitude is His Kingdom, because it was by means of the Cross that Jesus Christ was to enter upon His Kingdom. The persecuted share with Him its royal power, as the poor in spirit shared with Him its riches, and thus the cycle of Beatitudes is completed, and the last of the great principles of perfection falls on the ears of the disciples —'Blessed are the persecuted for justice' sake, for theirs is the Kingdom of Heaven.' And then, for the first time, our Lord turns and addresses them directly: 'Blessed are ye, when they shall revile you and persecute you, and speak all that is evil against you, untruly, for My sake. Be glad and rejoice, for your reward is very great in Heaven, for so they persecuted the Prophets who were before you.'

The Beatitude of the Persecuted differs in this from the rest, that it lies in suffering. The others lie in some internal disposition or act or attitude of the soul, as poverty of spirit, or in some external action, such as mercifulness or peacemaking. Persecution comes from without, and indeed, when we consider our Lord's language when He turned and addressed the disciples after giving the Beatitude, it would seem as if He meant us to understand that, according to the providence of His Father, it was the fact that others reviled them, persecuted them, and spoke all manner of evil against them untruly, which was to win them their reward. We shall see what the truth is which is expressed in this language when we speak more particularly of the reward with which this Beatitude is crowned. In the meantime it is enough to say that an interior disposition of willingness and faithfulness and charity and other virtues must be necessary in those who would gain this Beatitude. If such virtues were wanting, one of two things would happen. Either God would take care not to allow persecution to fall upon persons who were not worthy of suffering for His sake, or such persons would fail under the trial, and make peace with their persecutors. It still remains true that this Beatitude depends more than the rest upon the action of others. Not every one who would readily bear persecution may have the special crown which is here held out, but those only on whom God in His providence chooses that His Cross should fall in this particular form. Further, in order to distinguish the virtue here spoken of from patience, meekness, humility, submission, and other passive virtues, it must be remembered that not every kind of suffering which is patiently borne confers the crown of the persecuted, but only the suffering which is inflicted for the sake of justice. And it is a mark of our Lord's loving carefulness for those who belong to Him that He extends the cause through which this crown may be won so widely as justice of all kinds. By this, those who suffer ill-treatment in the cause of honesty or charity, or moral virtue of any kind, are put on a level with those whose persecutions are directly on account of the faith.

Persecution itself, strictly speaking, involves hatred of God, His law, His truth, His Church, on the part of those who inflict it, and in this it differs from tyranny and oppression of an ordinary kind. There is direct hatred of God in the measures which have been taken in so many countries in modern times against the practice of the Evangelical Counsels, or against the priesthood as such, against religious societies whose objects are works of charity or the propagation of the Faith, or again, against obedience to the authority of Councils and of the Holy See. Every measure which directly tends to fetter the free intercourse between the Head of the Christian Church and the members, or to interfere with Christian education at the hands of religious bodies, and the like, is in the eye of God a measure of persecution, even though some pretext of State policy be put forward as the ostensible motive of the enactment or the line of proceeding. And, as we have seen, our Lord extends the blessing in this case to all who suffer persecution of any kind, even though it be only the persecution of the evil tongue, obloquy, reviling, slander, calumny, and also to those who suffer for the maintenance, as has been said, of any moral virtue. All such persons are placed, as it were, under the direct protection of God by the act of their persecutors, who in truth assail God in them. And the reward and blessing promised to the persecuted must be measured by this, that it is God's cause that they maintain, and His business is to vindicate it and reward them. He takes into His own hands both the chastisement of the persecutor and the defence of the persecuted. If He does not choose, for their sake, to deliver them in this world, it is because He sees it better for them to have a special crown in the next.

W 2

In truth, the merit of the persecuted lies in this, that
their sufferings are an acknowledgment in the most loyal,
because in the most costly, manner, of His supreme
dominion and majesty, of the truth and holiness of His
law, and of the duty of obedience to the least of His
commandments. Those who undergo persecution for
the least thing which bears, as it were, the royal mark
that it comes from God, even if it be a ceremony of
the Church, such as St. Teresa said she would die for,
make the best public profession that is possible, that
they themselves, and all that they have and are, entirely
belong to Him, and are to be sacrificed without hesitation when it is for His honour that it should be so.
They bear witness before the world, at the cost of all
that is most dear to them, that the claims of His service
are paramount and imperative. God has an absolute
claim on us; all that we have, honour, position, substance, life itself, He may exact at any moment. He
does not go in any way beyond His rights when, by
allowing us to suffer even tortures and the most painful
death because we will not offend Him, He practically
forces on us the choice of obedience even unto death.
And, what is especially to be noticed in relation to this
Beatitude, He frequently allows this choice to be forced
by persecution, not on those alone who are His special
servants, such as ecclesiastics or religious persons, not
on the bishops of the Church alone, or those who have
the commission to preach His Word to the hostile world
or to carry the Gospel into parts of the earth where it
has hitherto been unknown, but on whole populations,
on lay men and women, on children, on the poor, on
the tenderest and weakest in sex and age. The powers
of evil rule the world, and our Lord allows the conflict
between evil and good, the Church and Satan, to be
carried on over the whole field of human society without

shrinking, as it were, from exposing multitudes of His children in every age to what seems to any eye but that of faith the hard choice between death and apostacy, the sacrifice of the Christian law or the sacrifice of all that makes life dear and pleasant. The world never unlearns the habit of persecution. Over and over again it is shown by experience that persecutors always end badly, that their sin is one of those which are chastised both in this world and in the next, and that the effect of their efforts is but to advance the cause against which they fight, even though they may succeed with a few who yield under persecution, and though the immediate effect of their cruelty may be to the detriment of religion for a time. Over and over again, therefore, is this same attempt repeated, and Christians in every generation have to remember what St. Paul calls the 'good confession' with which our Lord Himself 'gave testimony under Pontius Pilate,'[1] when He declared that for this He was born and came into the world, that He should give testimony unto the truth,[2] and that first confession of the Apostles, the pattern of all that have been subsequently in the Church, 'If it be just in the sight of God to hear you rather than God, judge ye.'[3] No generation in the Church is without its noble host of martyrs and confessors, and it is a part of God's providence that He exacts this service of, or rather grants this blessing in large proportions to, populations but lately converted to Christianity, as well as to the children of the Church in countries which have for ages been Catholic. Nowhere in the far East or among the Rocky Mountains or among the islands of the Pacific is the Gospel message carried by Catholic missioners, but simple peasants, girls and boys, or noble ladies, as well as men and priests, have the occasion of witnessing a good con-

---

[1] 1 Timothy vi. 13.   [2] St. John xviii. 37.   [3] Acts iv. 19.

fession in the face of persecution, and so of giving to God the highest honour which His creatures can render Him, that of sacrificing themselves for Him. 'Blessed are the persecuted for justice' sake, for theirs is the Kingdom of Heaven.'

These thoughts lead us to another kind of consideration concerning the blessedness of the persecuted, which may also explain how it is that though the crown is offered to so many, it is not all that gain it. For the confession of the Faith or of Christian principles and motives under persecution is in itself an exercise of very high graces. It requires, in the first place, a very vivid faith. St. Francis Xavier has left it on record in one of his letters how strange a cloud seems to come over the plain truth of certain passages of Scripture about the duty of losing our life in order to save it, and the like, when the moment of danger is upon us: as if there came at that moment quite a new and wonderfully strong sense of the value of life, as if all might well be given up in order to save it, while the truths of Faith seem to retire, as it were, behind a veil. It requires a robust and well exercised faith to rise above this trial. In truth, 'as gold and silver are tried in the fire, so are acceptable men in the furnace of humiliation;'[4] and there have been many instances in ancient and modern times in which men who have been put to the proof of persecution have failed when others who seemed far weaker have stood firm, and the failure in the former case can be traced to negligence, or tepidity, to some affection to human things, or some defect of charity. It is clear how much anything of this kind must be a clog on the soul which is called to make sacrifices for God, and how free and detached and simple in intention, on the other hand, those must

4 Ecclus. ii. 5.

be, who are to pass through the furnace unscathed, to have the blessed lot of giving to God, as it were, something of their own, in the tribulations which they voluntarily undergo for His sake, who, while they prove themselves His true subjects by the readiness of their sacrifice, prove themselves also to be His true children by the perfect charity which keeps all bitterness from their soul, and even gives them power, like St. Stephen and thousands of other martyrs, to pray for their persecutors. The stages of the perfection which is required in those who are to suffer with profit are traced by St. Paul when he says, 'We glory also in tribulation, knowing that tribulation worketh patience, and patience trial, and trial hope, and hope confoundeth not, because the charity of God is poured forth in our hearts by the Holy Ghost Who is given to us.'[5]

St. Paul has another doctrine with regard to this subject which seems to be too full of deep truth to be easily drawn out. Speaking of our Lord's sufferings and their rewards, he says: 'We see Jesus, Who was made a little lower than the angels, for the suffering of death, crowned with glory and honour, that through the grace of God He might taste death for all. For it became Him, for Whom are all things, and by Whom are all things, in bringing many children unto glory, to perfect the Author of their salvation, by His Passion.'[6] The doctrine of this passage seems to be that our Lord's humiliation was in order that He might taste death for all, and so be crowned with the glory and honour which are won by suffering in a manner more glorious to God than in any other way. For if God had chosen to use His might and majesty, instead of His condescension, He could have glorified our Lord, and His followers also, without their passing through the furnace of suffering,

[5] Romans v. 3—5. [6] Hebrews ii. 9, 10.

and drawing from their sufferings their crowns of glory. That might have been, for who could resist God or question what He should do? In the same way He might have given Heaven to the race of man without probation, instead of making them glorify Him by earning it as a reward of their correspondence with His grace. So it might have been. But St. Paul says that there was something which specially became God, as the Almighty Creator and Governor of all, in making the Author of the salvation of the vast multitude of His children, whom He was bringing to eternal glory, perfect in His office of Saviour by means of suffering and the Passion, rather than in any other way which cost Him less. It was, then, peculiarly glorious to God that our Lord should win our salvation by His Passion rather than otherwise, and we have but to consider the extreme beauty and perfection of the many virtues exercised by Him in the Passion in order to understand the contemplation of St. Paul. But he goes on to say that 'He that sanctifieth and they that are sanctified are all of one,' and that 'He is not ashamed to call them brethren.' It would seem, then, that if the virtues exercised by our Lord in His Passion were so singularly glorious to God that it was, as it were, becoming in the Father to ordain the Passion for the sake of them, the same truth must be extended so as to apply in its degree to the sufferings of His Church and of her children also, all of which are in a certain sense the echoes of our Lord's Passion, and ineffably pleasing to God on that account and because they are meritorious through it. There is something of the same thought in St. Peter, when he is speaking to some Christians on whom persecution was falling for the first time. He says, 'Dearly beloved, think not strange the burning heat which is to try you, as if some new thing happened to you. But if you partake of the sufferings of Christ, rejoice that when His glory shall be revealed, you also may be glad with exceeding joy. If you be reproached for the name of Christ you shall be blessed, for that which is of the honour, glory, and power of God and that which is His Spirit, resteth upon you.'[7] For it has ever been the way of God to conquer His enemies by weakness rather than by strength, to put down the rebel angels, and exalt the despised race of man over them by His grace. His children on earth have the privilege which the angels do not share, of suffering for Him after the example of their Lord, and it would seem as if, the more they suffered without being overthrown, the greater were their triumph and crown hereafter, and the greater the glory which He decrees for them : as if this, indeed, were the very choicest flower of all that earth and man can offer to Him—persecution for His sake.

Another element in the blessedness of persecution may be found in the truth which our Lord more than once expresses, that suffering is the condition of fruitfulness. St. John tells us, that after His triumphant entry into Jerusalem on Palm Sunday, some 'Greeks,' who may have been Gentile proselytes, wished to see our Lord and applied to St. Philip, who spoke of it to St. Andrew, and the two Apostles together went to our Lord. The occasion seems to have put before our Lord's Heart the fruit which was afterwards to be gathered in, to the glory of God, from the Gentile world ; much in the same way as the appearance of the Samaritans at Sychar, after His conversation with the woman by the well-side, suggested to Him the future labours of the Apostles among the people of that outcast nation. On the occasion of which we are speaking, our Lord answered the application of the two Apostles by what

7 1 St. Peter iv. 12—14.

seems a sort of soliloquy, if indeed it be not that St. John has only introduced the incident for the sake of reporting the words, and has in consequence omitted any direct answer which our Lord may have made. 'Amen, amen, I say to you, unless the grain of wheat, falling into the ground, die, itself remaineth alone. But if it die, it bringeth forth much fruit.'[8] This, then, is a principle in the Kingdom of God, represented, as in a parable, by the law of death and decay which is the condition which nature in the present system of the world requires in order that seeds may be fruitful. It need not have been so, but so it is, and the law holds good in the spiritual Kingdom of God, though the time will come when death shall have borne all its fruit, and this law shall no longer prevail. And our Lord applies the same principles to those who are to come after Him, at least as to the necessity of suffering to produce fruitfulness. 'I am the true Vine,' He says, 'and My Father is the husbandman. Every branch in Me that beareth not fruit, He will take away, and every one that beareth fruit, He will prune it, that it may bring forth more fruit.'[9] Here, then, we have the same rule applied to others as to our Lord Himself, and in this rule we see another of the blessings of the persecuted. The enemies of the faith, of Christian virtue, of loyalty to the Holy See, of the rights of the Church, are used by God in more than one way to execute His designs, and one of these many ways is that their violence and cruelty imparts to those whom they afflict the special grace of fruitfulness. The whole history of the Church is a commentary upon this, for the blood of the martyrs has from the beginning been, as one of the Fathers said, the seed of Christians. The first martyr whose life was taken in persecution was the blessed Stephen,

<hr>

[8] St. John xii. 24, 25.   [9] St. John xv. 1, 2.

and his intercession begat to the Church no less a son than St. Paul himself. The first propagation of the faith out of the Holy Land was at the time of the dispersion which was caused by the persecution in which St. Stephen's life was taken, and thus the Church which was oppressed in Jerusalem sprang up in a hundred new places at once. So it has ever been, and so it will ever be.

The last head on which we need dwell of the blessing which belongs to the persecuted, consists in the very special love with which God regards them and watches over them. He exercises His sovereign rights over them in requiring from them the sacrifice of their lives, or their substance, or their reputation, for His sake; but though He acts in this as a Lord and Master, He does this out of His Fatherly love to them, as when He refused the prayer of our Lord in the Garden, that the chalice might pass from Him, out of love, at the same time exacting, if we may say so, His perfect obedience to the precept laid upon Him. Certainly the Fatherly love of God is most especially shown in His dealings with the persecuted. In the first place, He is careful to assure them that 'not a hair of their head shall perish,' that they 'are of more value than many sparrows,' though not the smallest bird can fall to the ground without their Father, that is, that all that happens to them is exactly weighed out and permitted by Him. Then they are so entirely under His protection, that, as it were, He takes on Himself the care of their defence. They are not to premeditate what they are to say when they are taken before princes and kings, for He will give them 'a mouth and wisdom,' which none of their adversaries will be able to gainsay or to resist, for it is not they that speak, but the Spirit of the Father that speaketh in them. Again, He bids them rejoice 'in that day,'[10] at the very time when they are under persecution, and it frequently happens, so frequently that it may be said to be the ordinary rule in such cases, that their hearts are inundated by a joy from Heaven which makes all tortures seem nothing, even if He does not take away from them, as has sometimes been known, all sense of pain, and change it into pleasure.   And lastly, He gives a special power to their prayers, as we see in the instance of St. Stephen, which, like so many other incidents in the Acts of the Apostles, is a kind of type and norm of what is to be ordinary in the Church under the same circumstances.

CHAPTER XXV.

Persecution and the Kingdom of Heaven.

St. Matt. v. 10—12 ; *Vita Vitæ Nostræ*, § 31.

WHAT has been already said as to the blessedness of the persecuted for justice' sake is enough to show that, even if by possibility their sufferings were to lead to no special reward beyond themselves, they would still be abundantly repaid by the particular protection with which God favours them, the love with which He regards them, the virtues which their state enables them to exercise, and the fruitfulness which is accorded to them. It only remains, therefore, to consider the grounds of the connection which exists between the virtue of this Beatitude and the special crown which our Lord assigns to that virtue, which is nothing less than the Kingdom of God.

The first thought which meets us on this subject is that the reward of the persecuted is thus made by

[10] St. Luke vi. 23.

our Lord to be identical, at least in terms, with the reward of the poor in spirit. Something has already been said as to the multiplicity of ideas which are contained under the name of the Kingdom, and also as to the correspondence, in the case of the poor in spirit, between the virtue which they have practised and that particular feature in the Kingdom which seems to be allotted to them as their reward. If we are to proceed in the same manner as to the reward of those who are persecuted for the sake of justice, we must find that conception of the Kingdom which answers most directly to the sacrifice which they have made and the virtue which they have practised. It is not arranged, however, without a certain depth of meaning, that the series of the crowns of the Beatitudes should close as it began, with the Kingdom. The last note of the octave is, as it were, an echo of the first. Many writers have thought that our Lord here implies that the Kingdom of Heaven, which is given under various names and aspects to the virtues of the intermediate Beatitudes, is given simply and wholly and without qualification to the first and to the last. Poverty of spirit, again, is a kind of beginning of the active virtues which are practised in the Beatitudes, while persecution embraces the whole range of the passive Christian virtues, and thus these two Beatitudes correspond one to the other, each as the foundation of a distinct order of holy acts. Some other Christian writers think that in the first Beatitude the Kingdom is conferred as to the spirit, and in the last as to the body, inasmuch as the poor in spirit renounce what they renounce in spirit, and the persecuted suffer what they suffer in the body. Other similar contemplations need only be referred to.[1]

It has already been said that the special aspect of

---

[1] See Salmeron, vol. v. tr. 25.

the Kingdom of Heaven which seems to corresponds as a natural reward to the virtue of the persecuted, is the aspect of dominion, rule, power, victory, glory. They are trampled under foot very often by tyrannical and unjust laws, they are deprived of equal rights with others, and are treated as slaves and outlaws, violence and power of every kind are used to induce them to give up the right cause or not to adopt it. It seems natural, therefore, that they should find in the Kingdom of Heaven just what they have been deprived of for its sake. The Kingdom, in this sense, may be interior, as our Lord said—'the Kingdom of God is within you'—it may be that justice and peace and joy of the Holy Ghost in which the Apostle says that the Kingdom of God consists. In this sense the persecuted are rulers of themselves in patience and resignation, the concupiscences are kept subject to reason, the flesh to the spirit, the whole man to the law of God. External suffering has a direct tendency to help towards this result. Even tribulation of a more ordinary kind, such as that which comes to men in the course of God's Providence over them, sickness, poverty, loss, pain of every kind, helps to mortification and the subjugation of the lower parts of man. It brings practically home to him the lesson that he is here as a stranger and a pilgrim, that the world is a valley of tears, that he must look to higher things as the objects of his affections and hopes. There is no tribulation which is so much of a trial to virtue as persecution : because persecution is inflicted by man, and not merely by the chastening hand of God, about which there is always more or less of tenderness. Persecution has always given occasion for the display of more barbarous malice, more refined, and even diabolical ingenuity of torture, more faithlessness, treachery, a greater combination of cruelty and cunning, than men have ordinarily to suffer under afflictions of another kind. It is a sort of hellish sport in which the powers of evil delight, and in which, under their influence, passions seem to be unchained which are usually kept in restraint. The Passion of our Lord is the type of all persecutions in this respect; it is no common scene of depravity or barbarity, but an unexampled exhibition of both, such as it might have been thought would never have taken place, and yet it was brought about in the name of religion and law. When David had his choice of suffering, he said that he preferred falling into the hands of God rather than into the hands of man, and we see in many instances in the narratives of martyrdoms that the wild beasts forget their ferocity, and the elements of fire and water will not work their usual effects, while the malice of man is untamed even by miracles, and carries out its purpose to the end without remorse. In this way persecution is a more profitable trial than ordinary tribulation, because it bites deeper and more maliciously. The virtue which is put to the proof and comes out of the trial successfully must be perfect indeed kept up by a very high faith, and immense self-mastery. Then there is the additional provocation to anger which arises from the obvious injustice of the affliction, or the wickedness of the men who are the persecutors, their open hostility to God and to His law, and an ordinary faith is often sorely tried by their apparent success and the length of time during which their prosperity and tyranny are allowed to continue, to the loss of thousand of souls.

The consideration of these and other features of persecution makes it clear that the souls which can bear its fury in peace, resignation, and fortitude, must have the interior Kingdom of God very firmly rooted and established within them, and must advance rapidly in their path of perfection. Persecution, rightly borne, make them saints in a short time, and the growth of their interior graces is marvellous. In another way the Kingdom of Heaven is theirs, because they of all others are the men who, as our Lord says in another place, 'take it by force,' win it for themselves by great sufferings and exertions. Again, it is, as we have seen, the design of God that His Kingdom is to triumph and advance mainly by the Cross. Those, then, who suffer persecution are the soldiers of His Kingdom, and the issue of the war is mainly owing to their prowess. It is by them that it is spread over all the earth, for persecution always springs up as the shadow behind the footsteps of Evangelical preachers, and the sufferings of the persecuted are required to cement and hold together the fabric which the preachers raise. In the dispensation of the Incarnation, glory, power, victory, dominion, correspond to suffering as the fruit to the seed. It is therefore not wonderful that those who suffer after the example of the King of the new Kingdom should have a share in His triumph, and be made to sit on His throne in royal power like His. They are the instruments of its propagation, and thus they become its rulers.

Such seem to be, in general, the grounds why the Kingdom of Heaven, with respect of dominion, royal state, and glory, is assigned as the reward in the Beatitude of the Persecuted. It must, however, be remembered that this Beatitude immediately follows, and is in a way the supplement of, that of the peacemakers. It has been seen that the title of the peacemakers to be called the sons of God has a special ground in their share in that great work of peacemaking which was the object of the Incarnation of the Eternal Son. That, above all others, seems to be what is intended in the seventh Beatitude. It is natural to suppose that the eighth Beatitude has a close connection with that which precedes it, and that the position of the virtue of the persecuted at the very end, and as it may be considered, the very summit of the glorious chain to which it belongs, has a particular reference to that condition upon which alone it was ordained that the Son of God should 'enter into His glory,' after the accomplishment of His work of peace. It is as if in this last Beatitude we were told by anticipation what was to be the outward and apparent result of all the labours of our Lord. They were to end in the Cross. And yet, on the other hand, the Cross was not to involve defeat, but victory. It was to be the chosen instrument of the complete establishment of the Kingdom, and so of the most perfect glory of the King. Without the Cross the work of peace would not have been accomplished. And that which was to be the instrument of the Leader's victory, was also to be the instrument of the triumph of His followers. The making of the great peace between Heaven and earth, the establishment of the new reign of harmony and love was to be brought about at no less a sacrifice than that which was made on Calvary. Thus, the rich blessing which was to fall on all those who had a share in the work for which our Lord became Man, was naturally to extend itself still further to the participation of the condition on which alone the work itself, in the designs of God, was to prosper. The persecuted were to be blessed, because the peacemakers were to be persecuted, and to win their end by means of persecution. The blessing of the peacemakers was to be a share in the privilege which by nature belonged only to Him, Whose Father had sent Him into the world to work the work of peace. The blessing of the persecuted was to have a share, not only in the privilege of sonship, but first in the grace of suffering in the discharge of the great commission which was expressly that of the Son of God, and then in the victory by means of which the end intended by God was gained, and so in the royal dignity of Him Who was the Conqueror. They were to share first His sufferings and then His glory.

CHAPTER XXVI.

Our Lord and the Beatitudes.

St. Matt. v. 1—10 ; *Vita Vitæ Nostræ*, § 31.

OUR LORD has thus led us through the whole series of the Beatitudes, and although they are closely connected with the remainder of the Sermon on the Mount, it may not be amiss to conclude this volume with some general reflections concerning the Evangelical commandments which He has given, and His own relation thereto. They are as perfect as they are because they come from Him. They are based upon the conditions and circumstances of His Incarnation and Mission, as well as upon the essential relations between God and His free creatures. They have the power which they have to be the foundation of a new creation, to regenerate man and society, and to lead to the future blessedness of man and of society in Heaven, because they are His. They are creative laws, laws which carry with them to simple and humble hearts the high grace which is necessary for their accomplishment, because they are founded upon His work and upon His character.

The name of God is mentioned only twice in the course of the Beatitudes, when it is necessary to speak of it in connection with the rewards of the pure of heart and of the peacemakers. But the thought of God, of what He is, what He has done, His rights, and His ways of acting, lies at the very foundation of every one of these great principles. It is before the thought of God as the Creator, the Lord of all, the Owner of all, the one only Being worthy of honour, esteem, obedience, deference, that the poor in spirit lay down all claim to ownership for themselves in anything created, even in themselves, and the meek offer the sacrifice of all honour, esteem, independence, consideration, from creatures like themselves. If we put aside for the moment the dis-honour to God and the misery to mankind and all creatures which have been brought into the world by the misuse of the free-will with which God has endowed some of the beings which He has made, we have still enough to supply the mourners with subject-matter for their plaintive longings, and their elevation above all created joys, in the feeling of their present exile from Him for Whose possession they were made and directed by His mercy. The thought of the true service of God, and of the blessedness of the short span of human life during which such service is meritorious, urges on the hearts of the hungry and thirsty after justice to an irresistible and unceasing activity. The knowledge that He has made mercy the law of His creation, and given to each man a special commandment to practise mercy to his neighbour, leaving so large a part of the good things, which He has intended all to share, to be administered to them by men like themselves, lies at the foundation of the devotion to works of mercy which comes after the general love and practice of justice. The thought of God's ineffable purity, and of the like-ness to Himself which He requires in all who are to converse with Him and know Him, is the principle on which purity of heart is to be founded. The heart of man knows instinctively that it is open to His eye, which can read its hidden thoughts and interpret its slightest and subtlest emotions. It longs by nature and by grace, to know Him in return, and to practise as soon and as constantly as possible that intercourse with Him of thought, of affection, of prayer, of contemplation, of adoration, in which it knows that the noblest and most blessed occupation of its faculties must consist. But it knows also that He is of eyes too pure to look upon iniquity, and it yearns to be made clean enough for His sight with the 'unspeakable groanings' which the Holy Ghost forms with it.

Almost all that has been said might have been true of the Beatitudes, if our Lord had given them to a race of spiritual creatures who had never fallen from the eminence and grace in which their Creator had placed them. The fall of man, the miseries which it has brought in as its consequences, the condition of things which it has created, the wonderful contrivance of mercy and justice by which that condition has to be redeemed and replaced, give, however, a different colour even to those Beatitudes which might have been in any case the laws of human perfection. The poor in spirit not only renounce what does not belong to them, but what is fraught with danger to them, what has become the cause of endless perdition to man and dishonour to God. They renounce what God, when He came to save man, would not touch. The meek, in like manner, throw down before the throne of His Majesty, things which have been made the instruments of rebellion against Him; things, again, which He would have nothing to do with when He came to teach men the way to Heaven. The mourners have a heavy weight of grief laid upon their hearts, like in kind to that which broke the Heart of the Saviour of mankind, in consequence of the dishonour which sin has done for God, the ingratitude to Him which it involves, the cost at which it had to be ransomed, the defacement of the whole moral and physical creation which it has caused. The hungry and thirsty after justice have their cravings intensified with a consuming and insatiable fire, when they consider that justice is no longer the simple homage of an innocent creation of rational beings to their beneficent Father, the fulfilment of the plan which He has laid down for them for the use of their faculties and opportunities, which He wishes to reward in His own magnificent measure, but the reparation by His friends of the ruin made in His Kingdom by His enemies, the field of battle in which His faithful soldiers are to show their loyalty under His own eye, and with Him to teach them how to fight and how to conquer. So also the merciful find, in consequence of the Fall and all its issues, a world lying before them which is in ten-fold need of their ministrations, where the miseries which He looks to them to help in redeeming have terribly multiplied their malignity, where a law of cruelty has been set up by selfishness, which has nearly obliterated the original commandment of the Creator, where spiritual maladies which lead to eternal death can only be remedied by heroic sacrifices, and where God Himself, in His sojourn among men, has left behind Him the tenderest and most constraining example of the love which will give itself even unto death. And the clean of heart find that the work of their self-purification is now beset with difficulties which require immense patience, strenuous prayer, and relentless perseverance; and that they too have a perfect model of purity set before them as their example, which draws them after itself with irresistible attraction at the same time that it gives them the power to follow.

Thus, in all the Beatitudes which have been hitherto

enumerated, the two orders of God's providence, the order of Creation, and the order of Redemption, seem to be blended as the practical foundation on which the virtues and their rewards are built up. But in the earlier Beatitudes, if we may so speak, the first-named order seems to bear the principal part, while, as we proceed in the series, the order of Redemption seems to take the larger share. In truth, the Redemption and Restoration of man by means of the Incarnation, add, as we have seen, a wonderful intensity to the motives for poverty of spirit and for meekness, as well as for mourning and mercifulness, both on account of our fresh indebtedness to God for our salvation through His Son, and also on account of the immense increase of light thrown on all the natural duties of a creature to His Creator by the example of our Lord. When we pass on to the two last Beatitudes, we find ourselves reminded, not exclusively but in far larger measure, of the Incarnation, its object, and the means by which that object was to be gained. The work of peace which is set before us in the seventh Beatitude cannot be limited to the peacemaking which was carried out by the Incarnation and Passion, because, as has been seen, peace was the law of the universe and of all God's creatures, rational or irrational, from the beginning. But still the great 'Peacemaking' of the Son of God was in the Incarnation and Passion, and it is by the application of the fruits of these acts of God that all peace is now to be made in Heaven or on earth. Still more is the manner in which God made peace the ground and foundation of the last Beatitude, which to those who do not believe the Christian doctrine of the Atonement must seem as foolish as the preaching of the Cross to the Greeks of old. These two Beatitudes hold their position at the summit and as the climax of the advancing series which they close, because of the actual condition in which our Lord found the world when He came to it, because of the particular work which the Father gave Him to do, and because of the particular manner in which it was determined that that work should be accomplished. The Beatitudes begin with God the Creator, Who has made His rational creatures free, and has thereby given them the opportunity of rendering Him the homage of poverty and humility and obedience of spirit, and of seeking Him alone in the gifts which He has entrusted to them. At the end of the Beatitudes, we find God the Redeemer hanging on a Cross to atone for the mischief which has been done by the misuse of His creatures' free-will. The Kingdom of God is first established in the humiliation of creatures before His throne, and then it is restored by the humiliation of God Himself. The Passion and the Beatitude of the Persecuted repair a thousand-fold the harm incidentally involved in that permission of evil which the creation of rational beings brought about. For the wisdom of God 'reacheth from end to end mightily, and ordereth all things sweetly.'[1]

Thus the Beatitudes, if we may venture so to speak, write out the thoughts of our Lord's Sacred Heart as to the rights and ways of God. It is obvious to add that these sublime principles of truth could never have had the force in the world which they have actually exercised, except for the source from which they came. They form a few pregnant sentences, and if they had been mingled up with the apophthegms of philosophers, with no name given as of their author, they might perhaps have struck the admiration of a few thoughtful students —perhaps not all of them would have done even that— but they would never have become the foundation of a new order of ideas and a new system of life. Their

---

[1] Wisdom viii. 1.

power came from this, that they were the words of One, and He the Incarnate Son of God, Whose life they summarized and Whose character they described. Even in their sequence they seem to express a history, and that the history of a life which began in poverty at Bethlehem, and which went on in meekness and mourning in Egypt, which broke out into zeal for justice and mercifulness in Galilee and Judæa, while the Heart of Him Who led it was ever full of the utmost purity and of the vision of God, and which ended in the consummation of the work of peace and reconciliation on the Cross at Jerusalem. But whatever may be thought of such contemplations as to the order of the mysteries of our Lord's Life, it cannot be doubted that He was Himself from the very beginning the perfect example of the virtues commanded in the Beatitudes, and that, as the time came in the providence of the Father for the special and conspicuous display of this one or of that, He practised it in a manner which wrote it in letters of light on the memory of those who witnessed it. He was the truly poor in spirit, the truly meek, the true mourner. He was the Man Who hungered and thirsted after justice, and spent Himself in works of usefulness. He was the pure of Heart, the true maker of peace, the King Who through tribulation and persecution entered into His Kingdom. Thus the Beatitudes were not merely uttered by our Lord on this sacred mountain, as the Law had been given to Moses on Mount Sinai. The lesson and the commandments were repeated day after day for months, and even years, in the eyes of those who had the unspeakable blessing of seeing Him, conversing with Him, and being His friends and disciples. The law which was thus written in their hearts by His blessed example had the power and authority which always belongs to that Divine method of instruction, even when the pattern which is set before the eyes is one of the saints of God, a man like ourselves. But it had a far higher power and authority in that our Lord was the Incarnate God, and was sent into the world with the special commission to be our Teacher, and that both by precept and by example. When saints and prophets have been raised up for a particular purpose in the providence of God, there is always a special grace given both to them and to those to whom they are sent, to enable them to discharge their mission or to profit by it. Much more were the treasures of grace thrown open to men, when the messenger was the Incarnate Son Himself. But this does not exhaust the power of our Lord's example. His actions and His practice of virtues were not only exemplary, but life-giving and grace-giving. They won for those who belong to Him the grace to follow easily in His footsteps, they conquered the difficulties of the way, they weakened the enemies of our salvation, they, as it were, quelled temptations beforehand, and gave to the actions in which we imitate Him a special merit and a peculiar beauty in the eyes of His Father.

When our Lord had passed away from the sight of His disciples, to be no more their living Example and Teacher, but their Patron and Intercessor in Heaven, He sent the Holy Ghost to take up this part of His work, as well as the rest, and to bring to the remembrance of the Apostles, in the way not only of simple recollection, but also of powerful motive, whatsoever He Himself had said and done amongst them. Thus we find the teaching of the Beatitudes breaking out, as it were, in fruitfulness from the virgin soil of the infant Church, as the green shoots of the young corn spring up under the first warm rains of spring. The words of our Lord ring through the directions which survive to us of the Apostles to their converts, and the history of the early Churches is full of instances of virtue, which can be traced up to the words uttered on the Mountain of the Beatitudes. This is the account of the spontaneous growth of poverty in the first Church of Jerusalem, among whose members there must have been very many who had listened to the Sermon on the Mount. This is the account of the meekness, as well as of the courage, of the Apostles in the first persecution, when they went forth from the Council after their scourging, rejoicing, as our Lord had told them, because they had been 'counted worthy to suffer reproach for the name of Jesus.'[2] St. Paul, as far as we now know, had not seen our Lord while He was on earth before His Ascension; he is the Apostle who had never therefore been His intimate companion and associate, and yet we find him constantly echoing the teaching of the Beatitudes. You know the grace of our Lord Jesus Christ, he says, 'that being rich, He became poor for your sakes.'[3] 'Let this mind be in you which was also in Christ Jesus, Who, being in the form of God, thought it not robbery to be equal with God, but emptied Himself, taking the form of a servant, being made in the likeness of men, and in habit found as a man.'[4] He it is who uses the adjuration, 'I beseech you by the meekness and modesty of Christ.'[5] He it is who sums up the reasons for Christian mourning when he is recommending celibacy as one of its exercises. 'The time is short; it remaineth that they also that have wives be as if they had none, and they that weep as though they wept not, and they that rejoice as if they rejoiced not, and they that buy as though they possessed not, and they that use this world as if they used it not,

---

[2] Acts v. 41.   [3] 2 Cor. viii. 9.   [4] Philipp. ii. 5, 7.
[5] 1 Cor. vii. 29—31.

for the fashion of this world passeth away.'[6] We find him not less eager for the work of mercy than the other Apostles who had seen our Lord's examples. He dwells on this in particular in the Epistles written before his last visit to Jerusalem, when he was engaged in furthering the collection of alms for the poor Christians in Judæa. Almsdeeds form the last subject on which he dwells in his touching address to the priests of Ephesus. ' I have showed ye all things, how that so labouring you ought to support the weak, and to remember the word of the Lord Jesus, how He said, It is a more blessed thing to give rather than to receive'[7]—the only saying of our Lord which has come to us except through the Gospels. We gather from the words just quoted that St. Paul's practice of manual labour had a two-fold object, the practice of humility and poverty, and the practice of mercifulness. And he is the great Apostle who has spoken so much about the work of peace which our Lord accomplished on the Cross, as if it had been one of his great commissions to bring out the full theological meaning of the last two Beatitudes.

But, in truth, the whole moral teaching of the Apostles, as contained in the Epistles, is founded on the Beatitudes as expressed in our Lord's character; and it must be enough, in the present place, to have drawn but a few lines of what might be worked out into a large and crowded picture. The imitation of our Lord was practised in the early Churches at Jerusalem and elsewhere, before the Gospels were written, and if the Beatitudes had never been recorded, the outlines of their teaching would still have been traceable in the manners and principles of the Apostles and their disciples. Those manners and principles are the heritage of the Catholic Church ; they

---

'[6] 2 Cor. xi., he uses the word πρᾳότητος, which refers to the 'meek.'
[7] Acts xx. 35.

come to us as traditions which have been tested by the trials of ages—rich with the memories of thousands of saints who have reflected in their practice the image of our Lord. In the catacombs, in the Egyptian deserts, in the great cities of the Empire, in the monasteries which grew up round the sacred palaces of Palestine, the Beatitudes were the laws of life before the Western world fell under the invasion of the barbarians, or the Eastern bowed its neck to the yoke of the impure prophet. They were the rules by which the men lived who saved Europe and the Church from destruction, and painfully built up a new civilization out of the combination of the old and new races. As their practice has varied or increased, so has the Church been in decay or in vigour. When there has come a time of renovation and revival, the inspiration has always been caught from the Beatitudes; so it was when Francis and Dominic breathed a new strength into the Church; so it was in later days, when the names of her conspicuous saints were Ignatius or Teresa, or Vincent of Paul. In all ages and in every country, and for the children of every race, the law given on the mountain in Galilee has been the means of salvation and perfection and blessedness, because it has reflected the character of Him Who gave it. 'For God Who commanded the light to shine out of darkness, hath shined in our hearts, to give the light of the knowledge of the glory of God, in the face of Jesus Christ.'[8]

[8] 2 Cor. iv. 6.

APPENDIX.

Harmony of the Gospels.

§ 29.—*Beginning of the preaching in Galilee, and call of four disciples.*

<table>
<tr><td>

St. Matt. iv. 12—22.

Now when Jesus had heard that John was delivered up, He retired into Galilee. And leaving the city Nazareth He came and dwelt in Capharnaum on the sea-coast, in the confines of Zabulon and of Nephthalim ; that what was said by Isaias the Prophet might be fulfilled : The land of Zabulon and the land of Nephthalim, the way of the sea beyond the Jordan, Galilee of the Gentiles : The people that sat in darkness saw great light: and to them that sat in the region of the shadow of death, light is sprung up.[1] From that time Jesus began to preach, and to say : Do penance, for the Kingdom of Heaven is at hand.

And Jesus walking by the Sea of Galilee, saw two brothers, Simon who is called Peter, and Andrew his brother, casting a net into the sea (for they were fishers). And He saith to them : Come

</td><td>

St. Mark i. 14—20.

And after that John was delivered up, Jesus came into Galilee, preaching the Gospel of the Kingdom of God, and saying : The time is accomplished, and the Kingdom of God is at hand : repent and believe the Gospel.

And as He walked by the Sea of Galilee, He saw Simon and Andrew his brother casting nets into the sea (for they were fishermen). And Jesus said to them : Come after Me, and I will make you to

</td></tr>
</table>

[1] Isaias ix. 1, 2.

St. Matt. iv. 19—22.	St. Mark i. 18—20.
after Me, and I will make you to be fishers of men. And they immediately, leaving their nets, followed Him. And going on from thence, He saw other two brothers, James the son of Zebedee, and John his brother, in a ship with Zebedee their father, mending their nets : and He called them. And they immediately, leaving their nets and their father, followed Him.	become fishers of men. And immediately, leaving their nets, they followed Him. And going on from thence a little farther, He saw James the son of Zebedee, and John his brother, who also were in the ship mending their nets. And forthwith He called them. And they left their father Zebedee in the ship with his hired men, and followed Him.

§ 30.—*The Sabbath at Capharnaum.*

St. Matt. viii. 14—17 ; iv. 23—25.	St. Mark i. 21—39.	St. Luke iv. 31—44.
	And they came into Capharnaum : and forthwith on the Sabbath-day, going into the synagogue, He taught them. And they were astonished at His doctrine : for He taught them as one that had authority, and not as the scribes.	And He went down into Capharnaum, a city of Galilee, and there He taught them on the Sabbath-days. And they were astonished at His doctrine : for His word was with power.
	And there was in their synagogue a man with an unclean spirit ; and he cried out, saying : What have we to do with Thee, Jesus of Nazareth ? art Thou come to destroy us ? I know Who Thou art, the Holy One of God.	And in the synagogue there was a man who had an unclean devil, and he cried out with a loud voice, saying : Let us alone ; what have we to do with Thee, Jesus of Nazareth ? art Thou come to destroy us ? I know Thee Who Thou art, the Holy One of God. And Jesus
	And Jesus threat-	

St. Matt. viii. 14—16.	St. Mark i. 25—31.	St. Luke iv. 35—40.

St. Matt. viii. 14—16.

And when Jesus was come into Peter's house, He saw his mother-in-law lying, and sick of a fever : And He touched her hand, and the fever left her, and she arose and ministered to them.

And when evening was come they

St. Mark i. 25—31.

ened him, saying : Speak no more, and go out of the man. And the unclean spirit tearing him, and crying out with a loud voice, went out of him.

And they were all amazed, insomuch that they questioned among themselves, saying: What thing is this? what is this new doctrine? for with authority He commandeth even the unclean spirits, and they obey Him. And the fame of Him was spread forthwith through all the country of Galilee.

And immediately going out of the synagogue, they came into the house of Simon and Andrew, with James and John. And Simon's wife's mother lay sick of a fever : and forthwith they tell Him of her. And He came and lifted her up, taking her by the hand ; and immediately the fever left her, and she ministered unto them.

And when it was evening, after sun-

St. Luke iv. 35—40.

rebuked him, saying : Hold thy peace, and go out of him. And when the devil had thrown him into the midst, he went out of him, and hurt him not at all.

And there came fear upon all, and they talked among themselves, saying: What word is this, for with authority and power He commandeth the unclean spirits, and they go out ? And the fame of Him was published in every place of the country.

And Jesus rising up out of the synagogue, went into Simon's house. And Simon's wife's mother was taken with a great fever, and they besought Him for her. And standing over her, He commanded the fever, and it left her. And immediately rising, she ministered to them.

And when the sun was down, all

St. Matt. viii. 17; iv. 23.

St. Mark i. 32—39.

St. Luke iv. 40—44.

brought to Him many that were possessed with devils; and He cast out the spirit with His word: and all that were sick He healed. That it might be fulfilled, which was spoken by the Prophet Isaias, saying: He took our infirmities, and bore our diseases.[2]

set, they brought all to Him that were diseased, and that were possessed with devils. And all the city was gathered together at the door. And He healed many that were sick of divers diseases; and He cast out many devils; and He suffered them not to speak, because they knew Him.

And rising very early in the morning, going out He went into a desert place; and there He prayed. And Simon, and they who were with Him followed after Him. And when they had found Him they said to Him: All men seek for Thee. And He saith unto them: Let us go into the neighbouring towns and cities, that I may preach there also; for to this purpose am I come.

they that had any sick with divers diseases, brought them to Him. But He laying His hands on every one of them, healed them. And devils went out of many, crying out and saying: Thou art the Son of God. And He, rebuking them, suffered them not to speak: for they knew that He was Christ.

And when it was day, going out He went into a desert place, and the multitudes sought Him, and came unto Him: and they detained Him, that He should not depart from them. And He said to them: I must preach the Kingdom of God to other cities also: for therefore am I sent.

And Jesus went about all Galilee, teaching in their synagogues, and preaching the Gospel of the Kingdom, and healing all diseases and infir-

And He preached in their synagogues, and in all Galilee, casting out devils.

And He was preaching in the synagogues of Galilee.

<hr>

[2] Isaias liii. 4.

St. Matt. iv. 24, 25.	St. Mark i.	St. Luke iv.

mities among the people. And His fame went throughout all Syria, and they brought to Him all sick people that were taken with divers diseases and torments, and such as were possessed by devils, and lunatics, those that had the palsy, and He healed them : And great multitudes followed Him from Galilee, and from Decapolis, and from Jerusalem, and from Judæa, and from beyond the Jordan.

---

§ 31.—*The Eight Beatitudes and the Light of the World.*

St. Matt. v. 1—16.

Now Jesus seeing the multitudes, went up into a mountain : and when He had sat down, His disciples came to Him.

And opening His mouth He taught them, saying :

Blessed are the poor in spirit : for theirs is the Kingdom of Heaven.

Blessed are the meek : for they shall possess the land.

Blessed are they that mourn : for they shall be comforted.

Blessed are they that hunger and thirst after justice : for they shall be filled.

Blessed are the merciful : for they shall obtain mercy.

Blessed are the clean of heart : for they shall see God.

Blessed are the peacemakers : for they shall be called the children of God.

Blessed are they that suffer persecution for justice' sake : for theirs is the Kingdom of Heaven.

Blessed are you when men shall revile you, and persecute you, and shall say all manner of evil against you falsely, for My sake. Rejoice and be exceeding glad, because your reward is very great in Heaven : for so they persecuted the Prophets, that were before you.

You are the salt of the

earth. But if the salt lose its savour, with what shall it be salted? It is then good for nothing, but to be cast out, and to be trodden upon by men.

You are the light of the world. A city that is set on a mountain cannot be hid.

Neither do men light a candle, and put it under a bushel, but upon a candle-stick, that it may give light to all that are in the house. Let your light so shine before men, that they may see your good works, and glorify your Father Who is in Heaven.

§ 32.—*Evangelical Justice.*

Think not that I am come to destroy the Law, or the Prophets : I am not come to destroy but to fulfil. For Amen I say unto you, till Heaven and earth pass, one jot or one tittle shall not pass from the Law till all be fulfilled. Whosoever, there-fore, shall break one of these least commandments and shall teach men so, he shall be called the least in the Kingdom of Heaven : but whosoever shall do and teach, the same shall be called great in the Kingdom of Heaven. For I say unto you, that un-less your justice abound more than that of the Scribes and of the Pharisees, you shall not enter into the Kingdom of Heaven.

You have heard that it was said to them of old : Thou shalt not kill.[3] And whosoever shall kill, shall be guilty of the judgment. But I say to you, that who-soever is angry with his brother, shall be guilty of the judgment. And whoso-ever shall say to his brother, Raca, shall be guilty of the council. And whosoever shall say, Thou fool, shall be guilty of Hell fire. Therefore, if thou offerest thy gift at the altar, and there shalt remem-ber that thy brother hath anything against thee; Leave there thy gift before the altar, and first go to be re-conciled to thy brother ; and then come and offer thy gift.

Make an agreement with thy adversary quickly, whilst thou art in the way with him: lest, perhaps, the adversary deliver thee to the judge, and the judge deliver thee to the officer, and thou be cast into prison. Amen I say to thee, thou shalt not go out from thence till thou pay the last farthing.

You have heard that it was said to them of old : Thou shalt not commit adul-tery.[4] But I say unto you, that whosoever looketh on a woman to lust after her, hath

---

[3] Exodus xx. 13.

[4] Exodus xx. 14.

St. Matt. v. 28—48.

already committed adultery with her in his heart. And if thy right eye cause thee to offend, pluck it out, and cast it from thee : for it is better for thee that one of thy members should perish, than that thy whole body should be cast into Hell. And if thy right hand cause thee to offend, cut it off, and cast it from thee : for it is better for thee that one of thy members should perish, than that thy whole body should go into Hell.

It hath also been said : Whosoever shall put away his wife, let him give her a bill of divorce.[5] But I say to you, that whosoever shall put away his wife, excepting for the cause of fornication, causeth her to commit adultery : and whosoever shall marry her that is put away, committeth adultery.

Again, you have heard that it was said to them of old : Thou shalt not forswear thyself;[6] but thou shalt perform thy oaths to the Lord. But I say to you, not to swear at all ; neither by Heaven, for it is the throne of God ; nor by the earth, for it is His footstool ; nor by Jerusalem, for it is the city of the great King : Neither shalt thou swear by thy head, because thou canst not make one hair white or black. But let your speech be, Yea, yea ;

No,no: for whatsoever is more than these, cometh from evil.

You have heard that it hath been said :[7] An eye for an eye, a tooth for a tooth. But I say to you, not to resist evil : but if any man strike thee on thy right cheek, turn to him the other also. And if any man will go to law with thee, and take away thy coat, let him have thy cloak also. And whosoever shall force thee to go one mile, go with him other two. Give to him that asketh of thee, and from him that would borrow of thee, turn not away.

You have heard that it hath been said :[8] Thou shalt love thy neighbour, and hate thy enemy. But I say to you, love your enemies : do good to them that hate you : and pray for them that persecute and calumniate you : That you may be the children of your Father, Who is in Heaven : Who maketh His sun to rise upon the good and the bad, and raineth upon the just and the unjust. For if you love those that love you, what reward shall you have? do not even the publicans the same? And if you salute your brethren only, what do you more? do not also the heathen the same? Be you, therefore, perfect, as also your Heavenly Father is perfect.

[5] Deut. xxiv. 1.

[6] Numbers xxx. 2.

[7] Exodus xxi. 24.

[8] Levit. xix. 18.

Y 2

§ 33.—*Alms, Prayer, and Fasting.*

St. Matt. vi. 1—18.

Take heed that you do not your justice before men, that you may be seen by them : otherwise you shall not have a reward from your Father, Who is in Heaven.

Therefore, when thou doest an almsdeed, sound not a trumpet before thee, as the hypocrites do in the synagogues and in the streets, that they may be honoured by men. Amen I say to you, they have received their reward. But when thou doest alms, let not thy left hand know what thy right hand doeth : that thy alms may be in secret, and thy Father Who seeth in secret, will repay thee.

And when you pray, you shall not be as the hypocrites, who love to pray standing in the synagogues and at the corners of the streets, that they may be seen by men : Amen I say to you, they have received their reward. But thou, when thou shalt pray, enter into thy chamber, and having shut the door, pray to thy Father in secret : and thy Father, Who seeth in secret, will reward thee.

And when you are praying speak not much, as the heathens do : for they think that they are heard for their much speaking. Be not you, therefore, like them. For your Father knoweth what you stand in need of, before you ask Him. You, therefore, shall pray in this manner :

Our Father, Who art in Heaven, hallowed be Thy name.

Thy Kingdom come. Thy will be done on earth as it is in Heaven.

Give us this day our super-substantial bread.

And forgive us our debts, as we forgive our debtors.

And lead us not into temptation. But deliver us from evil. Amen.

For if you forgive men their offences, your Heavenly Father will also forgive you your offences. But if you will not forgive men, neither will your Father forgive you your sins.

And when you fast, be not, as the hypocrites, sad : for they disfigure their faces, that to men they may appear fasting. Amen I say to you, they have received their reward. But thou, when thou fastest, anoint thy head, and wash thy face : that thou appear not fasting to men, but to thy Father, Who is in secret : and thy Father, Who seeth in secret, will reward thee.

§ 34.—*Confidence in God our Father.*

St. Matt. vi. 19—34.

Lay not up for yourselves treasures on earth ; where the rust, and the moth consume, and where thieves dig through and steal. But lay up for yourselves treasures in Heaven ; where neither the rust nor the moth doth consume, and where thieves do not dig through, nor steal. For where thy treasure is, there is thy heart also.

The light of thy body is thy eye. If thy eye be simple, thy whole body will be lightsome. But if thy eye be evil, thy whole body shall be darksome. If, therefore, the light that is in thee be darkness, how great will the darkness itself be ?

No man can serve two masters : for either he will hate the one, and love the other ; or he will hold to the one, and despise the other. You cannot serve God and mammon. Therefore I say to you, be not solicitous for your life, what you shall eat, nor for your body what you shall put on. Is not the life more than the food, and the body more than the raiment ? Behold the fowls of the air, for they sow not, neither do they reap, nor gather into barns : yet your Heavenly Father feedeth them. Are not yon of much more value thau they ? And which of you, by thinking, can add to his stature one cubit ? And for raiment why are you solicitous ? Consider the lilies of the field, how they grow : they labour not, neither do they spin. And yet I say to you, that not even Solomon, in all his glory, was arrayed as one of these. Now, if God so clothe the grass of the field, which to-day is, and to-morrow is cast into the oven ; how much more you, O ye of little faith ? Be not solicitous, therefore, saying : What shall we eat, or what shall we drink, or wherewith shall we be clothed? For after all these things do the heathens seek. For your Father knoweth that you have need of all these things. Seek ye, therefore, first the Kingdom of God and His justice : and all these things shall be added unto you. Be not, therefore, solicitous for to-morrow ; for the morrow will be solicitous for itself. Sufficient for the day is the evil thereof.

---

§ 35.—*Against judging others, and of confidence in Prayer.*

St. Matt. vii. 1—12.

Judge not that you may not be judged. For with what judgment you have judged, you shall be judged : and with what measure you have measured, it shall be measured to you again. And why seest thou a mote in thy brother's eye, and seest not a beam in thy own eye? Or how sayest thou to thy brother: Let me cast the mote out of thy eye; and behold a beam is in thy own eye? Thou hypocrite, cast out first the beam out of thy own eye, and then shalt thou see to cast out the mote out of thy brother's eye.

Give not that which is holy to dogs: neither cast ye your pearls before swine; lest they trample them under their feet, and, turning upon you, tear you.

Ask, and it shall be given you: seek, and you shall find: knock, and it shall be opened to you. For every one that asketh, receiveth: and he that seeketh, findeth: and to him that knocketh, it shall be opened. Or what man is there among you, of whom if his son ask bread, will he reach him a stone? Or if he ask a fish, will he reach him a serpent? If you, then, being evil, know how to give good gifts to your children: how much more will your Father, Who is in Heaven, give good things to them that ask Him?

All things, therefore, whatsoever you would that men should do to you, do you also to them: for this is the Law and the Prophets.

---

§ 36.—*The Narrow way to Life.*

Enter ye in at the narrow gate; for wide is the gate, and broad is the way that leadeth to destruction; and many there are who enter by it. How narrow is the gate, and strait is the way, which leadeth to life: and few there are who find it!

Beware of false prophets, who come to you in the clothing of sheep, but inwardly they are ravenous wolves. By their fruits you shall know them. Do men gather grapes of thorns, or figs of thistles? Even so every good tree yieldeth good fruit, and the bad tree yieldeth bad fruit. A good tree cannot yield bad fruit; neither can a bad tree yield good fruit. Every tree that yieldeth not good fruit, shall be cut down, and shall be cast into the fire. Wherefore, by their fruits you shall know them.

Not every one that saith to Me, Lord, Lord, shall enter into the Kingdom of Heaven: but he that doeth the will of My Father, Who is in Heaven, he shall enter into the Kingdom of Heaven. Many will say to Me in that day: Lord, Lord, have we

St. Matt. vii. 22—29 ; viii. 1.

not prophesied in Thy name, and in Thy name cast out devils, and done many wonderful works in Thy name? And then will I profess unto them : I never knew you : depart from Me, you that work iniquity.[9]

Therefore, whosoever heareth these My words, and doeth them, shall be likened to a wise man, who built his house upon a rock. And the rain fell, and the floods came, and the winds blew, and they beat upon that house, and it fell not ; for it was founded upon a rock. And every one that heareth these My words, and doeth them not, shall be like a foolish man, who built his house upon the sand. And the rain fell, and the floods came, and the winds blew, and they beat upon that house, and it fell ; and great was the fall thereof.

And it came to pass, when Jesus had fully ended these words, the people were in admiration at His doctrine. For He was teaching them as one having authority, and not as the Scribes and Pharisees. And when He was come down from the mountain, great multitudes followed Him.

[9] Psalm vi. 9.

VOLUMES ON THE LIFE OF OUR LORD.

BY THE REV. H. J. COLERIDGE, S.J.

INTRODUCTORY VOLUMES.

The Life of our Life. Introduction and Harmony of the Gospels, new edition, with the Introduction re-written. Two vols. 15s.

The Works and Words of our Saviour, gathered from the Four Gospels. 7s. 6d.

The Story of the Gospels. Harmonized for Meditation. 7s. 6d.

THE HOLY INFANCY.

The Preparation of the Incarnation. 7s. 6d.

The Nine Months. The Life of our Lord in the Womb. 7s. 6d.

The Thirty Years. Our Lord's Infancy and Early Life. 7s. 6d.

THE PUBLIC LIFE OF OUR LORD.

The Ministry of St. John Baptist. 6s. 6d.

The Preaching of the Beatitudes. 6s. 6d.

The Sermon on the Mount. To the end of the Lord's Prayer. 6s. 6d.

The Sermon on the Mount. From the end of the Lord's Prayer. 6s. 6d.

The Training of the Apostles. Part I. 6s. 6d.

The Training of the Apostles. Part II. 6s. 6d.

The Training of the Apostles. Part III. 6s. 6d.

The Training of the Apostles. Part IV. 6s. 6d.

The Preaching of the Cross.   Part I.   6s. 6d.

The Preaching of the Cross.   Part II.   6s.

The Preaching of the Cross.   Part III.   6s.

THE FIRST DAYS OF HOLY WEEK.

Passiontide.   Part I.   6s. 6d.

Passiontide.   Part II.   6s. 6d.

Passiontide.   Part III.   6s. 6d.

CONCLUDING VOLUME.

The Passage of our Lord to the Father.   7s. 6d.

———

BY THE SAME.

The Return of the King.   Discourses on the Latter Days.   7s. 6d.

The Baptism of the King.   Considerations on the Sacred Passion.   7s. 6d.

The Mother of the King.   Mary during the Life of our Lord.   7s. 6d.

The Mother of the Church.   Mary during the first Apostolic Age.   6s.

The Prisoners of the King.   Thoughts on the Catholic Doctrine of Purgatory.   New Edition.   4s.

Chapters on the Parables.   7s. 6d.

The Seven Words of Mary.   2s.

EDITED BY THE SAME.

The History of the Sacred Passion.   By Father Luis de la Palma, S.J.   Translated from the Spanish.   5s.

The Hours of the Passion.   Taken from the "Life of Christ" by Ludolph the Saxon.   7s. 6d.

The Seven Words on the Cross.   By Cardinal Bellarmine. Translated from the Latin. Second Edition.   5s.

BOOKS FOR MEDITATION, &c.

The Manna of the Soul. By Father Paul Segneri.
Meditations for every day in the year. New edition in
two volumes, cloth, 12s.

The Christian Reformed in Mind and Manners.
By Father Benedict Rogacci, S.J. 7s. 6d.

Pious Affections towards God and the Saints.
Meditations for Every Day in the Year, and for the
principal Festivals. From the Latin of the Ven. Nicolas
Lancicius, S.J. 7s. 6d.

Select Works of the Ven. Father Nicolas
Lancicius, S.J.
> Vol. I. THE YEARLY EIGHT DAYS' RETREAT, AND HOW
> TO PROFIT BY IT. 6s. 6d.
> Vol. II. ON RASH JUDGMENTS AND ARIDITY. 6s. 6d.

The Life and Teaching of Jesus Christ in
Meditations for Every Day in the Year. By Father
Nicolas Avancino, S.J. Two vols. 10s. 6d.

Jesus, the All-Beautiful. A Devotional Treatise
on the Character and Actions of our Lord. By the
Author of *The Voice of the Sacred Heart* and *The Heart
of Jesus of Nazareth.*

The Adorable Heart of Jesus. By Father Joseph
de Galliffet, S.J. With Preface and Introduction by the
Rev. R. F. Clarke, S.J. Crown 8vo. 3s.

The Charity of Jesus Christ. By Father Francis
Arias, S.J. 3s.

The Virtues of Mary, the Mother of God.
By Father Francis Arias, S.J. With Preface by George
Porter, S.J., late Archbishop of Bombay. 2s.

The Spirit of St. Ignatius, Founder of the
Society of Jesus. Translated from the French of the
Rev. Father Xavier de Franciosi, of the same Society. 6s.

The Tribunal of Conscience. By Father Gaspar
Druzbicki, S.J. 3s. 6d.

Of Adoration in Spirit and Truth. By Father
J. Eusebius Nieremberg. With a Preface by the Rev.
P. Gallwey, S.J. 6s. 6d.

Daily Duties: An Instruction for Novices. By the
Rev. John Morris, S.J. 6d. net, by post 7d.

Meditation: An Instruction for Novices. By the
same. 6d. net, by post 7d.

Vocation: or Preparation for the Vows, with a
further Instruction on Mental Prayer. By the same.
6d. net, by post 7d.

Instructions for Novices. By the same. The three
above Instructions together, in cloth, post free, 2s. net.

BIOGRAPHIES.

St. Ignatius Loyola and the Early Jesuits. By
Stewart Rose. With about 100 Illustrations. Handsomely bound in cloth, extra gilt. Price 15s. net.

The Life of St. Ignatius of Loyola. By Father
Genelli, S.J. New Edition. 6s.

The Life and Letters of St. Francis Xavier.
By the Rev. H. J. Coleridge. Two vols. 10s. 6d.

The Life and Letters of St. Teresa. By the Rev.
H. J. Coleridge. Three Vols. 7s. 6d. each.

The Life of St. Francis di Geronimo, of the
Society of Jesus. By A. M. Clarke. 6s.

Life of St. Aloysius Gonzaga. By Father Virgil
Cepari, S.J. Edited by Rev. Francis Goldie, S.J. In
cloth, extra gilt, 12s. 6d.

The Life of St. John Berchmans. By the Rev.
Francis Goldie, S.J. 6s.

The Life of St. Alonso Rodriguez. By the Rev.
Francis Goldie, S.J. 7s. 6d.

The Life of Blessed Margaret Mary. By the
Rev. George Tickell, S.J. Third Edition. Cloth, 6s.

The Life of the Venerable Claude de la Colombiere.
Abridged from the French Life by Eugene Sequin, S.J. 5s.

Acts of English Martyrs, hitherto unpublished. By the Rev. John H. Pollen, S.J. With a Preface by the Rev. John Morris, S.J. 7s. 6d.

The Life and Martyrdom of St. Thomas Becket. By the Rev. John Morris, S.J. Second and Enlarged Edition. In one vol. large post 8vo, 12s. 6d. Or in two volumes, 13s.

The Venerable Sir Adrian Fortescue, Knight of the Bath, Knight of St. John, Martyr. By the Rev. John Morris, S.J. With Portrait and Autograph. 1s. 6d.

Two Missionaries under Elizabeth. By the Rev. John Morris, S.J. A Confessor and an Apostate. Demy 8vo, cloth. 14s.

The Catholics of York under Elizabeth. By the Rev. John Morris, S.J. Demy 8vo, cloth. 14s.

The Life of Father John Gerard, S.J. By the Rev. John Morris, S.J. Third Edition, re-written and enlarged, 14s.

The Life of St. Jane Frances Fremyot de Chantal. By Emily Bowles. 5s.

The Life of Dona Luisa de Carvajal. By Lady Georgiana Fullerton. Small Edition, 3s. 6d.

An English Carmelite. The Life of Catherine Burton, Mother Mary Xaveria of the Angels, of the English Teresian Convent at Antwerp. Collected from her own writings, and other sources, by Father Thomas Hunter, S.J. 6s.

The Life of Margaret Mostyn (Mother Margaret of Jesus), Religious of the Reformed Order of Our Blessed Lady of Mount Carmel (1625-1679). By the Very Rev. Edmund Bedingfield. 6s.

The Chronicle of St. Antony of Padua. "The Eldest Son of St. Francis." Edited by the Rev. H. J. Coleridge, S.J. In Four Books. 5s. 6d.

Three Catholic Reformers of the Fifteenth Century (St. Vincent Ferrer, St. Bernardine of Siena, St. John Capistran). By Mary H. Allies. 6s.

The Life of St. Thomas of Hereford. By Father L'Estrange, S.J. 6s.

The Life of St. Bridget of Sweden. By F. J. M. A. Partridge. 6s.

A Gracious Life (1566-1618); being the Life of Madame Acarie (Blessed Mary of the Incarnation), of the Reformed Order of Our Blessed Lady of Mount Carmel. By Emily Bowles. 6s.

The Life of Mary Ward. By Mary Catherine Elizabeth Chambers, of the Institute of the Blessed Virgin. Two Vols. 15s.

St. Mary's Convent, Micklegate Bar, York. A History of the Convent. 7s. 6d.

Gaston de Segur. A Biography. Condensed from the French Memoir by the Marquis de Segur, by F. J. M. A. Partridge. 3s. 6d.

Garcia Moreno, President of Ecuador. 1821—1875. From the French of the Rev. P. A. Berthe, C.SS.R. By The Lady Herbert. 7s. 6d.

A Martyr from the Quarter - Deck. Alexis Clerc, S.J. By The Lady Herbert. 5s.

Theodore Wibaux, Pontifical Zouave and Jesuit. By Father du Coëtlosquet, S.J., with an Introduction by the Rev. R. F. Clarke, S.J. Crown 8vo, handsomely bound in blue and gold. 5s.

Records of the English Province of the Society of Jesus. By Henry Foley, S.J. Vols. I. to VI., Six Guineas. Vol. VII., *The Collectanea*, in two Parts, price 21s. each. This Volume presents the History of the English Province, from its commencement to the year 1773, with Notices of Deceased Members to the year 1883. The entire set, £8 8s. net.

No living man is likely to see these *Records* superseded, or diminish in value. . . . The more widely they are known, the more highly will they be appreciated.—*The Athenæum.*

JAMES STANLEY, MANRESA PRESS, ROEHAMPTON.